1049
A 7R
бit gem

Morality and Language

Morality and Language

G. J. WARNOCK

Basil Blackwell · Oxford

© in this collection G. J. Warnock 1983

First published in this collection 1983
Basil Blackwell Publisher Limited
108 Cowley Road, Oxford OX4 1JF, England

British Library Cataloguing in Publication Data

Warnock, G. J.
    Morality and language.
    1. Philosophy
    I. Title
    192   BI674.W3/

    ISBN 0-631-13098-5

Typesetting by Oxford Verbatim Limited
Printed in Great Britain by
The Blackwell Press, Worcester

Contents

Historical

Introduction

The earliest of the essays that follow was written in 1950, the latest in 1980. The latest, not the last – they are not arranged here in strict chronological order but in groups, the items in each group being related by a certain broad kinship of subject matter – though the first group, in particular, might have to be described no more precisely than as being concerned with 'general philosophy'. I have left out a good many papers written (and some published) in those thirty years which seemed to me confused, or misguided, too hopelessly inconclusive, or in other ways defective, but the fact that any given paper is included should not be taken to imply that I believe it to be wholly without such defects; I have put in what seemed to me to be in some respect or other worth reading, either as making some point worth making, or at the least as providing a perhaps useful specimen of what was being written at a certain date by a certain kind of Oxford philosopher.

A good deal has been written about 'Oxford philosophy' of those years, and no doubt more will be. Not without reason. Gilbert Ryle said of the years just after the first war (*Ryle*, ed. O. P. Wood and G. W. Pitcher, Doubleday, 1970, p. 4) that 'during my time as an undergraduate and during my first few years as a teacher, the philosophic kettle in Oxford was barely lukewarm'. After 1945 – and owing perhaps even more than is generally recognized to Ryle himself - the picture could not have been more different. Writing of J. L. Austin after his death (in the *Proceedings of the British Academy*, vol. XLIX) I said that

The university to which he returned [in 1945] was, at any rate in the field of philosophy, in a remarkable condition at that time – and, one may well feel, looking back, an enviable one. As the war went on it had been, of course, progressively depopulated: afterwards, as it seemed in a moment, it was crammed and overflowing. Undergraduates, of whom now several generations were pressing into residence simultaneously, were anything up to ten years above the usual age; most had been in the services; and one had the impression that a large proportion knew, with more maturity and independence of judgement than is usually to be looked for among undergraduates, that after the war years work was what they wanted. . . . Senior members also wore something of a new look. Many had returned, like Austin, from distinguished war service; but also posts falling vacant in the previous six years had seldom been filled, so that there followed a sudden rush of new appointments. In philosophy there had not yet quite vanished the stimulating sense of an Old Guard opposition; but such pre-war 'radicals' as, conspicuously, Ryle and Ayer could now be regarded as advancing on what looked like a large and unmistakably winning side, with such names – perhaps somewhat heterogeneously assembled – as Waismann, Berlin, Paul, Hampshire, Hart, Urmson, and soon many others, on its muster-roll. No doubt such quasi-belligerent categories look, retrospectively, slightly absurd, even undesirable; no doubt the sharp sense of philosophical black-and-white was naïve, the optimism unfounded; but the sense of new things going on, of new starts being made towards what seemed quite attainable goals, was strongly invigorating, and by no means confined to, though common among, undergraduates of the period.

This sense of philosophical vitality was not wholly due to the mere release of energies pent up by the war: it was in large part a matter of the state of the subject itself. Ryle, who had succeeded Collingwood as Wayneflete Professor, was already making, in the work which led up to *The Concept of Mind*, what was perhaps the first systematic and really large-scale application of the new philo-sophical style to large traditional problems; and it was at this time also that the later work of Wittgenstein, long cloistrally prosecuted in Cambridge, came to be known in wider circles – and was, some may think, none the worse for a breath of fresh air. There really was, in the subject at that time, a good deal to be excited about.

Perhaps those who partook in, or were present in, this animated scene would have agreed most firmly in what they were against. There was a prevailing idea that most of the difficulty, of the unsatisfactoriness and disorder, of philosophy was attributable to obscurity, unclearness, and (consequently) confusion. (Some would have attributed to those defects the very existence of the subject itself.) Thus above all things obscurity was to be avoided; and from that certain more specific avoidances followed. First, literary pretension, rhetoric, the 'high style' of the Idealists, or the deep-mystery-mongering of (for example) Heidegger; a philosopher's first duty, prior even to that of being right and immeasur-ably prior to that of being eloquent, was to be clearly, plainly, and readily understood. Second, over-ambition and haste, biting off more than could be conclusively and thoroughly chewed, undertaking to settle too many questions too quickly – rather, small points clearly stated, limited aims clearly set out. Related to that was a certain distrust of 'theories', which were apt to be regarded – particularly by Austin – as both over-ambitious (because, in the current rudimentary state of the subject, premature) and potentially distorting, inhibiting clear and accurate perception of the actual phenomena under consideration.[1] And for partly the same reason – and against most markedly in Austin – there was much suspicion of technical terminology, of 'formalization' – partly because such terminology, though no doubt virtuously intended to be clearer than the supposedly rough-and-ready locutions of natural language, was often itself ill-defined and productive of obscurity; partly because the translation of a question into some formalized form, and the generation – even if formally impeccable – of a formalized 'solution', was liable to leave it unclear exactly what had been 'solved', to leave a doubt that simply something *else* had been allowed to take the place of the original question, and something irrelevant, consequently, to be obtruded as an answer.

I think I can say that such avoidances were at the back of my mind in writing all the pieces that follow, and I do not regret them – not that one can live by avoidances alone, or even succeed, always, in achieving them, merely because one wants to.

Perhaps I may mention one particular respect in which these essays seem to me less starkly heterogeneous than, when I agreed to the project of putting them together, I feared that they might be. There is one theme that, I found, tended to recur.

In the years between the wars progressive philosophy, under the influence of Russell and Moore and the Vienna Circle, was much dominated by the idea of 'analysis'. It was not indeed generally agreed exactly what the criteria of a correct analysis were; nor was it generally agreed –

---

[1] If I may quote again from the same piece about Austin: 'It was during the 30s that, in this country, the philosophical scene was first enlivened by the dismissive *brusqueries* of Logical Positivism. What did Austin make of this? He was sympathetic to the general intention. He disliked and distrusted (in this following Prichard and Moore) the rhetoric, pretension and obscurity that are apt to accompany metaphysical ambitions, and correspondingly approved the workshop, no-nonsense atmosphere of the Vienna Circle and its adherents. But he distrusted equally the positivistic addiction to quasi-scientific technical jargon; and though be believed that philosophical problems could in principle be definitively solved, he reacted instinctively (as well as for excellent reasons) against the production of alleged solutions with such staggering rapidity. Logical Positivism was itself, after all, just another ambitious philosophical theory, marked scarcely less, in Austin's view, for all its down-to-earth intentions, by mythology and obscurity than the theories it purported so confidently to demolish. It shared, as he thought, far too many of the defects of its intended victims.'

perhaps also it was too seldom considered – in what, when some analysis seemed both correct and philosophically useful, its philosophical usefulness actually consisted. But one can say nevertheless that, in much philosophy of that period, the object in view was to arrive at an 'analysis' in this sense: a sort of linguistic equation, with the 'analysandum' (an expression or sentence) on one side, and on the other the 'analysans' – the analysans being an expression or sentence such that it was (a) identical in meaning with – and usually longer than – the analysandum, but (b) in some philosophically relevant way *better* (for example clearer, more 'basic', epistemologically illuminating, less potentially misleading). For at least two reasons, post-war philosophy tended to move away, or had already moved away, from this programme. First, Wittgenstein, while agreeing in a way that the philosopher's object was a certain kind of elucidation, came to hold that that was not to be achieved only – perhaps not at all – in that particular, somewhat straitjacketed form: the solvent of philosophical perplexity was to be, not 'analysis' of trouble-making expressions or sentences, but a firm and clear grasp of their 'use'; so that the philosopher's proper undertaking was, not the quasi-definitional analysis of meaning, but the 'description' of use. Concurrently Austin (in particular) came to hold that analysis of meaning, even if quite successfully undertaken, might be philosophically unprofitable in that, in (again) the actual use of expressions and sentences, very much is involved beyond the bare meaning of the words; we may need to know, not only 'what was said' or the meaning of what was said, but why it was said, to whom, in what circumstances, when, to what actual or intended effect, and so on. 'Description of use', to be comprehensive, should bring in all these.

I appear to have been rather persistently preoccupied – more persistently than I had realized – with the thought that this notion of 'use' could itself become seriously misleading – could be taken to tell us more than it actually does, or even, and worse, could lead to substantial error. It is true that 'I know that . . .' is, sometimes, used in making a claim; but that correct observation does not tell us what 'I know that . . .' *means*, still less that that question somehow does not or cannot arise. It is true that '. . . is true' may be used in, say, expressing agreement; but that again neither tells us, nor debars us from asking, what '. . . is true' means. Conversely, 'I know that I have shoes on my feet' is 'not used' when there is no doubt, and no one has questioned or even mentioned in any way, that I have shoes on my feet; but it does not follow that, in such a case, I do *not* know that I have shoes on my feet, or that if, however oddly, I were to say so, I should not have given linguistically unobjectionable expression to a truth. I find this preoccupation in many of the pieces that follow, in various degrees of explicitness – in the pieces, of course, about truth and knowledge, but also in two of the three pieces about ethics, and in the one about performative utterances. (Roughly – that sentences of moral discourse are sometimes used 'to prescribe', though it is some sort of fact about their 'use', tells us, I argue, a good deal less than it has been supposed to; that 'promise', in 'I promise', is 'used differently' from the same word in 'He promises' – that is, in making, not reporting, a promise – does not justify the conclusion that it does not have the same meaning, or that, whereas 'He promises' can be true or false, 'I promise' cannot.) I think I had the fairly unformulated idea that meaning – and much preferably, for any given word or expression, *constancy* of meaning – stood in need of defence, of being brought back into view, amidst the encroaching welter of different 'uses', and the dangerously over-accommodating vagueness of 'use' itself. I was also interested (but I am not sure that many others have been) in the case, that of imperative sentences, in which I found this, I thought, impossible to do – in which to assign to a given sentence a constant meaning, detachable from the different 'uses' to which it might be put, was a programme that could not in fact be made to work.

About the papers themselves. The first needs no comment: it was written in 1950 and appeared in *Mind* in January 1951. The second, 'Perception', was written, I believe, in 1954, and was used as the starting-point of a long series of seminars given over the next couple of years by myself and H. P. Grice: it was never published, largely because we had the idea, arising from those seminars, of jointly writing something on perception on a much larger scale; nothing came of that, but by the time the idea had been tacitly abandoned there seemed to be no occasion for publishing this piece in particular. The next, 'Seeing', was published in the Aristotelian Society's *Proceedings* in 1955; I certainly discussed it with Grice, and probably read something like it – though not, I think, it – to one of our seminars. It was included in the collection *Perceiving, Sensing and Knowing* (ed. R. J. Swartz, Doubleday, 1965) – appearing there with a one-page postscript which I have here omitted (on the advice of F. I. Dretske, the author of that admirable book *Seeing and Knowing*, University of Chicago Press, 1969).

The paper 'Claims to Knowledge' was the first piece (the second was by L. J. Cohen) in a symposium at the Joint Session of the Mind Association and Aristotelian Society in 1962. It has one rather curious feature. I was preoccupied in this piece, as noted above, by the potential misleadingness of the notion of 'use'. In this particular case, I thought that some philosophers had been misled, by the undoubted fact that 'I know . . .' can be 'used' – and in that sense *is* used – in making a claim to knowledge, firstly into seeming to believe that the expression is *always* so used, and secondly into taking that fact to be far more revelatory than it actually is of what knowing *is*, of what 'know' *means*. I mentioned A. D. Woozley and A. R. White as targets of this criticism, and Austin, in a footnote to the second part of the paper, as having provided at least much of the required and salutary discrimination among the uses of 'use' itself. The latter point is not wrong; but I must, I think, have been aware nevertheless that by far the most conspicuous and influential instance of the very mistake (as I took it to be) that I was reprehending was to be found in Austin's own paper in the symposium *Other Minds* of 1946. I must have been, I suppose, not very creditably, simply unwilling to embark on the admittedly very perilous business of charging Austin with error, and for that reason set up less formidable targets to shoot at. I hope I was not entirely *clearly* conscious of doing that.

The final paper in the first section, 'Every event has a cause', was written for a joint seminar (with D. F. Pears) on the general topic of synthetic necessary truth, and was published by A. G. N. Flew in his collection *Logic and Language* (Blackwell) in 1953.

In the next section, the paper 'A Problem about Truth' was written and read at Princeton in 1962, and published by G. W. Pitcher in his collection *Truth* (Prentice-Hall, 1964). It is followed in that collection by a reply by P. F. (now Sir Peter) Strawson; and it is pertinent to mention also his 'Truth: A Reconsideration of Austin's Views', in his *Logico-Linguistic Papers* (Methuen, 1971). The next piece, which was a response at the Joint Session of 1973 to a paper by C. J. F. Williams, is included partly because it has a common origin; the symposium was given (by Williams) the subtitle 'Bristol Revisited' because it was at Bristol that there occurred, in 1950, the important symposium on Truth which prompted his paper in 1973, as it had prompted mine in 1962.

Of the other four pieces in this section, I think nothing need be said except where and when they were published – 'Words and Sentences' in the collection *Ryle* (ed. O. P. Wood and G. W. Pitcher, Doubleday, 1970); 'Some Types of Performative Utterance' in *Essays on J. L. Austin* (ed. I. Berlin *et al.*, Oxford University Press, 1973); 'Imperatives and Meaning' in *Contemporary British Philosophy* (ed. H. D. Lewis, Allen and Unwin, 1976). 'A Question about Illocutions' was written for a special issue of *Philosophia* (vol. 10, nos. 1–2), brought out in 1979 as a tribute to Sir Peter Strawson.

I think it is true to say that I paid almost no attention to moral philosophy until 1962, when I was asked – because, I can only think, of temporary shortage of local manpower – to do a seminar called *Systematic Ethics* at Princeton. As an undergraduate I had read with admiration C. L. Stevenson's *Ethics and Language* (1944) and a little later R. M. Hare's *The Language of Morals* (1952), and felt secure in the belief that (then) modern sophistications about language would illuminate, and were illuminating, that branch of philosophy along with others. But after 1962 I came to think not only that this was not true, but that it was the reverse of the truth – that in this case attachment to, and belief in the illuminating power of, certain doctrines about language were actually retarding progress by directing attention the wrong way. The paper 'Ethics and Language', which argues this case in a rather small nutshell, was given as a lecture in 1967 to the Royal Institute of Philosophy, and afterwards published in a collection entitled *The Human Agent* (ed. G. N. A. Vesey Macmillan, 1968). The piece called 'Morality and Language' argues much the same case in a particular instance, against the claim made by R. M. Hare that philosophical doctrines about 'moral language' are of central importance in moral education. This was included with, and written as a reply to, a piece by Hare called 'Language and Moral Education', in a collection called *The Domain of Moral Education* (ed. D. B. Cochrane, C. M. Hamm and A. C. Kazepides, Paulist Press and Ontario Institute for Studies in Education, 1979). I rather feel that in this instance my (unusual) confidence in the cogency of my case led me into a perhaps excessively polemical, even aggressive style of arguing. It is some comfort, if so, that Hare very fairly supplied to the same collection a 'Rejoinder' to my piece, the manner of which is also rather markedly crisp.

The other piece on moral philosophy, called 'Comments on Frankena's *Three Questions*', sits here a little uncomfortably, in the inevitable absence of the long text on which it comments. I think, however, that it just deserves its place, partly because it does contain at least a summary statement of the relevant part of Frankena's position, and partly because it gave me the chance to say shortly and simply some things about morality that I believe to be worth saying (not things about its 'language') and which otherwise I have said only in books. Frankena's three lectures, my comment and two others, and a 'Reply' by Frankena were all published in *The Monist* in 1980 (vol. 63, no. 1).

The three remaining pieces need no special comments. 'The Primacy of Practical Reason' was a Dawes Hicks lecture delivered to the British Academy in 1966 and published in its *Proceedings* (vol. LII). 'Liberty', not

published before, was the last in a series of lectures on Hobbes delivered
in Oxford in 1979, to mark the tercentenary of his death. The final piece,
'Saturday Mornings', was written for the collection, mentioned above, of
Essays on J. L. Austin. Its presence here could be objected to on the ground
that it is not, except in the most oblique and glancing way, about philosophy;
but I hope it may nevertheless be of interest to philosophers; and in any
case I should have been sorry not to include in this book at least something
directly about Austin, still, to my mind, the most impressive and enliven-
ing philosopher I ever met.

Perception and Other Matters

1

Empirical Propositions
and Hypothetical Statements

I should like to add to Mr Isaiah Berlin's many-weaponed attack on phenomenalism (in Mind, July 1950) one further point, the importance of which seems to me to have been generally overlooked. This will not perhaps 'refute' that resilient theory, but it will, I think, be seen to necessitate yet another dilution of its claims, and in this way to hasten its eventual disappearance.

I

There is one preliminary matter to be settled. It seems to me rather undesirable – though not, for Mr Berlin's case, importantly so – to say as he does that (some) categorical sentences 'point' (to things, events, etc.). For such sentences out of context are like sign-posts lying on the ground in the middle of a field; we should not say that these sign-posts point to anything, but rather that they *could* do so – i.e. they would if they were put up in appropriate places. An unerected sign-post marked 'Dunley 1½' does not, though it could be made to, point the way to Dunley; and a contextless sentence such as 'This table is brown' is in a similar but even worse case, for we cannot even say what table it *could* be used to point to. It could in fact be used to point to any table; but it seems very queer to say that it actually does so.

If for these reasons we distinguish, in Mr P. F. Strawson's way (Mind, July 1950, p. 325), between a sentence (which could be used to point) and a use of a sentence (in order to point), part of Mr Berlin's case can without difficulty be restated as follows: Some categorical sentences can be and are used to point to actual objects, states of affairs, etc.; but the chief characteristic of hypothetical sentences is that they are not, cannot be, are

From *Mind*, NS vol. LX, 1951.

specifically not *meant* to be, used in this way. It follows that hypothetical sentences, and *a fortiori* hypothetical sentences about sense-data, cannot in every case be used to do the same job as is done by categorical sentences. Even if (as Professor Ayer holds[1] is never the case) our categorical and hypothetical sentences entail each other, substitution without loss is impossible.

It may be worth noticing that it may also be inadvisable to use the word 'point'. For it is true to say that I cannot literally point *at*, but only towards, or in the direction of, what is out of sight; and this seems to make it necessary to give a special explanation of the use of sentences to 'point' to objects in absence. Mr Berlin describes this use of 'point' as 'semi-metaphorical'. But his use of 'point' is wholly metaphorical in any case; and might we not avoid some unnecessary difficulties by substituting for 'point' some other expression, the *literal* use of which implies no restriction to present, visible objects?

II

To return now to the distinction between a sentence and the use of a sentence, and the point of making it.

Mr Berlin indicates the phenomenalist's programme in (among others) the following ways (p. 291): (1) he offers an 'analysis of how material object sentences ae to be "reduced" (without residue) to sentences describing both what the observer does, or did, or will observe, as well as what he would, or would have, might or might have, observed under appropriate conditions': and (2) he proposes 'the reduction of material object sentences into what we may, for short, call sense-datum sentences'. These are, I think, fair descriptions. And we may add a version from Professor Ayer: 'What is being claimed is simply that the propositions which are ordinarily expressed by sentences which refer to material things could also be expressed by sentences which referred exclusively to sense-data.' (*Foundations*, p. 232) This version is slightly complicated by the use in it of 'proposition'; but if we take it that Professor Ayer is here using 'proposition' as, roughly, a way of referring to a class of sentences having the same meaning, we may rewrite his claim thus: 'For any sentence which can be used to refer to a material thing, there is a set of sentences having the same meaning which can be used to refer exclusively to

---

[1] *The Foundations of Empirical Knowledge* (1940), pp. 239–41.

sense-data.' This is no doubt what is meant by saying that phenomenalism offers an 'alternative language'.

It seems to me that Mr Berlin's two versions, and Professor Ayer's version, reveal even in this (already diluted) form of phenomenalism a special absurdity, which although not recondite has not, I think, been previously emphasized; and which can be avoided only at the cost of still further and possibly fatal dilution.

It must be noticed that the claim is to analyse (reduce, translate) *sentences* (or propositions = classes of sentences). Let us take, then, the sentence 'This table is brown.' Now, so long as it is the sentence that we are considering, and not some particular use of it by a particular person, the questions 'What table is being referred to?', 'By whom?', and 'In what circumstances?' are not in point. This sentence *could* be used, by some person or persons, to refer to some particular table in some particular circumstances; but the unused, out-of-context sentence specifies no speaker or writer, no table, and no situation. Suppose then that we invite a phenomenalist to analyse (reduce, translate) the material object sentence 'This table is brown': his reply must inevitably take the following form – 'If an observer [who?] were to do something or other [what?], or were in some situation or other [which?], there would occur some sense-data [which?].' Now it is perfectly clear that it would be no good trying to answer the bracketed questions. For as soon as we seek to specify who is to do what, or how he is to be situated, to achieve what result, we require information about some particular occasion on which the material object sentence may be supposed to be used; and thereafter we are not analysing (etc.) the *sentence*, but making possibly true statements about the circumstances of some one occasion of its use; and these possibly true statements will certainly be false of almost every other such occasion. But at the same time it is no good refusing to answer them; for unless we do so, we cannot even begin to compose sense-datum sentences; we can only hint that, in rather different circumstances, we could have done so.

A parallel absurdity can be seen inevitably to arise out of attempts to reduce, in this sense, even sentences offering better *prima facie* opportunities for this treatment. It would, for example, be generally admitted that an infantry battalion is composed of men. But consider the sentence 'The battalion is on a night exercise.' It is clearly impossible to maintain that any set of sentences, containing the proper names of individual men, means the same as this sentence. For by inspection of the sentence alone, we do not discover what battalion is in question, at what stage of its history, nor which of its members are supposed to be present, nor what they are supposed to be doing. Of course, given some particular occasion on which this sentence was used, we might laboriously attempt to compile some list of sentences, using the proper names of individuals, and describing their activities. But it is clear that the statements made by the use of this list of sentences would almost certainly be false, if made on any other occasion of use of the sentence 'The battalion is on a night exercise' – even if the battalion referred to happened to be the same battalion. Thus, unless we are prepared to adopt the desperate and fantastic view that the meaning of the sentence 'The battalion is on a night exercise' is (or is almost certain to be) different on each occasion of the use of this sentence, and remains quite indefinite until some such occasion is specified, it is necessary to conclude that the sentence is not susceptible of analysis in the way proposed.

The root of the matter can be revealed in this way. Any list of proper names, however long, supplies us with a means of referring to *some* particular persons, however numerous; whereas it is the chief (and of course the intended) merit of such expressions as 'the battalion' that they do *not* do this. Of course the doings and undergoings to which I may refer by statements about the battalion are in fact the doings and undergoings of individuals; but by using the expression 'the battalion' I do not say *which* individuals, and it is for precisely this reason that sentences in which this expression occurs can be used on many very different occasions. The respects in which such occasions must be broadly of the same *sort*, in order to allow correct uses of the expression 'the battalion', or of such sentences as 'The battalion is on a night exercise' – these are the very respects which *cannot* be brought out by the compiling of any list of sentences containing the proper names of individuals and descriptions of their doings. In just the same way, any list of sentences mentioning the particular conditions in which certain sense-data are or could be had by somebody, can at best supply us only with the means of referring to some particular occasion of use of such a sentence as 'This table is brown.' The *sort* of situation in which the sentence may be used, the very general respects in which each situation must resemble at least some of the others – this (which is what we know when we know the *meaning* of the sentence) is precisely what cannot be indicated by any list, however vast, of fatally specific, particularizing sense-datum sentences.

From the hopeless attempt to analyse the sentence 'The battalion is on a night exercise', we can gather only that battalions consist of men: and from the even more hopeless attempt to analyse the sentence 'This table is brown', we can gather only that tables are visible.

III

It seems clear that for these reasons, which I think are different from and additional to Mr Berlin's, the phenomenalist's claim to provide a general analysis of material object sentences must be disallowed; and historically it is certain that this claim has been advanced, and not in any trivial, unimportant way that could plausibly be ascribed to mere terminological carelessness. However, it might I suppose, be retracted, and replaced by the less ambitious claim to provide, whenever a material object sentence is actually used, some substitutable set of sense-datum sentences – these sets being admittedly very different from each other even where, on the various occasions on which they are offered, the very same material object sentence is used. No doubt there is a surprising number of further reasons for rejecting even this more modest claim; but even if it could be allowed, much orthodox phenomenalist doctrine would still be objectionable. In particular, it would be highly misleading to maintain that phenomenalism offers an 'alternative language', or some sort of translation. For in the normal, honest use of 'translate' it is possible to translate accurately 'This table is brown' without knowing which table, when, where, and referred to by whom. But the fact is that, in a 'sense-datum language', there would be nothing to which we could point as *the* translation of 'The table is brown'; for no collection of analyses of particular uses of this sentence would mean the same as the sentence itself. There is thus no genuine inter-translate-ability. This is similar to the point which Mr Berlin expresses materially by saying (p. 296) that phenomenalism offers 'a different picture of the world . . . and in no sense merely a description of the old picture'. If 'alternative' language means 'totally different' language, very well; but surely the suggestion has usually been that the new language would be not only similar, but just as good or better – even, it has been said, for some purposes more convenient. This last is perhaps the oddest suggestion of all.

2

Perception

1. One of the propositions which writers on perception have been commonly concerned to establish is that we are never directly aware of material things. Now this, if we attach any natural sense to the words, is obviously untrue: and of course, if we give the words a sufficient twist, we can make it not only true but also necessary. However, some philosophers have taken quite a different view of this proposition. The statement that we are never directly aware of material things has seemed to them to be neither patently false nor a contrived tautology, but a statement which we can find good *reason* to accept if we stop to reflect upon it. One line that such reflection is supposed to take leads into the so-called 'argument from illusion', where I shall not follow it on this occasion. Another device is to suggest that seeing is closely analogous to hearing: that we are all ready 'if pressed' to admit that we do not directly *hear* material things; and hence that there is good reason to deny that we ever directly see material things, however strongly we are at first inclined to assert that we do. (Berkeley argues in this way in his *New Theory of Vision*; and H. A. Prichard and C. D. Broad have sometimes used similar arguments.) The case of touching raises some difficulty for this procedure. Berkeley allows in the *New Theory of Vision* that we do really (directly) touch material things. But Prichard found the verb 'touch' difficult to deal with, and so 'pitched on' the verb 'to feel' instead: and Broad has put forward the modified contention that the 'experience of touching' is closely analogous with the 'experience of hearing'.

At the same time many philosophers have observed that seeing and hearing at any rate *seem* to be unlike each other. Broad says that 'phenomenologically' they *are* unlike, though in his view 'epistemologically' not so. One striking difference between them has been brought out by O. K. Bouwsma in the following way. We say 'I see a rat' and 'I hear a

---

Unpublished paper, *c.* 1954.

rat': we could also say 'I hear a gnawing sound.' But there seems to be no sentence beginning 'I see . . .' which corresponds to 'I see a rat' in the way in which 'I hear a gnawing sound' corresponds to 'I hear a rat.' That is, there seems to be no noun in the vocabulary of seeing analogous with the noun 'sound' in the vocabulary of hearing. Similarly, the verbs 'taste' and 'smell' have their nouns, namely 'taste' and 'smell', but with the verb 'touch' no noun is associated in this way.

Why is this? Perhaps it is merely a troublesome accident, to be set right by straightforward invention of suitable new nouns. Or perhaps there is (as Bouwsma suggests) a 'deficiency in the facts', so that there would simply be nothing for any new nouns to refer to. I do not think that either of these is quite the appropriate comment: though the second is more nearly appropriate than the first.

2. First of all let me deal very briefly with the verb 'touch'. I say, for example, 'I touch the table', or 'I am touching the table', or 'My hand is touching the table.' Can we replace the expression 'the table' by some expression of the form 'the x of the table', as we might put the expression 'the sound of the clock', in place of the expression 'the clock', in 'I can hear the clock'? Now we could, of course, use a variety of expressions referring to parts, or parts of the surface, of the table – 'the leg', 'the top', 'the corner', 'the edge'. But these expressions are not like 'the sound'. For whereas to say that I hear the clock entails that I hear the sound of the clock, to say that I touch the table does not entail that I touch the leg of it, nor the corner, nor any other *particular* part of it or of its surface. 'We hear sounds' is a truism, but 'We touch tops (edges, etc.)' is not. It might be suggested that we touch *surfaces*: but this is either false or pointless. In fact it is natural to speak of touching surfaces only in cases where we might have touched something else – the inside, for instance, what lies beneath or below the surface. (It would be odd to assure a miner that he touches only the surface of the earth.) And if we exercise our undoubted right to turn 'We touch surfaces' into a tautology, it becomes a particulary point-less one – it has much less point than the remark that we hear sounds. For one might insist that we hear *sounds* in order to emphasize the fact that we can only be said to hear *things* if they make (as they very often do not make) sounds. But one could not similarly seek to emphasize that we can only be said to touch things if they have (as they often do not have?) surfaces. For this implies that, just as some physical objects do not make sounds, some physical objects have no surfaces. And even if we took this last odd-looking statement to be true (and *is* it true? Fogs and flames, perhaps, do

not have surfaces, they are not sufficiently clearly bounded, but then would we call them 'physical *objects*'? And we do not say that we *touch* fogs or flames) we still have no analogy with sounds. For an object might be of the kind that we can sometimes hear, and yet might elude the sense of hearing on particular occasions by making no sound: but an object of the kind that we sometimes touch could not be said, on some particular occasion, to elude the sense of touch by having no surface. A clock, while remaining the same kind of thing, can sometimes make sounds and sometimes make none: but it cannot, while remaining the same kind of thing, have a surface sometimes and at other times not. Things cannot be from time to time intangible as they can from time to time be soundless: still less could they be *always* intangible, though many things are always silent.

Further, it is only animate and sentient beings that can be said to hear things: whereas the limbs or bodies of animate beings, and also inanimate things and their parts, may quite properly be said to touch things. There is no eccentricity in saying that my feet touch the floor, as there would be in saying that my ears hear the clock; nor is there any eccentricity in saying that the tyres of the car touch the kerb.

It is not, I think, difficult to see why this should be so. For consider what the verb 'touch' actually means. It means 'to be in or come into "physical contact" with' something. And of course it should occasion no surprise that it is only with physical objects, their parts or their surfaces, that we, our limbs, or anything else, can be said to be in or come into physical contact. The verb 'touch', in fact, is not really a verb of *perception* at all. Two inanimate objects that are touching do not perceive anything: and we ourselves do not perceive anything 'by touch' unless we not only touch but also feel. We often do touch things and 'perceive' nothing: anaesthesia certainly inhibits our sensitivity, but it does not reduce our ability, or the ability of our bodies, to *touch* things.

No doubt there is more to be said about the verb 'touch'. There are differences between 'I touched the floor' and 'My feet touched the floor'; also of course between '. . . touches' and '. . . is touching'. We would not always *say* that we touched all the things (our clothes?) with which we were in contact, though we would not deny it either. There are also many extended and figurative and abnormal uses. But we need not go into these matters now. For it is, I believe, sufficiently clear already that the verb 'touch' means *literally*, and *at least*, 'to be in or come into physical contact with . . .', and from this it follows at once that grammatical objects of the verb must be expressions that refer to physical things, their surfaces or insides, or their parts – things of which it makes sense to say that physical contact is made with them. And there is thus no room in the vocabulary of touching for any further expression, playing the role that the noun 'sound' plays in the vocabulary of hearing. There is no room for any intermediary, since to touch is to make *literally* that direct contact with the world, to which the other senses are sometimes said (metaphorically) to aspire. Roughly speaking – the verb 'touch' could not occur except in a language permitting mention of physical objects; whereas the verb 'hear' could certainly occur – for we hear sounds, and are not obliged to mention what makes them, or even to say whether anything makes them at all.

It would be natural at this point to say something about the verb 'to feel', and about the nouns 'feeling' and 'sensation'; for touching and feeling are of course closely associated. Indeed, perception by touch is the *only* sort of perception in which it is natural to say that sensations are involved. However, though we may have sensations when we touch things, we certainly do not touch sensations. 'Sensation' and 'feeling' are not nouns that could be employed as grammatical objects of the verb 'touch'. And I have been concerned with the verb 'touch' only; feeling raises too many new questions to be dealt with here.

3. We must next consider the case of *seeing*. In this case, I think, it is less obvious why there should be no 'intermediary' noun like 'sound'; perhaps it is not even clear that there is none. For though it is certainly usual for expressions used to refer to physical things (or events, or states of affairs) to occur as grammatical objects to the verb 'see', this is not necessarily so, and very often it is not so. We use very numerous expressions of a different kind. We see sunsets, rainbows, the sky, flames, steam, and showers of rain – things which we should hardly describe as 'physical objects'. And though it is fairly obvious that none of these are at all like sounds – we could not be said to see such things whenever we see anything at all – there are yet other expressions which may seem to resemble 'sound' quite closely. I will mention a few.

(a) Berkeley suggested that 'We see light and colours' is the proper analogue to 'We hear sounds.' And to some small extent this is not wholly wrong. He was impressed by the point that, if I hear anything at all, I *can* be said (though often I would not be said) to hear a sound: and he took it, reasonably enough, to be also true that, if I see anything at all, I *can* be said (though I hardly ever would be said) to see light and colours. But in other respects the analogy soon breaks down. I may say that I hear the sound *of* a car; also, that I see the light *of* a car, or the colour *of* a car. But whereas, if I hear a car, I hear the sound of a car, it cannot be inferred that, if I see a car, then I see the light of a car, or the colour of a car. For we see the light of something only if it is or incorporates a source of illumination; and to see the colour of something is not simply to see it, but also to see what colour it is. 'I heard the sound of his footsteps' means the same as 'I heard his footsteps'; but 'I saw the colour of his hair' does not mean the same as 'I saw his hair.' For perhaps I saw his hair only by moonlight. And 'I saw the light of his hair' means nothing at all.

(b) We hear sounds: we see sights. But these are not analogous and equally natural remarks. For the noun 'sight' has quite special uses, much narrower than those of the noun 'sound'. The adjectives that typically qualify 'sight' are for instance 'amusing', 'puzzling', 'entertaining', 'impressive', 'shocking', 'unpleasant', or 'beautiful'. And this reveals the use of the noun. When I say that I saw a disgusting sight, I am not in fact giving either a preliminary or tentative report or description of *what* I saw, but rather indicating that, whatever it was that I saw, it disgusted me. In this use the noun 'sight' occurs in remarks that indicate the speaker's *reactions* to what he saw, but do not *tell* what he saw. Sounds, on the other hand, can be as it were impersonally described: I can say what I heard, what sort of sound I heard, without stating or betraying how I felt when I heard it, but simply saying what I heard. In another use, 'sight' is to be compared, not with 'sound', but with 'hearing' – we say 'at first sight', 'at first hearing', and so on.

(c) I have heard it maintained that, whenever we see anything, we see a *view*. But this is hardly acceptable. To see a high brick wall at a range of three feet is not to see a view; I may indeed see the wall itself with ideal clarity, but this is still not to *see* a view, but rather to *have* a good view – namely, of the wall. We say that we have a good or a bad view of things that we can or cannot see clearly, without obstruction, and so on; but to *see* a view is to survey a reasonably extensive prospect. A book of pictures called *Views of Venice* would be ill-named if it contained only close-ups of architectural details; for though we undoubtedly see these things, and perhaps have excellent views of them, we do not, in seeing them, see views.

(d) Fourth and last, although such phrases as 'the look of a saxophone' are just as common as 'the sound of a saxophone', and though they have many similar uses, they also diverge in obvious ways. For though we hear sounds, it would be exceedingly odd to say that we see looks. I may say that someone looks prosperous, or that he has a prosperous look about him, but not that, in seeing him, I see prosperous looks.

I do not want to go on with this tedious process of elimination; it may be that no one wants seriously to maintain that any existing and common word could occur as object to the verb 'see', the use of which would be truly analogous to the use of 'sound'. In any case I venture to take it as now established that there is no such analogue to be found; indeed, if there were, one would naturally expect that it would come to mind immediately, and not require to be hunted out. We do not have to think very hard or long to reach the conclusion that we hear sounds, smell smells, or taste tastes.

4. Next, I want to point out a respect in which hearing and seeing are *partially* analogous, this partial analogy serving to emphasize the lack of any general analogy. It is a familiar but also rather striking fact that there is, besides the noun 'sound' itself, an enormous number of words for particular sounds – such as 'bang', 'crash', 'boom', 'roar', 'whine', 'whistle', 'squeak' and many others. Now these nouns certainly are very like some nouns in the vocabulary of seeing. We hear the boom, and we see the flash, of guns; we hear the crackle, and we see the glow, of fires; we hear the clash, and we see the glint, of cold steel. The list of 'visual' nouns of this kind is not lengthy – certainly it in no way rivals the rich profusion of words for sounds – but the analogy between these lists is genuine. It is particularly to be observed that each noun corresponds to a particular verb, usually identical in form with the noun itself – 'roar', 'crash', 'tinkle' and the rest, occur both as nouns and as verbs. So also do 'glitter', 'glare', 'gleam', 'glow', 'flash' and the rest. We hear roars (as a rule) only when something is roaring, a shriek when somebody shrieks; similarly we see a glow (as a rule) only when something is glowing, a flash when something flashes; and so on. Most sounds are thought of as emanating from, or being *made* by, things; for a thing to be heard it has to do or be done by, to make or be caused to make a sound, a tinkle or thud, rattle or scream or buzz; a glow (as a rule) is also emitted, made or given off by something glowing; the guns must be flashing if we are to see the flash of guns. However, it is clear that in the case of sight these are entirely *special cases*. We do not think in the *ordinary* way that an object has to give off something, to make or do something, if it is to be seen. We may see the guns when they are no longer in action, or the lighthouse when it closes down for the day. And here is the point at which this analogy fails. To hear the boom of the guns is to hear the guns, but we can say that we see the *flash* of the guns and say also that we do *not* see the guns themselves. For seeing the guns may be something different from, and better than, seeing

the flashes they make: whereas to hear the boom of guns is an *ordinary*, normal case of hearing the guns. Hearing the guns is not something either different from, or better than, hearing the booms; to hear things is *only* to hear the noises they make; there is nothing different from this to be called hearing *them*.

5. This richness and variety of words for sounds suggests a question about tasting and smelling. Here we have a pair of nouns, namely 'taste' and 'smell', whose use is very similar to that of 'sound'; but we conspicuously lack any further list of nouns for particular *sorts* of taste and smell, nor have we more than a handful of adjectives with which to characterize tastes and smells. Why should this be so?

One might be inclined to suppose that part of the explanation lies in the comparatively meagre and intermittent character of our experiences of tastes and smells. Certainly, we see and hear far more *continuously* than we taste and smell. But there is a better reason than this. It is not only that we have less *occasion* to talk about tastes and smells than of sounds and things seen, it is rather that, when we have reason to do this, we can do it most conveniently by reference to the various things which *have* the tastes and smells in question. For those things which do have tastes and smells have (on the whole) reasonably *characteristic* tastes and smells. For referring, for example, to the taste of an orange, we do not need an expression referring to the taste without mentioning the orange, since (a) this particular taste is not possessed by any common objects *except* oranges, and (b) almost all oranges have more or less exactly this taste. So also for smells. It is also partly for this reason that we say things *have* smells and tastes – they nearly always taste and smell roughly the same – and we do not need to say merely that they give off, make, convey, etc., a taste or a smell – perhaps different tastes and smells on different occasions. (Of course we do sometimes say that things emit or give off smells; and if they do this with sufficiently troublesome vigour, we call in a verb – we say that they stink, or reek.) On the other hand, almost any object may make, or be concerned in the making of, a wide variety of sounds, and most sounds may also be made by a very wide variety of objects. Hence, such an expression as 'the sound of a dog' would seldom be of much use – do we mean barking, growling, whining, scratching, pattering, bumping, howling, or what? And most of these sounds are in any case not specially associated with dogs. Accordingly, since most sounds are not *characteristic* of particular sorts of things, we need a number of ways of referring to sounds without reference to the things that make them – a number of nouns for particular sounds;

but we have no such good reason for requiring a lot of nouns for tastes and smells. (If different sorts of things were hardly ever similar in colour, it would be reasonable to expect that one way of referring to colours might be by way of reference to the things that had them. But as it is, in *this* respect, colours are more like sounds than like tastes or smells.)

6. We have, then, a very large number of words for sounds; and though we have few (if any) words for particular tastes and smells, we do still have the words 'taste' and 'smell'. But for seeing, though we use a few partially analogous words in special circumstances, we have no similar *general* word; and for touching we have no similar words at all. I want now to say that these linguistic facts reflect certain straightforward but very important *non*-linguistic facts – that in this case, as of course in other cases, how language is serves to remind us of how things are. There are three connected points to be made:

(1) that we *identify* common objects predominantly by the sense of sight;

(2) that (if necessary) we make sure that an object is 'really there' by the sense of touch; and

(3) that by the use of both these senses together we not only *judge* distances, shapes, sizes and positions, but acquire by them our spatial concepts.

(1) I take it that the *fact* that we identify common objects mostly by the sense of sight will not be disputed. But perhaps I should try to make it clear how this fact bears on the linguistic facts (or vice versa). Here there are two points.

(a) Since a predominant use of the sense of sight is for the purpose of identifying *things* (or, we may add, events and states of affairs), it is only to be expected that the question 'What do you see?' is *normally, naturally* to be answered by mentioning the name of some thing, or referring to some event or state of affairs. This is what the sense of sight is *for*. To answer with some expression analogous with 'sounds' (if there were one), i.e. to answer *without* mentioning or attempting to mention any physical object, would be to refrain from putting the sense of sight to its predominant use; it should not therefore seem at all surprising that we have no standard linguistic means for supplying a general answer of this kind. *Of course* we do not have linguistic devices for doing things which we do not wish in the least to do. On the other hand, if I am asked what I *hear*, certainly I may, and often I would, mention by way of answer some physical object; but very often I might be quite unable to do this – so many things might be making the sound that I hear – and in any case it is not normally by *hearing* that we expect to identify physical objects. Hence we have, and we need to have, some normal way of answering without mentioning or seeking to mention any physical object, i.e. we have a large number of words for sounds.

(b) If I say that I hear the sound *of* a car, I am claiming that the sound I can hear is made by, or comes from, a car. And, clearly enough, in saying this I imply that there is something, a car, which is identifiable *independently* of what I hear, of the sound that it makes. I may be quite sure about the sound, but prepared to regard as still open to question whether it is, as I say it is, made by a car. And of course this open question is not answerable solely by more assiduous listening – I can look and *see* whether there is in fact a car making this sound. It is by hearing such sounds and also seeing cars that I come to be able to *recognize* such sounds as being of cars. Thus, when we make use of non-thing nouns such as 'sound' and 'smell', and report the perception of the sounds and smells of things, there is the implication that the presence and identity of these things would be decisively established by other means. So that *of course* there are, for the verbs 'see' and 'touch', no non-thing nouns as objects, like 'sound' and 'smell'; for we could not in saying what we see or touch use a form of words with the implication that *other* sensory means would be better and more decisive.

Here it is worth comparing such expressions as 'a deafening racket' or 'a pungent aroma', expressions whose application *is* determined by the senses of hearing and smell. For the expressions 'sound of' and 'smell of' now becomes wholly out of place. The implications in the phrase 'the *sound* of a deafening racket' – namely that something *other* than hearing would establish the actual occurrence of a deafening racket – renders the phrase an obvious otiosity. So also for the phrase 'the smell of a pungent aroma'. The aroma just *is* what I smell, as what I see when I see a bus is the bus itself. I do not smell the *smell* of an aroma to be otherwise identified; nor do I see (say) the '*look*' of something whose identity or existence is to be established in some other and better way.

(2) I take it again that argument will not be needed to establish the *fact* that, if we seem to see something and yet wonder whether it is really there, we call in (if possible) the sense of touch. If we seem to see a dagger but have our doubts, we naturally proceed to say 'Come, let me clutch thee'; and we make up our minds according to whether we touch (say) a dagger, a painted canvas, a mirror, or nothing. Touching, it is clear, is not of very

much use in the tasks of identification, of recognition; even quite small things, and still more obviously large things, are difficult or impossible to identify by this means alone; and with objects out of reach we cannot even begin. However, the sense of sight is notoriously liable to all sorts of tricks and vagaries, illusions, deceptions, and delusions; and touching is not only less fallible – it is *peculiarly* well suited to the business of deciding such questions as whether there is, as there may seem to be, a dagger before me. For I regard my own body (of course) as a physical object; and if I do see, as I seem to see, a dagger, then this object will be able to act on, bump into, resist, be clutched by, that other physical object, my hand. We have in our own limbs a conveniently mobile physical object which, by bumping about among other physical objects, enables us to tell that there *really are* such objects about us. We do not thus learn much of what *sort* of objects these are (though if we are blind we may come to know a good deal); but *that* there really are such objects is shown by the occurrence of physical contacts. Incidentally, our limbs would still be serviceable for this purpose even if we were wholly or partly insensitive; for we can *see* (and sometimes hear) our limbs touching things, as well as having the ordinary sensations. This special importance of touching shows itself, I think, in the fact that material things (which may *of course* be tasteless, odourless, and soundless) could conceivably be also invisible, but could *not* conceivably be intangible. We seem to understand well enough stories about real but quite invisible men, but stories about visible but intangible men would not be about *real* men, but about ghosts, or visions, or simulacra of men.

(3) I want to put forward a few remarks about the senses and space, spatial properties and positions. The sense of taste is here in a curious position. For either we have simply (as we say) a taste in our mouths, from which we learn nothing of the whereabouts of that thing (if there is such a thing) whose taste it is; or we actually have the *thing* in our mouths, and hence know exactly where it is by the sense of touch. But in either case it is obvious enough that the sense of taste is of no use for locating things or finding our way about. Sounds and smells are not quite so useless; but still they are not very much use. Smells in particular are apt to be drifting, diffused, and pervasive; even the sensitive nose of a foxhound is easily defeated by wind, or by a confused but directionless concentration of scents. *We* are in any case far less alive to smells, and would almost always have great difficulty in tracking an object down by smell alone. Most smells, to our detecting, do not carry very far. Most sounds carry further, but still not *very* far, and here there are other serious limitations. As we noted before, few sounds are specially *characteristic* of particular things;

and sounds go round corners, they too are subject to distortion by wind, and they interfere with one another. They are on the whole poor guides to the position, and still poorer guides to the character, of their sources. We do not have a clear and distinct, highly discriminable 'auditory field'. We can, for instance, count the players in an orchestra easily enough by looking at them, and tell where the violas or the clarinets are seated; but only a prodigy in specially favourable circumstances could do the same thing with his eyes shut. We ought, I think, to *emphasize* the enormous differences between the behaviour of sounds and the behaviour of light, for of course they are of great practical importance to us. If seeing were to be at all really like hearing, there would have to occur at least these five major disasters – (a) the atmosphere would have to become so dense that no ordinary light could penetrate very far through it; (b) light would have to lose the property of travelling in straight lines; (c) most surfaces would have to be fairly efficient mirrors; (d) most objects would have to become to some extent transparent; and (e) there would have to be no continuous sources of light like the sun or moon, but intermittent flashes, gleams, glares and glows from all around us. This *is* exactly how sounds behave. They do not carry very far; they go round corners; they go through walls; they are reflected from almost any surface; and they are highly intermittent. It is thus no whim or caprice of ours that we attach far more importance to the sense of sight. We should indeed be in a nasty mess if light began to behave as sounds now do.

Finally, consider these two suppositions. If we could taste and hear and smell, but neither feel nor see, it is (I believe) clear that we should form no concepts of space, of distance or shape or size or movement or position; hence we should form no concepts in any way resembling our concepts of physical objects. If, on the other hand, we could see and feel, but neither hear nor taste nor smell, we should be worse off undoubtedly, but not so wholly and fantastically worse off as before. Our problems would be practical ones; how to keep out of the way of cars and avalanches, how to attract the attention of people looking away from us, and so on. Our general concepts of space, shape, position, and even our concepts of particular physical objects, would not be seriously affected. There is really nothing very strange in the notion of odourless and silent aeroplanes, rivers or people; so long as we can see these things and touch them, we could get along without very much change. We might well hear sounds, smell smells, and taste tastes and have no conception of any 'external', material world; if, however, we see and feel, this need not be so. For it *is* the external world that we see and touch; it *is* by sight and touch that we get the ideas of externality, of position in space, of shapes and sizes and movement.

7. Finally, I want very briefly to consider the question whether we could *invent* a pair of new nouns, to stand to 'see' and 'touch' as 'sound' stands to 'hear'. Now I suppose we could do this, up to a point and in a way. We could certainly devise two new words, say 'visa' and 'tacta', and assign to them suitable grammatical constructions. 'We see visa' and 'We touch tacta' become necessary truths. We see the visa, and touch the tacta, *of* things. Visible things are said to *have* (rather, I think, than to *make*) visa, and tangible things are said to have tacta. Presumably any number of people may see the same visa and touch the same tacta, just as any number of people may hear the same sound; and presumably the *esse* of visa and tacta is not *percipi*, any more than it is of sounds or tastes or smells. So far (conceivably) so good. But I think a difficulty must arise in the following way. Suppose I say 'I can see the visum of cats in the garden.' Now if I had said 'I can hear the noise of cats in the garden', I might have been asked 'How do you know? How do you know it's the noise of *cats*? Lots of things after all might make a noise like that.' And here I can say 'I know that it's cats, because I saw them all in the garden a moment ago.' But now let us ask the analogous question – 'How do you know? How do you know it's the visum of cats? Lots of things might have visa exactly like that.' In reply to this, it seems to me we have to take one of two courses. We might feel constrained, wrongly I suppose, to admit that we never *really* know – we only see visa and yet more visa, we only touch tacta, we can never get to grips with or really witness the very things themselves; or else we reply, as I think we should reply, that seeing visa of cats does settle the question that there are *cats*, and that touching the tacta as well makes this absolutely certain. But this is to say that seeing visa is really not at all like hearing sounds, but *is exactly* like what we now call seeing things. The question, what the visa we see are the visa *of*, is not regarded as a question which may always be seriously asked – inevitably, for if it *is* seriously asked, there appears to be no way of answering it. So what is the *point* of our new phrase 'seeing visa'? If the *fact* is that the senses of sight and touch predominate enormously over the other senses, so that their verdict on what there is about us is normally taken to be decisive, there cannot be any point whatever in attempting to assimilate the uses of 'see' and 'touch' to those of 'hear', and 'taste', and 'smell', in attempting, that is, to make our language conceal this predominance. For either it really conceals it, and we come to think that material things have escaped us and all is uncertain;

or it fails to conceal it, and then we see that there is no point in the change. To say that we see only visa of cats is perilously like saying that we see only *signs* of bread; to say the second is indeed to say something false, whereas to say the first is to say something neologistic; but all the same, the neologism is either wrong in the same way, or without point.

I suggest two general morals. The first is that, when we undertake to write about 'perception', we ought not to discourse, as philosophers seem strangely prone to do, exclusively about seeing; or to write as if human beings had only one sense (perhaps without even making clear what sort of sense that is supposed to be); or as if (recognizing that humans have more than one sense) one sense is very much like another – all being used in 'perceiving'. And specifically, if for any reason one wishes to deny that people are 'directly aware' of material things, it is injudicious to attempt to support that denial by comparing seeing with hearing; for that comparison tends in fact to exactly the opposite conclusion. Other modes of arguing may be efficacious for the purpose, but not that one.

3

Seeing

It is in some ways an unfortunate fact that many, perhaps most, of those philosophers who have written about perception have in fact been primarily interested in knowledge – in the principles of human knowledge, in our knowledge of the external world, in the foundations of empirical knowledge. It may be that the theory of knowledge presents more interesting problems than perception does, but in discussing them perception itself cannot be ignored, and ought not to be treated in too perfunctory a manner. In this paper I wish to call attention to some points about seeing which have not perhaps been sufficiently remarked. Indeed, in the discussions of perceiving, observing, sensing, apprehending and the rest, it appears that simple seeing has often been neglected.

In the actual employment of the verb 'to see' there appears at first sight to be a mere chaos of constructions and indeed of categories. In the case of most transitive verbs there are fairly clear and fairly close restrictions on the types of expressions which can properly occur as their objects, or on the other constructions, if any, by which they can be followed. By contrast one is inclined to say[1] that one may be said to see at least (1) things (not necessarily material objects); (2) events, happenings, performances; (3)

---

[1] I say only that one is *inclined* to say this, since it is not clearly a proper thing to say. One may say that, e.g., I saw the colour of his tie, that the colour of his tie is a quality of his tie, and hence that I saw a quality; or that I saw the untidiness of his room, i.e., the untidy state of his room, and hence that I saw a state. But the reverse argument that one may see a quality, that redness is a quality, and hence that one may see redness, seems to lead to an uncomfortable conclusion. Similarly, that one may see the relation between the windows and the door suggests that one may see a relation, but one does not wish to say that one sees, say, proximity. The rather bald expressions in the text should be interpreted in terms of the various constructions which we do employ, not as licensing constructions which we do not. The need for caution here was pointed out to me by Mr H. P. Grice, to whom I am indebted also at many other points.

From *Proceedings of the Aristotelian Society*, NS vol. LV, 1954–55.

qualities; (4) relations; (5) states or conditions; and (6) facts (including negative facts). One may further be said to see where things are, how things are done or how to do things, why things happen, and whether things are happening. The list is not exhaustive, but it seems to me to be already extensive enough to make it clear that the verb 'to see' is in some way an oddity; we need to investigate its seeming grammatical and categorical sprawl. It will appear also that the implications of its uses are by no means simple.

I

1. Consider first the statement that I once saw Lloyd George. Now if we take Lloyd George to have been what H. A. Prichard used to call a body, this statement entails that on at least one occasion I saw a body. It is now relevant to consider one of the reasons for which Prichard, and others, used to maintain that such a statement 'will not stand examination'. It was urged that, if ever a body were 'really seen', it would necessarily appear as it really was; there are however admittedly cases in which this is not so, and, by a rather indefinite appeal to some sort of 'continuity', it was concluded that in no case is it really so. Similarly C. D. Broad has maintained (in *Philosophy*, January 1952) that 'in view of the continuity between the most normal and the most abnormal cases of seeing', it is necessary to conclude that in no case at all is seeing really 'prehensive of bodies', or of the surfaces of bodies; and it appears that this conclusion is taken to refute any ordinary claim to see a body, at least as that claim would be commonly understood.

If I understand these arguments rightly, they turn on the point that, if A really prehends (or apprehends) X, it is impossible that X should appear to him as it is not; I am not sure whether it would have been asserted also, what is not the same thing, that it is impossible that A should take X to be what it is not. Broad appears to incline to this latter assertion, since he does not think it clearly mistaken to suggest that 'prehending might properly be described as a form of "knowing" '; but Prichard, at some apparent risk of inconsistency, maintains that we do habitually *mis*take the entities that we apprehend for bodies. However, we need not settle this point precisely; for it is in any case now possible to conclude that seeing is in fact neither prehending nor apprehending, nor is it commonly thought to be so. For, so far from its being impossible that, if I really saw Lloyd George, he should have appeared to me otherwise than he really was, perhaps impossible also that I should have been mistaken as to his identity or character, there is no need to deny that I saw Lloyd George even if every possible mistake[2] were actually made, or even if he appeared in the most unnatural guise.

Suppose for example, that I saw Lloyd George standing lost in meditation in Madame Tussaud's, and mistook him for a wax model of Winston Churchill; suppose, if you like, that he was actually pretending to be a wax model of Winston Churchill, and had disguised himself for the purpose; there would be in all this no reason at all to deny that I then saw Lloyd George. For to say that I saw Lloyd George does not entail either that I was then, or that I am now, able to describe his appearance correctly or even at all, that at the time I identified him correctly or even at all; it does not entail that he appeared to me to be Lloyd George, or that he appeared as Lloyd George normally did. Certainly if I now say that I saw Lloyd George, I do at least claim to have now, by whatever means and in spite of whatever disguises, identified as Lloyd George the person that I saw; but others might truly say of me, even though I would not say of myself, that I saw Lloyd George, even if I have not now, and had not then, any notion that it was Lloyd George that I saw. We may consider a more extreme case still. Suppose that, when I saw Lloyd George, I made no mistake only through making no judgement whatever, that I was not misled by appearances only because I was not led by appearances at all; suppose that I was an infant in arms. Even so, so long as there is reason to hold that I did, as we might say, 'set eyes on' the man who was in fact Lloyd George, then there is reason to say that I saw him, even though I then neither made, nor could have made, any judgement at all, either right or wrong, about who or what it was that I saw.

2. I suspect that some philosophers have been misled in this matter by confining their attention to uses of the verb 'to see' in the present tense and the first person singular. It has been rightly emphasized that the statement that one sees, say, a fox, is true only if there is a fox to be seen, and if what is seen is actually a fox. It follows from this that I would myself ordinarily say that I see a fox only if I not only believe with some reason, but believe that I know, that what I see is a fox. But the question whether I actually do see a fox is not the same question as whether I myself would say

[2] This is, I fear, a rhetorical exaggeration. Mistakes exceeding a certain degree of wildness would justify the view that I was the victim of hallucination or in some other way in no fit state to see things.

that I do. Not only might I falsely say that I do when I do not; others might truly say of me that I do, even though I would not say this or would actually deny it. If I say that I see a fox and am asked how I know that it is a fox, I cannot consistently say 'I don't know – perhaps it isn't'; but if I say of someone else that he sees a fox and am asked how he knows that it is a fox, I may properly say 'He doesn't know – he thinks it's a dog' – though of course I still imply that I know that it is a fox. Similarly with the past tense; if I now say that I saw a fox, although I thus purport to know now that it was a fox that I saw, I may quite properly deny that I knew this when I saw it. One who says that he sees purports to know; but one who does not know does not, for that reason, not see.

It is of course true that very often the best way to identify something, or to put one's self in a position to describe it correctly, is to see it, to have a look at it; it is however a mistake to suppose that seeing things essentially involves knowing, or getting to know, what they are, or what they are like, or even how they appear.

3. We must now consider some of the qualifications required by this rather bald conclusion. We need not go into the question whether it is necessary that one who is to be said to see should have eyes (though of course it is in any case a highly important fact that we do have eyes, that we have two of them, that they are as they are, and that they both point the same way); for without answering this question, we may say for a start that one who sees must have a field of vision, and that what he may rightly be said to see must be in it. Now what more than this ought we to say?

(a) The obvious point that one who sees must not only have his eyes open and in working order, but must also be conscious, is not quite so simple as it might seem. The infant of whom we say rightly that he saw Lloyd George doubtless set eyes on him in a normal, though non-adult, condition of consciousness; it is however clearly not necessary that the condition of consciousness should be normal. The taker of mescalin presumably sees what he looks at; but the open-eyed sleep-walker presumably does not; and there is room for many intermediate conditions. How far, then, may one deviate from normal conditions of consciousness without its for that reason being called in question whether one sees those things on which one's eyes are set? I do not know what can be said in general on this point, if anything can; it may be that only *ad hoc*, and probably sometimes rather arbitrary, decisions are possible for particular cases.

(b) It would, I imagine, be easily admitted, though some philosophers have seemed to deny, that the truth of the statement that Jones saw a fox is not impugned by Jones' misidentification of what he saw, nor by his failing either to identify or misidentify it, nor by his being mistaken as to its character or qualities. But, it might be said, not only must one who sees be conscious, he must in some way and degree be conscious *of* what he sees. If Jones sees a fox, he must at least be conscious of a – perhaps by him unidentified and unconsidered – *something* in his field of vision; if not, it must surely be absurd to say that he sees it.

Now let us widen the scope of this question by bringing in the notion of noticing. 'Notice' appears to have at least two (relevant) uses; roughly, it means sometimes 'to be struck by', sometimes 'to pick out'. Suppose that I am asked 'Did you notice his tie?', in a context such that the question suggests that there was something noteworthy about it. Now I might be in no doubt that I did see his tie, but if I was not particularly struck by and perhaps cannot recall anything about it, I might answer the question in the words 'No, not particularly.' On the other hand, if asked 'Did you see Lloyd George?' (e.g., in the audience) I might reply that I did not, for the reason that I had not noticed him, picked him out in the crowd. It seems to me to follow from this that it scarcely makes sense to ask *in general* whether one who sees also notices. It is, I suppose, not inconceivable that a person should be of so enthusiastic or sensitively observant a nature that he noticed, was in some degree struck by, absolutely everything that he saw; but this is certainly not the common case, and indeed one might say that for most of us there is, about most of the things that we see, simply nothing to notice (particularly). It is even clearer that not every case of seeing is a case of picking something out; in this sense, when for instance one sees a large building from close at hand, one neither notices it nor fails to do so. Thus, when it is true that X saw Y, the question whether X noticed Y may, not be in place at all; if it is in place, the answer may be 'Yes' or 'No', depending on the sense in which the question is to be understood.

What then of 'being conscious of'? Clearly there are some cases, and some senses, in which one may be said to see what one is not conscious of. One may, for instance, be quite unconscious of the dust on one's furniture, idiomatically 'blind' to it, but one need not be said not to see it; one may indeed become unconscious of it precisely because one sees it so often. I think too that it would be intelligible to say that someone's attention was occupied so exclusively with, e.g., what he was listening to, that he was quite unconscious of what he saw; perhaps also one may be said sometimes to remember seeing something that one was not conscious of at the time. But in absolutely ordinary cases the question is certainly obscure and perhaps unreal; if I report that Jones saw Lloyd George at a meeting yesterday, what could prompt you to ask me 'Was Jones conscious of him?' If Jones were an ambitious Liberal of the appropriate date, it might indeed be said of him that he was agreeably conscious of his leader's presence in the front row; but one is not in this sense conscious of all that one sees, nor indeed is it necessary that one should see what one is thus conscious of. I suspect that, if there is a sense of 'being conscious of' so different from that of 'noticing' that one is in general and always conscious of what one sees, it is such that it is to be simply analytic that what one sees one is conscious of; but whether there is any utility in such a sense seems to me doubtful. One might be inclined to sponsor such a use of 'conscious of' in the hope of evading an apparent dilemma: if one abandons, as clearly one must abandon, the idea that one who sees must have actual knowledge of what is before his eyes, it may appear that seeing is in peril of becoming attenuated to the object's merely being before his eyes; it is however a mere physical fact that this is so, and it is rightly felt that seeing must amount to more than this. At this point, then, one may be inclined to say that one must be conscious of what one sees, thus bringing in more than the thing's merely being before one's eyes, yet less than one's having actual knowledge of it. This is, however, too obscure to be the solution of any difficulty, and should be regarded only as an incentive to the examination of particular cases. Certainly, if someone appears to be, and later sincerely asserts that he was, unconscious of something clearly before his eyes, there must always be a serious question whether he saw it; but such cases will differ, and we should not assume that in all it must be impossible so to explain his being unconscious of it as not necessarily to exclude saying also that he saw it.

(c) There is a variety of curious questions which might be raised about the thing seen, turning upon the question, where this is appropriate, *how much* of it must be seen for it to be true that simply the thing itself is seen. It used at one time to be urged that one never sees, at a given moment, the whole of any object at which one looks, and hence that one cannot be said simply to see it. This contention appears to overlook the seeing of, for example, rainbows. More seriously, it seems to confuse seeing only part of (the proper contrast with the whole of) an object, with seeing it only from one point of view – seeing only Lloyd George's left leg, for example, with seeing him only from the side. This is not unimportant, for whereas one might well hesitate to say that one had seen Lloyd George if one had seen, unfortunately, only his left leg, one would not so hesitate if one had seen him, naturally enough, only from one's place in the auditorium. It would be minute and tedious to elaborate this question very far; I would like to make only four general comments upon it. (i) It is clearly not in general necessary that one should see the whole of what one sees, even in cases where to speak thus is appropriate, for it to be simply true that one sees it. I have never seen the whole of Blenheim Palace, but there is no question that I have seen it. (ii) It is important to bear in mind the conditions in which particular types of things are customarily seen. We are accustomed to seeing people, for instance, partly covered by clothing, but do not feel inclined, since this is how we ordinarily see them, to complain that we see only part of them. Even if they were totally covered up, still, so long as what they were covered with was clothing or at least something commonly worn such as armour, we might say that we had seen them without qualification. The case would be altered if they were encased in boxes, particularly if these were quite rigid, and it is of course different also for objects which are not ordinarily covered at all. (iii) Some parts of some objects are more significant than others. One would be readier to say simply that one had seen Lloyd George, if one had seen only his face, than if one had seen only his feet. (iv) The question what it is proper to say will often depend also on the conversational context. For example, where the task is to find some object, it will not mislead to say that one sees it as soon as one has located it; but where the interest is in an object's appearance, inability to give an account of this might call for qualification of the claim to have seen it. Thus, if one were trying to locate the cricket pavilion on a very dark night, one might say that one saw it (implying 'Now I know where it is') on seeing only a very small though recognizable part; but if one had seen only the top left-hand corner of a painting otherwise completely covered, to say simply that one had seen it (suggesting 'I know what it looks like') would be improper. This is not of course to say that inability to describe an object's appearance is *always* a reason for qualifying the claim to have seen it.

So far, we have been considering the seeing of things, objects – not necessarily, of course, material objects. The case of seeing happenings, events, occurrences must be briefly dealt with, and in any case is similar in most respects, not quite in all. If, for example, I say truly that Smith saw the robbery committed, it does not follow that he then knew, or now knows, that that is what he saw happening, that any robbery was committed. He may have failed to realize, or perhaps not particularly noticed, what was going on; if so, he will not be a good witness to the event, but he still was a witness of it – he did see it happen. Again, one might properly say that the only witness of some occurrence was, unluckily, an infant, who had no idea what was going on and could not give any account of what he saw. The only important new point, I think, is this: one may not only fail to realize the nature of, or fail to notice, an event that occurs before one's eyes – it may be that the event occurs too quickly to be seen at all; so that even if warned and watching, and although the event does certainly occur before one, one cannot say that one sees it happen, or happening. It might reasonably be suggested, however, that there is an analogue to this in the case of an object which is in one's field of vision too briefly to be seen; in such a case it is clear that one simply does not see it; it is not a case of seeing but failing to notice. The conjuror sometimes eludes one's vigilance by diverting one's attention; but sometimes the quickness of the hand defeats the eye.

The argument so far can be summed up as follows. In any of the cases so far considered, we may take it that, if it is to be true that A saw X, then at least A must have set eyes on X, being conscious and with eyes in reasonable working order. It may in some cases be further required that A should have noticed X, picked X out; but this point does not arise in every case; and certainly it cannot be always required that A should have taken particular note of X. It may be that in some sense – which deserves more consideration than I have given it – it must be true that A was conscious of X; however, there is certainly *a* sense in which this is not necessary. It is in no case necessary that A should have identified X, or made a correct judgement of X's character or qualities, or even that he should have known how X appeared to him; on this last point, one might say vaguely that he always could have known this, but certainly he need not actually have done so.

It seems to me that these contentions have often been denied, perhaps inadvertently, and indeed that they must be denied in most attempts to exhibit seeing as consisting in, or even including, any sort of 'apprehending' or 'direct awareness'; for these latter expressions have commonly been defined by reference to what the percipient knows, in some cases 'incorrigibly', to be true. One who sees, however, need not know anything at all.

II

1. The case is radically altered when we pass to the other constructions which I listed at the beginning. This is most obviously so in the case of (6), the seeing of facts; and this case can usefully be contrasted with those that

we have just been considering. Suppose that I, who do not play chess, and a competent chess-player are watching together a game in progress. It is clear that, in the senses so far considered, he sees what I see, no more and no less; we both see the board, the pieces, the players, the movements made. But suppose that at a certain stage of the game my companion sees that White's bishop is dangerously exposed. Now although in a sense I still see what he sees, I certainly do not see this; and clearly the reason for saying that I do not see it is that I do not realize, and in my ignorance am not in a position to realize, that the piece in question is dangerously exposed. The facts that it is so, and that I have a good view of the game in which that is true, do not together add up to my seeing that it is so; for in this there would be essentially involved my noticing, realizing, getting to know that it is so. Nor, if I later learn how to play chess, can I say retrospectively that I saw White's bishop was dangerously exposed; for I did not realize this at the time, and hence did not then see it.

One can say 'I saw a fox but I did not know that it was one', or 'He sees a fox but he does not know that it is one.' By contrast one cannot say either 'I saw that it was raining but I did not realize that it was', or 'He sees that it is raining but he does not realize that it is.'

2. Now of the other cases not yet considered I think one can say, not only that they share this feature, but also that they share it in virtue of being essentially variants of the same case. Consider a simple case of what we called, with hesitation, seeing a quality, for example seeing the colour of Lloyd George's tie. It is clear that one could not rightly say that one saw the colour of his tie, if one did not get to know at the time what colour it was. At first sight this might seem anomalous. Why, one might ask, if I can rightly say that I saw the tie though I did not know what it was, can I not say that I saw the colour of the tie though I did not realize what it was? I imagine that the answer to this question – the question why we should speak in this way – would be that, unless I noticed the colour of his tie and hence knew what colour it was, there would be no point in making particular mention of the colour in saying what I saw. Similarly, there would be no point in asking the particular question 'Did you see the colour of his tie?', if an affirmative answer to this question were compatible with the answerer's not knowing what colour it was. It is worth noticing that, if asked whether one could see, say, the shape of a building, it would be natural to reply in the words 'No, I could not really *tell* from where I was standing.' It would by contrast be plainly outrageous to reply 'Yes, but I could not tell what shape it was.'

Similar considerations apply to the seeing of relations, and states or conditions. To say 'I thought he was a very tidy person until I saw the state of his room' is clearly to imply that I saw *that* his room was untidy; the point of making particular mention of the *state* of his room would be lost unless I meant to convey that I got to know what his room was like. Similarly, a newly immigrant Eskimo taken on a tour of my garden might certainly be said to see my garden, but hardly the neglected condition of my garden; for his general ignorance of gardens would preclude him from realizing that it was, by comparison with other gardens, neglected. An expert who looks at the engine of a car might possibly see its condition at a glance, but I, though I see the same engine, do not see this. Again, suppose that an architect directs one's attention to the relation between the upper and lower windows of a façade; if one does not know what he has in mind, what exactly it is that he sees to be true of these windows, one would be guilty of some dishonesty if one claimed to see the relation in question. One might indeed say simply 'No, I don't see it.'

We may simplify the remaining cases by saying briefly: to see why the engine stopped is to see *that* it stopped for a particular reason; to see where the fault was is to see *that* it was in a particular place; to see how to cure it is to see *that* it could be cured in a particular way; to see whether there is petrol in the tank is to see *that* there is some (or is not). In effect, in all these instances alike it is the 'see that . . .' construction which must be regarded as fundamental. It thus becomes important to examine this construction more closely. Perhaps it will be useful to consider the ways in which a claim to see that so-and-so might be attacked, since this should serve to bring out what it is that is claimed.

3. First, then, and very obviously, any such claim might be attacked by denying or questioning the fact alleged in the subordinate clause. If for instance I say 'I had hoped to have a word with Jones, but I see that he isn't here', I would be conclusively shown to have been mistaken if it were shown that in fact Jones was present. One cannot claim or be said to see that *p*, if not-*p*, just as in such a case one cannot rightly claim or be said to know that *p*; and this is of course more than a chance analogy.

Next, such a claim might be attacked on the ground that although what one claims to see to be the case is the case, yet one does not know that it is the case. Suppose that I say 'I saw at once that he was seriously ill.' It might be objected that I had not in fact realized this. 'You did nothing about it for days; I don't believe you knew'; or that I lacked the necessary qualifications – 'You're not a doctor; how could you have told that he was seriously ill?'; or that nobody could have known – 'There weren't any particular symptoms at that time'; or again, that I ought not to speak so confidently – 'You couldn't possibly have been sure.' It is not in these cases disputed either that I saw him, or that he was ill; it is contended that, when I saw him, I did not or could not have *known*, and hence did not see, that he was ill.

Slightly different from this is the further objection that, although what one claims to see to be the case is the case, and although one may know that it is the case, still one does not *see* that it is the case. For example: 'You knew he was ill from what the nurse told you; there weren't any visible symptoms.' Similarly, if someone were to make the absurd remark 'I see that the moon is 250,000 miles away' (and were to say this as if making a judgement of distance by eye, not reporting something that he had read), it would not be necessary to question either the fact or his knowledge of the fact; the absurdity would consist in the impossibility of discovering, or even estimating, just by looking, the distance away of such a distant object.

Thus the claim to see that *p* – *mutatis mutandis* for other tenses – appears to involve (i) that *p* is the case; (ii) that the claimant knows that *p* is the case; (iii) that there are in what he sees sufficient grounds for concluding that *p*; and (iv) that he so concludes on those grounds.

4. It will be advisable to correct at once a possible wrong impression that might be conveyed by speaking, almost unavoidably, of 'grounds' and 'conclusions'. We tend, no doubt, and in general quite properly, to think of the grounds for a conclusion as being appreciably different from the conclusion, and of a conclusion as being drawn, reached, or arrived at, after at least some thought. In the discussion of seeing that *p*, however, all this may be inappropriate. The 'ground' for saying, for instance, 'I saw that he was mowing the lawn' may be simply that one saw him mowing the lawn; and in such a case that he was mowing the lawn would not be a 'conclusion' drawn at length or with difficulty – nor, one might add, arrived at by inference. If the question be raised why in this case one should bother to say 'I saw that he was mowing the lawn' at all, when one might have said simply 'I saw him mowing the lawn', an important part of the answer would be that, however verbally alike, these constructions may have very different conversational points. Roughly, if what is of concern is what happened to the lawn, the former construction is the more natural; if what is of concern is what he was doing, then the latter. There would often be hardly anything to choose between them, but this is not to say that there would never be any reason to pick one rather than the other.

Furthermore, in spite of the close verbal similarity between 'I saw that he was mowing the lawn' and 'I saw him mowing the lawn', there are important logical differences. Certainly neither sentence entails the other. For if he had a very strange sort of mowing machine I might see him mowing the lawn without seeing that that was what he was doing; and I might possibly, on seeing, say, cut grass flying into the air on the other side of a wall, be justified in saying that I saw that he was mowing the lawn, though it would scarcely be proper to say that I saw him mowing it.

Of course the 'conclusion' *may* sometimes be quite remote from the 'grounds'. For example, on seeing chairs, tables, crockery, etc., being carried out into my neighbour's garden at about 4 p.m., I might say 'I see that they're going to have tea in the garden.' On seeing the flag at half-mast I might say 'I see that someone has died.' And there is also the rather special case of, for instance, seeing in the newspaper that income tax is to be raised.

5.   This last case raises a question of some interest. One can well imagine the protest being made 'But you don't literally *see* that income tax is to be raised.' But why not? It might be said that all one literally sees is that the paper says so. But what if the paper is absolutely reliable, so that one can reasonably claim to know that what it says is true? Or again it might be said that all one literally sees are the *words* 'Income tax is to be raised'. But does one not literally see that those words are on the page? And if one sees this and knows what they mean, does one not see that a certain assertion is made, and hence – if the paper is known to be reliable – that something is the case? Or if the extreme position is taken that one literally sees only black marks on a white ground, one might ask why, if these marks are in fact printed words, it should be non-literal to say that one sees the words. There is surely nothing non-literal in the statement that one sees, say, a drawing of Lloyd George, though this too may consist only of black marks on paper.

I believe that what this train of argument shows is not perhaps that it either is or is not correct to say that one literally sees that income tax is to be raised, but rather that the distinction here between literal and non-literal uses is less clear, or more arbitrary, than one might have supposed. No doubt it would be safe to say that such locutions as 'seeing the solution', 'seeing no hope', or 'seeing prosperity ahead' are simply visual metaphors, that here there is no question of literal seeing. One might on the other hand be tempted to say that only visible objects can be literally seen. To say this, however, is not safe at all; for it appears to entail that *all* cases of 'seeing that . . .' are cases only of metaphorical seeing; and this is too extreme. But if one accepts some such cases as cases of literal seeing, a series could be devised from these to the metaphorical cases a fair stretch of which would be indeterminate. To see Jones mowing his lawn gives so plain a reason for saying that he is mowing his lawn that one must surely concede that one literally sees that he is doing so; to see certain words in a newspaper gives a very different sort of reason for saying, for instance, that income tax is to be raised; but there are other sorts of reasons from which it is not so different, and it is also a reason which a blind man could not have.

It is less important, perhaps, to settle this question than to notice how this sort of doubt as to the propriety of saying 'I see that . . .' differs from other sorts. It might be objected that, whatever sort of reason seeing certain words in a newspaper may give, it in no case gives a sufficiently good reason for saying that one sees that income tax is to be raised. But to say this would be to object to the statement as being credulous, ill-founded, unwarranted, not as being non-literal. This is of course an entirely different objection, which would be rebutted, if at all, on quite different grounds; the dispute would concern, not linguistic propriety, but the strength of evidence.

My aim in this paper has been to call attention in the first instance to the wide variety of constructions in which the verb 'to see' can occur, and then to clarify so far as possible the complex and confusing picture thus displayed at first sight. I have concentrated mainly on establishing one distinction, which can be briefly summed up as follows. If there is a sense, as there is, in which we speak of the ability to see as a physical capacity, in which to be able to see better than others is not to enjoy any superiority of wits, skill, talent, or experience, then there must be a sense in which seeing does not involve the acquired abilities to identify, recognize, name, describe, and so on. The recruit to the Observer Corps must learn how to identify aircraft, but he is already as well able to see them as he ever will be. By contrast, if only the comparatively expert is able to see why the engine stopped, what is wrong with the carburettor, how to put it right, and so on, then there must be as it were another sort of seeing in which the wits are essentially exercised, which requires experience or judgement, talent or skill. There is on either side of this broad division considerable complexity and some flexibility, distinctions which should certainly not be neglected; but I believe that those distinctions are neither so great nor so sharp as is the main distinction itself, nor so liable to generate confusion, if they are ignored, in philosophical argument about perception and knowledge.

I would like to append two final remarks. First, it is clear that much of what I have said of seeing could *not* be truly said of hearing or smelling, tasting or feeling. And second, it is a curious fact that, if I am right, the familiar philosophical distinction between sensing and observing does not fit the case of seeing at all; for though there are doubtless many cases in which seeing is a good deal more than sensing, there are many also in which it is much less than observing.

4

Claims to Knowledge

In the first part of this paper my aim is to establish what is really not more than one point, both small and negative, about knowledge: in the second part I shall allude to a somewhat wider matter, of which my small negative point provides, if sound, a particular illustration.

I

I thing I am right in saying, and the title chosen for this paper might seem to confirm, that the idea is current that, if one is going to talk about knowledge, then it is particularly well to the point to talk about claims: it seems not uncommonly to be hinted, or even affirmed, that knowing and claiming in some way are near allied. Professor A. D. Woozley, in his paper called 'Knowing and Not Knowing' (*Proceedings of the Aristotelian Society*, 1952–53), is properly careful to distinguish knowing from claiming to know: but he seems often to imply that saying one knows, at any rate, is claiming to know; and at one point he goes so far as to say that he uses the phrase 'claim to know' as meaning the same as the phrase 'statement that one knows'. Professor A. R. White, in his paper called 'On Claiming to Know' (*Philosophical Review*, 1957), is more explicit. He says indeed in his last paragraph, 'I do not wish to say that "I know" is always used to make a claim'; but in his third paragraph he does say this, or something remarkably like it, viz., ' "I know" is used to make a claim': and in his last sentence he particularly desiderates 'a detailed investigation into the logic of claims', as likely to be specially pertinent to problems about knowing. All this seems to me misguided, and not quite trivially so.

It is, to begin with, so obvious as scarcely to be worth saying that knowing is not claiming, or making a claim. For to make a claim is *inter*

From *Proceedings of the Aristotelian Society*, supp. vol. XXXVI, 1962.

alia to say or do something – to say 'Mine', for instance, or to submit forms in triplicate – while to know something is not, either in itself or necessarily in its consequences, to say or do anything. One usually knows, for instance, what day of the week it is; but one quite seldom has occasion to say what day of the week it is, or that one knows this: and no doubt it is true that we all know many things which we have not spoken or even, perhaps, thought about for years and years – though, naturally, there is a certain difficulty in producing examples to support this. In any case it is, I take it, beyond dispute that one who knows that *p* may or may not have occasion to say that *p*, and may or may not have occasion to say that he knows that *p*. If he does have occasion to say that he knows that *p*, then perhaps he may in so saying be making some claim: but, if so, he makes the claim because (he thinks) he knows that *p*; his knowing that *p* neither consists in nor requires his making the claim.

But, it will be said, no one has ever been so absurd as to suggest that knowing just is making a claim, not even a thoroughly well justified claim; the connection between knowing and claiming has never been thought to be so peculiarly intimate as that; of course, claiming comes in only when one *says* that one knows, when one says 'I know . . .'. And this, no doubt, is what falls chiefly to be considered.

If, then, it is said that one who says 'I know . . .' is, thereby or therein, making a claim, we naturally wish to enquire what claim he is said to be making. Some recent texts, including that already cited, by Professor Woozley, seem to sponsor the idea that to say that one knows is to claim *to know*. We may consider this first, and some variant doctrines in due course.

Well, certainly to say that one knows may be to claim to know. In applying for a job, for instance, I may, in the words 'I know Russian', claim to know Russian: in conversation with a colleague I may claim to know, perhaps to have known for years, something which he is vaingloriously attempting to represent as a discovery of his own: in seeking to convince the court that I am indeed the long-lost heir, I may claim to know the names and personal peculiarities of long-dead members of the testator's family circle. In these cases (which differ from one another in familiar ways) to say 'I know . . .' would indeed be to make a claim – specifically, to claim to know something, or to claim that I know it.

But why is this? What is it about these cases of saying 'I know . . .' which makes my so saying a *claim* to know? Is the use of 'I know . . .' sufficient in itself to account for this, or is there some further claim-constituting feature in these cases?

I suggest that there is here a special claim-constituting feature. In claiming to know Russian in the circumstances supposed, I am not just saying that I know Russian, but positively demanding, or appealing for, *recognition* of this accomplishment by those to whom my words are addressed – on the ground, presumably, that they have professed to regard it as relevant to and desirable for the purpose in hand, and I wish to secure the job that is on offer. In claiming to know what my colleague retails as his own discovery, I demand recognition by the company of the fact that it is not news to me; I wish it to be known that I know, if only for the purpose of putting him in his place. In claiming to know the names of the testator's deceased relations, I wish the court to take note of and acknowledge this highly relevant circumstance – much as, indeed, in laying claim to the testator's estate, I am asking for the court's recognition of my title to it. In each of these cases in which I say 'I know . . .', the circumstances are such that I particularly wish it to be realized, or at least believed, that I know: that realization or belief will help me to get the job, put my colleague in his place or money in my purse; but further, if I am properly to be said to be claiming to know, it must be supposed that, in saying 'I know . . .', I am not merely giving my interlocutors to understand that I know but, so to speak, obtruding my putative knowledge upon their attention, demanding that it be recognized, that appropriate notice be taken of it by those concerned. Rather similarly, if in the words 'That's mine' I am *claiming* my umbrella, then I am not merely avowing or disclosing my ownership of it, but bringing my rights in the matter to the notice of my audience for the specific purpose of repossessing the umbrella.

But if so, it becomes obvious that there are many cases of an altogether different kind. If the police were to find my umbrella crushed beneath a battered corpse, so far from demanding recognition by them of the fact that it is mine, I might well be exceedingly reluctant to have that fact publicized; I would by no means hurry forward to claim my umbrella. When subsequently my finger-prints are identified on the handle and questions are asked, I may well be constrained to mumble 'Yes, it's mine'; but this is to make a reluctant admission, and not a claim. Rather similarly, when, standing trial with my confederate, I say 'Yes, I knew he had a gun, but I never thought he'd use it', I am not claiming knowledge of the fact that he had a gun: so far from demanding that the court take due note of this circumstance, it may well be no more than the certainty of being disbelieved that prevents me from posing as a stranger to this item of knowledge. I may be forced to admit, but I do not *claim*, that I knew. Guilty knowledge, after all, is scarcely a thing that a reasonable man would claim, though a scrupulous man might confess to it, an unwary man reveal it, or a cornered man be obliged to admit it. Less dramatically, I neither claim nor confess nor admit that I know when, offered some item of current news, I say 'Yes, I know'; it is hard to see what this case could be said to be, if not that of simply saying I know, just telling him I know, or that, in an old-fashioned phrase, 'I am not now to learn . . .'. This use, I find, is particularly common in conversation with or among children, who are both more eager than most adults are to impart information, and less attentive to the likely news-value of what they say; their interlocutors frequently have occasion to indicate that they were actually already possessed of the information purveyed.

Knowledge by me that *p*, then, may indeed be claimed in the words 'I know that *p*'; but it may also, in the same words, be admitted, confessed to, conceded, avowed, revealed, disclosed, or just asserted. Claiming to know is just one way of saying 'I know . . .', or rather is saying this in certain special circumstances for particular reasons. The question whether saying 'I know . . .' is claiming to know has nothing to do with the question whether the speaker does know, but only with the question why, to what end, and in what setting, he *says* he knows. Furthermore, that he says he *knows* is, in a sense, neither here nor there; that is, his saying just this specifies what claim it is that he is making, if indeed he is making a claim; but it does not establish that he is making any claim at all. He may be, of course, as may be one who says 'I am an Archduke'; but also he may be making a painful confession, a damaging admission, or just a casual remark.[1]

It may be noted here by the way that, if it is not the case that to say 'I know . . .' is necessarily to make a claim to know, then it is also not the case, as Professor White seems to hold that it is, that to say 'He knows . . .' is, always or characteristically, 'used to allow, endorse, or favourably judge' a claim. For one thing, one of whom we could rightly say 'He knows . . .' may

---

[1] I suspect that we sometimes say of someone that he claimed to know when, although he did not envisage himself as making a claim, as parading his knowledge for recognition, *we* wish to deny that, or raise the question whether, he *did* know. To say that he *claimed* . . . is to call attention to the possibility, and perhaps the imminence, of an objection. There is, of course, a dialectical point in doing this, and I suggest below that the case is of some relevance here: but it seems, strictly, a bit dishonest to represent a speaker retrospectively as having made a claim when perhaps nothing whatever in the circumstances in which he spoke justifies this description of what he did. When the police witness says of me 'He alleged . . .', I feel some understandable resentment if all I did was to say 'I live here'.

never have had occasion to say 'I know . . .', and may for that reason have proffered no claim to knowledge for our endorsement or appraisal. I may say, 'He knows that no courses on theatrical designing are available in this university', not on the ground that he has laid claim to possession of this piece of information and I judge his claim a sound one, but on the ground that I, knowing the ropes, have told him that such courses are not available, and suppose my statement to have been neither forgotten nor disbelieved; I told him, he took my point, and so now he knows. But further, even if he has had occasion to say 'I know . . .', yet, since he may not thereby have been making a claim, we may not be in any position to be endorsing (etc.) a claim when we say 'He knows . . .'. The MP says to his local committee, 'I know that, since I have abandoned the CND, you no longer regard me as an acceptable representative, but I have no intention whatever of resigning my seat'; the naïve constituent, eager for a change, says 'He must be told that we no longer want him as our representative'; and the better-informed committee-man replies 'He knows.' In so saying he does not endorse a claim made by the MP; he intimates, on the strength of his own admission, that the MP is not unaware of the fact which his constituent urges should be brought to his attention.

It may be noted also that, just as Professor White's account of 'He knows . . .' is not right in all cases, Professor Woozley's account, to which he opposes it, is not in all cases wrong. Professor Woozley holds, as reported by Professor White, that to say 'He knows . . .' is not to endorse, but to make, a claim, namely the claim that he knows; and so, not always of course, but sometimes, it is. If I say proudly of my schoolboy son, 'He knows the dates of every important battle in English history', I make a claim which not only, perhaps, has he never made for himself, but which he may well be too modest, or too candid, ever to have thought of making. Professor White, in fact, himself refers to this sort of case, but seems to maintain that it does not really count – it is not, I think he means, *the typical* use of 'He knows . . .'. Well, perhaps not; but such a use is at least entirely legitimate; and is the claim-endorsing case, which of course also does occur, any *more* typical? Is there really such a thing as *the* typical case?

However, as was noted above, some may say that the relation between knowing and claiming should be differently conceived. To say that one knows, it may be said, is indeed not always, not necessarily, to claim *to know*, but it is all the same to make a claim of some kind. This must be considered.

Well, do I perhaps, in saying that I know that *p*, claim that *p*? 'I know that *p*', it might be argued, does entail that *p*; so, in saying that I know that *p*, I must, perhaps by implication, be claiming that p. But it is plain enough that there is not much sense in this. That I am claiming that p is not in any way established by the fact that I say something which entails that p. It is unhappily true for one thing, though scarcely relevant here, that one may be unaware of what one's remarks entail; and one could hardly be said to claim that a proposition was true which, perhaps, one had never entertained at all. But suppose that I say, 'I know his mother was a Russian, but I regard his loyalty to the Parish Council as unquestionable': I am thereby committed, of course, to the proposition that his mother was Russian, and of this I could scarcely, in the circumstances, be unaware; all the same, it is plain that I am not, however implicitly, *claiming* that his mother was Russian. I am conceding the point to his, or perhaps to my, possible critics, and letting it be understood that I have not, in appraising his loyalty, overlooked it. Or suppose that I say, 'I know how anxious you are to help, but really I'd rather try to manage on my own'; my words certainly entail that you are anxious to help, but this is not *claimed*; it is rather, perhaps simple-mindedly, assumed, accepted, or taken for granted, in what I say.

In saying 'I know that p', then, I am not necessarily claiming that p – though, indeed, I may be. Am I then claiming the right to affirm that p, or to be sure that p, or to be an authoritative spokesman on the question whether p or not-p? To know that p, as has often and very properly been contended, is not just to be completely confident in the view that p, nor yet is it to be this with the further proviso that 'p' be true. One knows that p only if one's confidence in the truth that p is well-grounded or justified, only if one is properly entitled to be sure that p, has the right and not merely the readiness to affirm that p. This question of entitlement or justification must, or at any rate may, always come up, for only thus is knowledge to be distinguished from full and – perhaps just luckily – correct conviction. But, it may here be said, that one is entitled to or justified in the view that p is precisely the sort of thing that one could and would *claim*: this is not only very like, but in a sense actually is, the claiming of a right, the demand for due recognition; is there not, then, always *this* claim – the claim to be justified or entitled – made, 'implicitly' if you like, in saying that one knows?

A moment's thought, however, will show that even this, which has some slight plausibility, is not really correct. It is, perhaps with marginal qualifications, true enough that one knows that p only if, *inter alia*, one has some sufficient ground or justification – which however one may not always be able to state – for one's view that p. But that one must, if one knows that p, have some such ground is very far from requiring the conclusion that, in saying that one knows that p, one must be claiming that one has it. If I say to you sceptically, after some discussion of the matter, 'Do you *know* that this medicine is harmless to children?' and you reply, 'Yes, I do', then perhaps you are thereby claiming, in the face of my implied dubiety, to be justified in believing and pronouncing the stuff to be harmless. But if the historian says, 'I know that Napoleon was of less than average height, but I question the relevance of that fact to his military career', he is surely not claiming to be, but taking for granted, assuming, or presupposing that he is, justified in the view that Napoleon was of less than average height. Certainly I might argue that he was not so justified, and therefore that at least he should not have said 'I know that . . .'; but to argue thus, in such a setting, would be to question or attack an assumption, not to oppose a claim. If an informative stranger tells me that there are philosophers in Oxford and I reply 'Yes, I know', I am not, I think, claiming, but quietly exercising, the right to be sure that what he says is indeed the case. To claim them, in short, is not all that we ever do with the rights we have.

I venture to suggest, then, that no good reason can really be produced for supposing that 'a detailed investigation into the logic of claims' would be particularly helpful with problems about knowledge. Such an investigation might certainly be illustrated from the case of knowledge, since knowledge is undoubtedly among the immense variety of things which can be claimed; but why come at it in this way? Is there any reason why the chronicler of umbrellas should devote particular attention to the business of *claiming* umbrellas? The central topic, it would seem, should be the question what to know something is, what 'knowing' means; the question whether possession of a given item of putative knowledge is, on this or that occasion, claimed or disclosed, admitted or avowed, presupposed or advertised, seems to be by comparison neither here nor there.

Not indeed that it would be uninteresting, or not worth the trouble to raise the question what these diverse performances are and how they differ from each other: far from it: but this question has nothing in particular to do with *knowledge*. That one is a vegetarian, no less than that one knows that the earth is round and the sun will rise to-morrow, can be claimed, confessed, disputed, admitted, or revealed – depending, roughly speaking, on the course and tactical exigencies of the tract of discourse in which allusion to that fact may occur. The question what it is to claim to know has actually two parts – What is it to *know*? What is it to *claim*? – both excellent questions but not, I think, intimately related.

II

I come now to the wider matter, which, I think, this business about knowing and claiming illustrates. The confused notion, as I take it to be, that the making of claims is *specially* pertinent to problems about knowledge derives in large part, I think, from a more general, and perhaps more prevalent, confusion in the notion of the *use* of words – in particular from loose, though not in all respects unbeneficial, talk about how words 'work', about their 'jobs', about how people 'operate' with them, and so on.[2]

That, at some period in the fairly recent past, philosophers by degrees began to talk less and less about the meaning or analysis, and more and more about the use or uses of words and phrases, is by now a familiar story. I think that there can be no doubt that this trend was beneficial. The philosopher wedded to the metaphor of analysis was perhaps, among other things, liable to take too seriously the attendant images of constructions and their parts, wholes and their elements, of taking things to pieces and putting them together again. The philosopher zealous in the pursuit of meanings seems to have been prone to engage in a form of inward gazing and groping which made it nearly impossible for him to find what he was in search of. By contrast, the question how a word or phrase is used seems calculated at least to get the enquirer facing in the right direction, looking for his quarry where he has some prospect of finding it, namely, among actual uses of the word or phrase in question. It may be added that the notion of the *use* of a word or phrase is somewhat wider, comprises more, than the notion of its *meaning*; and since it may sometimes be just this extra bit that is really interesting, it is as well not to have it excluded by one's terms of reference.

In spite of these benefits, however, and in spite of occasional cautionary utterances by individuals, it seems to me that the use made of the notion of use has been often uncertain, and at times is still regrettably confused. One might say that the notion has proved to be over-accommodating: one may discuss, under the general rubric 'how the word is used', the meaning of a word, what is typically or characteristically done in or by its use, what is deviantly or fortuitously done in or by certain uses of it, or even for what

---

[2] My sketchy remarks on this topic are derived entirely, I hope not distortingly, from the late Professor Austin's systematic investigations of 'speech-acts', or of what he sometimes called the *forces* of utterances as distinct from their meanings.

purpose it is used, with what end in view or to what intended effect; and since these quite different matters may all be discussed under the same general rubric, it has been insufficiently remarked that they are quite different. The possible permutations and combinations of confusion between them are very numerous; but I will here mention only two, which are perhaps the most prevalent.

First, there appears to me to have been a tendency for the question, how some word or phrase is used, to be discussed and dealt with in some *one* of its numerous aspects or senses, and thereafter for the assumption to be tacitly made that the question, how that word or phrase is used, has been comprehensively answered. For example (not an uncontroversial example), it has been very properly observed that the word 'true' is used in executing a variety of linguistic performances – in indicating agreement or acceptance, in corroborating or confirming, in admitting or conceding, and (rather differently) in expressing favourable appraisal of statements and some other things. Now these are undeniably ways in which the word is used. But some who have said so, quite correctly, seem thereupon either to have overlooked the existence of the – on the face of it – quite different question, what the word *means*; or perhaps to have supposed that they have actually answered this question; or even, perhaps, that since they have already explained 'how the word is used', there simply cannot be any *further* question to be asked. It is true, of course, that a distinction between the question what a word or phrase means, and the question what is or may be done by one who uses it, cannot well be drawn in every case; to say, for instance, what the words 'I promise' mean, and what is standardly done by one who utters those words, seem to come to the same, namely, to saying what is to make a promise. But this is the special case of a phrase or formula designed (as one may say) specially, and employed solely, for the execution of a quite specific linguistic peformance; and there are comparatively few words or phrases of which this is true. Far more commonly, the question what some word or phrase means is quite clearly distinguishable from the question what one who uses it is, or may be, doing thereby; it is not the whole truth about the word 'imbecile' that it is often employed as a term of abuse, or about 'virtuous' that it is commonly a term of tepid praise. Now it might be that the predicative phrase 'is true' has *no* meaning in any sense which can be distinguished from its use or function as an indication of agreement (etc.); but this seems implausible, and has never, I believe, been seriously argued for; the question what its meaning may be has, I suspect, tended to be crowded out by concentration on its 'use' in another sense or other senses, and by the notion that description of its use in this sense or those senses *completely* answers the question how the phrase is used.

Secondly, I believe that there has also been a tendency for some features of *one* species of the 'use' of words to be, unwittingly and erroneously, transferred to another. Philosophers who have discussed, for instance, the words 'good' and 'ought' have often held, and probably rightly held, that these words are not ambiguous; they do not, in diverse standard contexts, have different *meanings;* in this sense, then, one might say that they do not have, in this context or that, different uses. But from this point there seems quite often to have occurred an unnoticed transition to the view that these words have just one use, in the quite different sense that there is just one thing which one who uses those words thereby does. Thus, one finds it apparently maintained that one who uses the word 'good' is, specifically and always, *commending,* or that 'ought' always gives expression to a *recommendation.* Now it is in general exceedingly unlikely that any word should have, in *this* sense, only one use; there are very few words of which this is true; and it seems to me likely that the tendency to believe, and even obstinately to maintain in the teeth of plain counter-examples, that in this sense 'good' and 'ought' have just one use apiece is due to failure to distinguish their use in this sense, from their use in that other sense which involves their – as is plausibly supposed – non-multiple *meanings.* It is perhaps felt, and quite wrongly felt, that to admit that the words 'good' and 'ought' may be used in doing a quite wide variety of different (thought probably not unrelated) things would be to open the door to the properly unwelcome contention that they have many meanings; but it would not be; a term that is used in just one way, that is, with one meaning, may quite well be used in many different ways, that is, to do or in doing many different things.

But now to return to the case of knowing and claiming. Those who have recently taken to speaking as if claiming were in some way *specially* germane to knowing, and as if the study of claiming would illuminate knowing in some way, have, I would conjecture, not abstained from either of the types of confusion I have just baldly outlined. They may have been tempted to suppose that, since the term 'know', at least in the locution 'know that . . .', is not ambiguous, then it must have one, or at any rate one central and dominant, use; it must 'work ' (as Professor White puts it) in just one way, namely, in a 'claim-making rôle'. At least, I cannot see why it should have been supposed that the locution 'I know that . . .' has just this one – or even this one central and dominant – use, *unless* this idea had been confused with, or not properly distinguished from, the quite correct view that the phrase in question has one standard meaning. Rather similarly, the suggestion that a general study of claim-making would illuminate knowing in some way may, I think, owe something to the idea that, since making claims is a use of 'I know that . . .', a study of that activity would be a study of the use, in the sense of the *meaning*, of 'I know that . . .'. But it would not be; two quite different senses of 'use' are involved here; and the one has nothing (in particular) to do with the other.

One point remains to be, perhaps rather speculatively, explained. Why should it have been the case that, among the actual wide variety of things which one who says 'I know that . . .' may in so saying be doing, philosophers should have been prone to pick on *claiming* to the exclusion of all else?

Presumably they have wished to have some way of referring to actual or possible uses of the words 'I know that . . .' which would leave open the question whether the actual or possible speaker of these words *does* know that. . . . This would be reasonable enough; and it is certainly the case that, while I can say that *A* claimed to know that *p* and then myself either assert or deny that he did know that *p*, if I say that *A* admitted, confessed, or disclosed that he knew that *p*, I thereby debar myself from denying that he knew that *p*. For, roughly speaking, only truths can be admitted, confessed to, or disclosed (which does not mean, of course, that everything incorporated in seriously proffered admissions, confessions, or disclosures is true). But the need for the non-committal style of reference to uses of the words 'I know that . . .' is scarcely sufficient to explain why claiming alone should be picked on; for assuming, presupposing, taking for granted, alleging, avowing, stating, asserting, and just *saying* that one knows that *p* are, on the question whether one does know that *p*, every bit as non-committal as claiming is.

What more, then? It is not, I think, that uses of 'I know that . . .' to make, or in making, claims are in general more common, more typical, more central, etc., than are uses of those words to do, or in doing, quite other things; I can see, as I have said, no reason to suppose that that is true. But what *is* perhaps true is that claim-making uses are typical of the situations in which philosophers pass much of their time. For most philosophers professionally, and some no doubt temperamentally, are addicted to disputation; when they think about knowledge, they think naturally of plain men unguardedly, rival theorists ambitiously, or pupils with timidity laying claims to knowledge, and of other philosophers, perhaps themselves, subtly insinuating or proving that those claims are without foundation – they envisage an *argument*. They do not think, understandably enough, of that vast and perhaps philosophically unexciting territory in which communication, not disputation, is ordinarily conducted, and in which knowledge, if alluded to at all, does not need to be claimed since its possession is not in dispute. A philosopher's saying that 'I know . . .' is for making claims is rather like a garage-hand's saying that water is for cooling engines; one can see why it is said, but one should note that it is not the whole story.

5

'Every Event has a Cause'

I

There is obviously something strange about the sentence 'Every event has a cause.' It is natural enough that there should sometimes be disagreement over the question whether some statement is true or false. Less commonly, but still understandably, there occur disputes about what some sentences mean, or whether they really mean anything. But in this case the situation is more complicated. Some in saying that every event has a cause (or in using more or less sophisticated variants of this) have believed without question that they were making a true statement. Others have adduced from widely diverse fields considerations which lead them to say that it is false. But views quite different from either of these have been put forward. It has been held that the statement that every event has a cause is not merely true in fact, but *necessarily* true; also that, though perhaps it is not in the ordinary way necessarily true, it is yet in some special way *unquestionable*; and also, perhaps most paradoxically, that despite appearances it is neither a true statement nor a false one, neither necessary nor unquestionable – indeed not a statement at all, but a kind of maxim, or precept, or exhortation. All this seems to show that the sentence 'Every event has a cause' is not understood as clearly as could be wished; for if it were understood it should surely be possible to decide whether what it says is contingent or necessary; or at least whether one who utters it is making a statement, adopting or commending a maxim, issuing an exhortation or expressing a resolution. Or perhaps it would be found that he is doing none of these things.

From *Logic and Language,* Second Series, ed. A. G. N. Flew (Blackwell, 1953).

II

Those who have argued the question whether it is true or false to say that every event has a cause were often, certainly, at cross purposes. The motive for maintaining that it was true was usually the belief that every event is an instance of some scientific law, or law of nature, and could thus in principle at least be causally explained. And the motive for maintaining the contrary was not primarily the belief that this was not the case, but rather the conviction that at least some happenings can be explained by reference to the intentions, choices, and decisions of intelligent and responsible beings, or 'agents'. The contention that some events have no causes was sponsored on the assumption that only if this were so could it really be held that some events occur *because* responsible beings choose or decide to act in certain ways. However, it is by no means a clearly correct assumption that explanation of an event in terms of an agent's decision must exclude the possibility of giving a causal explanation of it as well. In order to maintain that the occupant of the next room *decided* to turn on the lights it is not necessary, nor indeed is it possible, to deny that their lighting up was an ordinary instance of the laws of electricity. And to say that the golf-ball finished short of the green because the player wanted to keep out of the bunkers does not make it either incorrect or impossible to explain its flight in terms of the elasticity of ball and club-face, the velocity of impact, and the state of atmosphere and ground.

III

This particular dispute might be continued into many further complications; but it has sometimes been swept aside as wholly misguided and inappropriate. It is, it has been argued, quite mistaken to ask whether it is true or false that every event has a cause, or what would be the consequences of affirming or denying its truth; for the alleged statement in dispute is not really a statement at all, so that questions of truth and falsity do not arise. Kant for example (in criticizing certain metaphysical arguments about a First Cause) found difficulties both in the claim that the alleged statement was true, and also in the assertion that it was false; and accordingly suggested that it must be regarded as an *injunction* to extend the search for causes as far as possible, and to seek always to make more coherent and comprehensive our formulations of natural laws.[1] Earlier, however, he had himself written as if the law of causation were a necessary truth; and indeed it does not seem at all to resemble what would ordinarily be thought of as maxims, injunctions, or rules. 'Do not rely on defective apparatus'; 'Do not draw general conclusions from a few observations made in unfavourable conditions'; or (cf. Darwin) 'Always pay special attention to instances apparently contradicting your hypotheses' – these for example would naturally be regarded as maxims for scientists, hints on how to succeed. To attempt to formulate coherent and comprehensive statements of law, on the other hand, seems to be rather what scientists actually do (almost, what scientists do *by definition*) than something which they should be enjoined or encouraged to do. To affirm the law of causation would be, on this view, to urge them to carry on with their activities, not to give them maxims or tips on how to succeed. And in any case, although one who says that every event has a cause would naturally be regarded as thereby *displaying* determination to carry on the search for laws, or perhaps as urging his audience not to give up, it is still the natural view to take that he is *stating* that, if he or they persist, success will be achieved. It at least looks as if he were urging the continued search for laws only by way of stating that there are in every field natural laws to be found. There is thus no case for adopting this Kantian view, unless the natural belief that we are dealing with some kind of statement turns out to be utterly untenable; and if if turns out to be untenable, the statement-like form 'Every event has a cause' must be abandoned as muddling.

IV

Some others who have held that it is out of place to argue about the truth or falsity of this alleged statement have, I think, had the idea that the law of causation is to the natural sciences what the laws of logic are to deductive disciplines. It is in this sense, I believe, that one must understand the contention that this law is and must be 'presupposed' in all scientific investigation – that it must be accepted and cannot sensibly (or 'rationally') be questioned. It might be urged that, just as one cannot profitably engage in deductive argument without accepting rules specifying the difference between valid and invalid reasoning, so one cannot engage in scientific inquiry without accepting the law of causation. Put thus, how-

[1] *Critique of Pure Reason*, A498 (B526).

ever, this contention looks obviously wrong. The proper analogy would be that between the laws of logic and the canons of inductive argument. The pursuit of scientific inquiry certainly requires pretty general agreement on the difference between good evidence and bad, between well-established conclusions and rash hypotheses, between properly conducted tests and random gropings. But the law of causation has not much to do with this. For one who wishes to reject this law need not, it would seem, deny that the grounds offered in support of most scientific conclusions are adequate; he need only maintain that there are or very well might be some cases in which no similar conclusions can be reached. This is certainly to reject the common assumption that the canons of inductive argument must be regarded as worthless unless one also accepts the law of causation; but this assumption is surely mistaken. It amounts to suggesting that the canons of inductive argument essentially require the guarantee, or at least the presupposition, that their observance will in principle always ensure success; but they do not in fact require so much as this. One might well recognize that to pay assiduous attention to inductive evidence is the best thing that one can do in attempting to formulate statements of law, and yet not assume that there are no cases at all in which the best attempts would be utterly baffled. It is probably true that most people who use inductive arguments do assume, or perhaps half-unconsciously take for granted, that if they try hard enough they will succeed in their quest; but it is not by any means *necessary* that they should assume this. One might well continue to do the best that one could, with failure accepted as a constant lurking possibility; and certainly one might accept without any disquiet the idea that inquirers in other fields might always fail. H. W. B. Joseph's assertion that to accept this idea is to 'despair of reason and thought' is dramatic, but an exaggeration.[2] Failure and despair in some cases are compatible with optimism and success in others.

So far, then, we have noted that the sentence 'Every event has a cause' has (often for extraneous and dubious reasons) given rise to debates about whether, as a statement, it is true or false; that it has been held to express a sort of precept or injunction – a paradoxical claim on which we suspended judgement; and that it has been held to be 'unquestionable' by rational persons who wish to use inductive arguments – a suggestion that we have rejected. I wish now to examine the suggestion with which I shall be mainly concerned – the suggestion, namely, that the statement that every event has a cause is *synthetic a priori*, a *synthetic necessary truth*. I hope that in

---

[2] *Introduction to Logic* (1906), p. 420.

the assessment of this suggestion the main source, or sources, of the difficulty will be discovered.

V

The question of synthetic necessary truth has been for some time a storm-centre in philosophy. That there should be disagreement here is understandable; but it seems that this question engages the emotions also. This is, I think, because upon this issue philosophers of sharply different casts of mind, however they may agree on this point or that, find themselves strongly inclined to take opposite sides. It appears to matter enormously which side is taken, and as if, here at least, the line between two opposing camps were clearly drawn out. This however is, most strikingly, not the case. Those who aver that there are synthetic necessary truths are apt to put forward the baffling contention that by some sort of insight, or intellectual gazing, we can see that some truths of fact are necessary truths; while those who contend that no synthetic truths are necessary maintain the hardly less cloudy doctrine that truths of fact can only be based on, and so might at any time be or might have been falsified by, Experience. These are large issues, and they excite strong feelings; but we must not at once range ourselves with one party or the other. Nothing but confusion can result (as it has often resulted) from considering this topic in wholly general terms, or from assuming that, whenever a claim to synthetic necessary truth is made or denied, some simple and single question is presented for decision.

To the sorts of statements which are most comfortably called synthetic it is natural also to apply such predicates as 'contingent', 'factual', 'empirical', or '*a posteriori*'; and we expect the contradictories of these to be of exactly the same logical character. To expressions naturally regarded as analytic we are apt to attach also such predicates as 'logically necessary', 'true by definition', and '*a priori*'; and here we expect the contradictories to be logically impossible, self-contradictory. We would hesitate to say that a statement was quite ordinarily synthetic unless it appeared also to rank as contingent, factual, and empirical; we feel uneasy in labelling an expression 'analytic' unless we can show that it is somehow necessary, true by definition; and we expect the normal behaviour of contradictories. Thus, if one refuses to submit to this dichotomy and seeks to bridge it by the phrase 'synthetic *a priori*', one's refusal may be due to a variety of discomforts. Perhaps the statement that it is proposed to call synthetic *a priori* is, though not analytic, not contingent either; perhaps it appears to be empirical but not *a posteriori*; it may seem to be necessary but not true by definition, or logically necessary and factual at the same time. The notions involved in all this are numerous, related no doubt, but nevertheless diverse. There is accordingly scope for a good many difficulties in the customary attempt to divide all significant indicative sentences into two classes; there is no good reason to suppose that in all cases we can effect a single, orderly, exhaustive, and satisfying classification; and so there are correspondingly numerous and various reasons for clutching at some such straw as 'synthetic *a priori*'. Or perhaps it resembles a smoke-screen rather than a straw; the phrase is nobody's salvation, but it serves to cloak many a tangle behind the lines.

In this case we shall consider the claim made for the sentence 'Every event has a cause', without insisting that what is said of this case has necessarily any application to other cases, and allowing that other sentences for which this claim is made may well require a very different treatment.

VI

First we must try to make clear what is or might be involved in the claim that the law of causation is a synthetic *a priori* truth. For saying that it is synthetic there seem to be two (related) reasons. First, the sentence 'Every event has a cause' cannot plausibly be represented as analytic; it is not like 'Every bicycle has two wheels.' For whereas, in giving the meaning of the word 'bicycle' it would be necessary to make it clear that a bicycle has two wheels, it does not seem that, in defining the word 'event', it would be correct or necessary to stipulate that every event has a cause. There is no definition of 'event' by the help of which 'Every event has a cause' can be transformed into a manifest tautology. Conversely, the sentence 'Some events have no causes' is not self-contradictory. H. A. Prichard, indeed, claimed that to realize the truth of the law of causation we need only consider what we mean by 'a physical event'; but this is for several reasons peculiar.[3] His claim was intended, but even if correct would fail, to support the idea that this law is synthetic *a priori*; it does not in any case seem to be true that 'having a cause' is part of what is *meant* by 'a physical event'; and there seems to be no good reason why the events of which the

---

[3] *Kant's Theory of Knowledge* (1909), p. 300.

law says that every one has a cause should be only *physical* events. However, the point at present is only this – that it seems impossible to hold that 'Every event has a cause' is analytic, tautologous, true by definition; and this inclines us to conclude that it must be synthetic. For if it is not analytic what else could it be?

A second reason for inclining to this conclusion is that the law of causation appears to make a statement, and indeed a fundamentally important statement, about the course of nature – about what actually occurs in the universe we inhabit. It does not appear merely to illustrate, or to analyse, what we mean by the word 'event', but rather to say something of enormous importance about the way things actually are. Is it not a fundamental fact about the universe that we find in it the rule of law?

Such, then, are the main considerations that may lead us to say that the law of causation is a synthetic statement. Some would say that, if we allow these considerations to have weight, we thereby make it impossible to hold that the law is also *a priori*; for it is sometimes argued that the expression '*a priori*' can only mean the very same as 'analytic', and hence that the expression 'synthetic *a priori*' is self-contradictory. This contention, however, is not acceptable. There may be reasons, even if not good reasons, for saying that some statements are synthetic *a priori*, and it is unhelpful, whatever suspicions we may have, to dismiss this suggestion at the outset as logically absurd; but also it is by no means obvious that 'analytic' and '*a priori*' do mean the same. Neither term is in fact quite unambiguous, but the first seems to be somewhat narrower than the second. Certainly, if we define the term 'analytic' so that only those sentences are rightly so called which can, with the help of definitions, be transformed into formal tautologies, it will be an error to hold that only analytic sentences are *a priori*. For there are sentences (e.g. 'Nothing can be red and green all over') which it would be natural and proper to regard as *a priori* – anyone who knows English knows that they are necessarily true – but which cannot be shown to be tautologous by the use of *definitions*. In a sense, certainly, they owe their necessary truth to linguistic rules; but the rules governing the use of 'red' and 'green' cannot be expressed as definitions. But quite apart from such cases as these, there are, reasons for holding that 'analytic' and '*a priori*' do not mean the same. For to say of a statement that it is true *a priori* is to say that it can be seen or shown to be true without appeal to empirical evidence or tests; and though it might be that this could rightly be said only of expressions that are in fact analytic, still to say this would not be to say the very same thing as is said when we say that those expressions are analytic. I suggest, then, that those who say that the law of causation is, as well as a synthetic, an *a priori* truth, may be taken to mean that what it states about the course of nature can be seen to be true without appeal to empirical evidence; or perhaps (though this as will be seen is a very different matter) that we can see that no empirical evidence against it could be found. There is no denying that this is a curious claim. If the law really tells us something about the course of nature, surely we must find out whether or not it is true by discovering what the course of nature actually is; and surely there must be something that could count against it – namely nature's not pursuing the course that the law says that nature does in fact pursue. Certainly the claim is strange; but it is worth examining.

In what follows I shall try to show that, although there are considerations that might incline us to say that the law of causation is true *a priori*, these considerations in fact cancel completely the reasons that there seemed to be for saying that the law was a synthetic statement. This is not to say that the expression 'synthetic *a priori*' is in general and in every case self-contradictory (though I think it is always unhelpful); it is only to say that, in the present instance, the case for applying the predicate 'synthetic' is destroyed by the case for applying the predicate '*a priori*'; there may be a case for each, but not for both at once.

VII

As a preliminary move it will be desirable to rephrase the sentence 'Every event has a cause.' For this sentence has many rather misleading features, some of which (by no means all) it will be helpful here to eliminate. It is in particular, as has often been pointed out, misleading to suggest that for any event there is some *one* other event to be described, and alone described, as its cause. Suppose, for example, that I cause my house to collapse by improvidently removing an oak beam from the cellar. Although we should no doubt ordinarily say that it collapsed *because* I thus interfered with its structure, it is obvious enough that it would not have collapsed unless the whole house was actually so constructed as to depend for its stability upon this beam. It was thus not merely my removal of the beam which occasioned its collapse, but this removal combined with the other structural features of the house. A full account of the disaster would have to include an account of these other features, as well as the statement that the beam was removed – just as a full report on an outbreak of fire would have to include an account of the inflammable materials in the area and perhaps of the conditions of atmosphere, as well as the statement that a cigarette was dropped into a waste-paper basket. The event in question (the collapse, the outbreak of fire) occurred because certain quite complex conditions were present; from these we might, as we often do, pick out as *the* cause that which was brought about immediately before the event occured, or (sometimes) that which was unusual. (It might be said that my house collapsed *when* I removed the beam *because* I had taken to storing several tons of books in the attic.) But not uncommonly it is pointless or impossible to pick out any one occurrence as *the* cause of an event – not because the event is random or inexplicable or mysterious, but because there is no case for stressing any one in particular of the numerous conditions sufficient for its occurrence. What is important is that there should *be* conditions sufficient for its occurrence, not that it should be always possible to select some one of these as the single cause; and the statement that every event has a cause does not, presumably, claim that this is always possible. (If it did so it would be clearly synthetic, and false.)

Suppose, then, that we re-write the sentence 'Every event has a cause' in some such way as this: 'For any event E, there is some set of antecedent conditions such that, whenever these conditions obtain, an event of the kind E occurs.' (I refer to this hereafter as S.)

This is still a comparatively unsophisticated formula, and it might be criticized on various grounds which, however, are here of no great importance. Some might say that it fails to distinguish between causal and coincidental connections – might it not happen, by sheer coincidence, that whenever certain conditions obtain a certain kind of event occurs? This version allows also the possibility that more than one set of conditions may be sufficient for the occurrence of some kinds of events, and it might be held that ideally this should be ruled out. It might also be said that, at least in some of the sciences, there is no reason for being specially interested in antecedent conditions; what we require are statements of law permitting inference from any state of a given system at any time to its state at any other time, with no special bias towards prediction or interest in the future. It might be held, too, that the vague word 'event' should be eliminated as ill-suited to scientific exactitude. All these are reasonable points in their way; but I think there is at present no reason why we should seek to translate 'Every event has a cause' into a form and vocabulary acceptable to scientists; for in the present argument nothing turns on this. The version adopted above will serve well enough, though I certainly would not deny that it might be improved upon.

VIII

Suppose one were to ask how the alleged statement S is to be verified; this
at once brings out one curious feature of it. First, it is in a comparatively
ordinary way of unrestricted generality. It appears to make a statement
about any and every event that ever occurred, occurs, or will occur. It
might thus be thought that, while we have no doubt some reason for
inclining to the view that S is true, we could not possibly have good reason
for affirming positively that it is true. How could we rightly venture to
make positive assertions about absolutely every event? But then there is
worse still to come. For it will be seen that S also makes a statement of
unrestricted generality about each of an unrestricted number of events –
namely that for each event there are conditions such that, whenever they
obtain, an event of that kind occurs. It would thus seem that causal
statements really are, as all empirical statements were once supposed to
be, indefinitely vulnerable to time. If we say that conditions ABC are
sufficient for the occurrence of an event E (or that A, or B, or C, is the
cause of E), what we say now will have to be retracted if at any time these
conditions obtain and E does not occur. We can say 'There really was a
telephone here, but now it's vanished'; we cannot say 'This was the cause
of E, but now it isn't'. For to say that conditions ABC may now obtain and
event E not occur is to admit that we were wrong in saying earlier that
ABC were its sufficient conditions. It would thus appear that even
particular causal statements are indefinitely exposed to falsification; far
more so then the doubly general assertion that of every event some such
statement could be truly made. By this line of argument we might be led to
the view that it would be unpardonably rash, almost a mere act of faith, to
affirm S with confidence; one can understand why this affirmation is
made, but one cannot feel much confidence in its truth.

IX

But now there is quite another side to the case. Suppose that there are
indefinitely many cats, and that someone says (of all cats there ever were,
are, or will be) that every cat has a tail. Here we might say that there could
hardly be good reason for accepting this statement with confidence as true
– after all we can only actually inspect a finite and rather small number of

cats. Furthermore, we have no difficulty in saying what would show this universal statement to be false – namely the discovery of a cat without a tail – and such a discovery might be made at any time. Now it was suggested in the previous paragraph that S, being of doubly unrestricted generality, is doubly and indefinitely exposed to the risk of falsification. Suppose then that we now raise the question what would have to occur in order to establish that S is false?

A verbal answer – 'an uncaused event' – of course springs to mind. But this answer raises obvious difficulties. It is easy enough to imagine an event E, conditions sufficient for the occurrence of which have always been supposed to be ABC; and that some day these conditions may obtain and yet the event E does not occur. But clearly this has no tendency to falsify S. For it was said in S only that there are *some* conditions sufficient for the occurrence of any event; it was not specified what these conditions actually are in any instance, nor was it implied that anyone necessarily knows in any instance what conditions are sufficient. To say that there are some laws of nature does not imply that anyone knows, or indeed ever will know, what exactly they are. And thus the affirmation of S is compatible with the rejection of every particular statement of law, and every causal statement, that is or ever has been or will be asserted. If I say 'Someone now in this house has green hair', it can be shown that what I say is untrue; for everyone now in this house can be paraded and none observed to have green hair. But if I say 'There once was or is or will be, somewhere in the universe, a person who has green hair', I need never admit that I am wrong. For it could never be said that every part of the universe at every possible date had been inspected and found to contain no green-haired person. Similarly, if I were to say 'Some set of the conditions ABCDF is sufficient for the occurrence of E', it could be shown that I am mistaken. For all of the finite number of combinations could be tried and none found to be sufficient for the occurrence of E. But if I merely affirm that there are *some* conditions, and do not delimit the area of search for them at all, I need never admit that I am mistaken. For it could never be said that every conceivable factor and set of factors that might be conditions of E had been tried and rejected; and so it could always be said that the right combination of conditions had not yet been found.

Thus, there could never occur any event which it would be necessary, or even natural, to describe as an uncaused event. (There are of course events whose causes are not known.) It could never be said that among its complex and indefinitely numerous antecedents *none* could be said to be sufficient for its occurrence. And this is to say that nothing could occur which would require us to hold that S is false. Whatever occurred we might still affirm that S.

It is in this way that S resembles a tautology, an *a priori* truth. It is completely independent of the actual course of events, compatible with anything and everything that does or might happen. It calls indeed for no supporting empirical evidence, for none could count against it. It cannot be empirically tested, for no test could fail – or rather nothing could be made to count as a test. But, clearly enough, if these points were brought to support the contention that S is *a priori*, they would tell conclusively against the claim that it is synthetic. For if S can be affirmed whatever may be the course of events, it says nothing of what the course of events in fact is. It does not tell us what we shall find in our experience, for whatever we find we may assert it without fear of mistake. This is not to say, what I think is plainly untrue, that S is tautologous or analytic. It resembles a tautology in being compatible with any and every state of affairs; but it escapes the possibility of falsification not because it is necessary, but rather because it is vacuous. It is more like the assertion that there are invisible, intangible, odourless, soundless, and otherwise indetectable tigers in the garden – though it is less conspicuously vacuous than this, the reasons for its unfalsifiability being different and much less obvious.

X

All this, I think, shows that there must be something wrong with, for example, the sort of argument that Kant brings in favour of the view that S (or something like S) is a synthetic *a priori* truth.[4] Very roughly, the argument is that S lays down what is almost a defining property of human experience – unless it were the case that every event has a cause, our experience would be so unimaginably different that we could not think or speak about it in any way, there would merely be chaos and confusion. Thus, it might be contended, the fact that we can *say* that every event has a cause, and be understood, itself shows that what we say is actually the case; for if it were not, neither this nor anything else could intelligibly be said. This sort of argument is, I believe, an exaggeration of something interesting and important. It is true that if there were *too many* random, inexplicable, quite unforeseeable happenings, we should find ourselves not merely in practical but also in linguistic difficulties. If, for example, it

---

[4] *Critique of Pure Reason,* Second Analogy.

were the case that objects frequently changed colour in a seemingly quite random manner, we could no longer say what colour things really were, but only what colour they looked at some particular time; and this would be a nuisance, particularly in cases where colour is a criterion of identity. (There would then be no Cabbage Whites or Scarlet Ramblers.) And we could not say with confidence 'This is an apple' unless we could be sure that the object of which we spoke would behave and respond to treatment as apples do. What this shows, however, is that we could not speak and act as we do if there were *too much* disorder and chaos in our environment; it does not show that we could not tolerate any at all. Nor, of course, does it show that it must be *true* that every event has a cause; for, as we have seen, to affirm that S is compatible with any sort of happenings whatever. We would presumably be unable to speak and act as we now do if, though there were in fact conditions sufficient for the occurrence of any event, these conditions were too complex or too numerous for us to discover them. A world whose behaviour could only be rightly described in statements of law too complicated for us to formulate or comprehend would be, for our purposes, every bit as intractable as a world whose behaviour was merely random and chaotic – it would in fact be indistinguishable from such a world. There are, no doubt, some statements of fact about the world which would only be falsified by some radical change in the whole character of our experience; and it may be that some of these statements state conditions essential to the use of language (or at least to the use of any languages now used). If so, there will indeed be certain statements which, if they can be uttered at all, are thereby verified; for if their contradictories were true they could not be said. But the supposed statement that every event has a cause cannot rightly be regarded as a statement of this kind. It lays down no essential conditions; for it lays down nothing.

XI

The suggestion that the expression 'Every event has a cause' is – owing to the impossibility of describing any circumstance that could show it to be false – vacuous and utterly uninformative, may well cause some dissatisfaction. There is a natural feeling that it does say something, and furthermore something of the greatest importance. However, this feeling arises, I believe, from confusion. There are indeed certain matters of importance that abut, so to speak, on the territory of the law of causation;

but these important matters are its neighbours, not identical with it, nor yet are they its dependants. And thus they need neither be ignored nor rejected when the Law itself is accused of vacuousness.

It is, first of all, a patently important fact that there are many people nowadays who do seek for statements of law, who do not attempt to understand, control, or alter the course of events entirely by prayers or spells or ritual performances, and who do not merely wait indifferently for what may occur. This is an important, synthetic and true statement about what many people actually do. If they did not do this or did not do it with conviction, we might properly (not by saying 'Every event has a cause') urge or encourage them to persist in their inquiries. It is a different but equally important synthetic true statement that those who seek to formulate statements of law meet with considerable, and on the whole with constantly increasing, success. (Human beings might have been much less intelligent, and the course of events might have been much more complicated.) But to say that for every event there are some conditions sufficient for its occurrence is clearly not to say that people often succeed in discovering them, nor is it to say that none will constantly elude discovery; to say that every crime is committed by somebody is not to say that no criminals go undetected nor to say that the record of the police force is good. Again, to say that correct statements of law are 'simple' is clearly to say something synthetic; and as the physicists multiply 'fundamental particles' it may well cease to be regarded as true. (A single sort of 'corpuscle' or 'atom' is not, of course, nowadays thought to be enough for all purposes). It is also synthetic to say of natural laws that they are spatially and temporally invariant; and this also, I believe, is no longer universally taken to be the case. And that the sufficient conditions for any event are to be found within a certain limited area of space and among some quite small number of possibilities, though usually and no doubt reasonably assumed, is also clearly not necessarily true.

These, then, are some of the important matters which belong in the same area as the law of causation; and there are no doubt others. I believe that those who attach fundamental importance to the so-called rule of law often have in mind some of these, and do not mean merely to utter the vacuous phrase that 'every event has a cause'. Or rather they do not think of this phrase as vacuous. It suggests that the universe is like a well-ordered house where everything runs exactly to plan and up to time; there is nothing just random and therefore unintelligible; what seems inexplicable will one day be explained. Certainly there is, as a rule, an important disagreement between one who says, and one who denies, that every event has a cause; they *intend* at any rate, to state different things. But what they actually *say* cannot be plausibly represented as stating any of the important facts mentioned in the last paragraph; and confusion is apt to result from not noticing this. For whereas these facts are indeed important and interesting, they are not necessary facts; and if we confuse them with the vacuous law of causation, we may come to attach to them, with resulting bewilderment, the property of being invulnerable to falsification which properly attaches alone to that vacuous law.

XII

In conclusion, and with some trepidation, I must say something of the 'indeterminacy principle'; for it has often been said that, here at any rate, we find something that counts against the law of causation. It is extremely difficult for those who are not physicists to come to grips with this perplexing affair; and physicists often seem to feel a similar difficulty. The suggestion that I would offer is merely this – that although certain features of quantum physics might make it even more than usually *pointless* to insist that every event has a cause, they could not establish that this is actually a false statement. To support this I submit the following considerations. It may be that, given certain conditions, it is sometimes impossible for us actually to predict what will occur; and this may be a theoretical and not a merely practical difficulty. It may be (and this is really the same point again) that the determination of a certain quantity theoretically precludes us from determining another; and perhaps in this case we should even refuse to speak of both quantities as being determinate – what point is there in this if we cannot discover both? However, this is not to say that, given certain conditions, sometimes one thing and sometimes another occurs; it is only to say that we cannot discover whether or not this is so nor what will occur; and hence perhaps we refuse to regard the question as a proper one. But one who says that for any event at all there are some conditions sufficient for its occurrence, need not assert, as we have already seen, that anyone does or could know what these conditions are; and he need not hold that every event is in fact, or even in theory, predictable. Perhaps then he is, though doubtless rightly ignored, not flatly refuted by the contemporary physicist. If he is prepared to speak of what admittedly cannot be experimentally tested, he may remain invulnerable. I need hardly say that no great value attaches to this type of invulnerability; but I would suggest that the law of causation is vacuous enough to elude the attack even of this unusual and well-armed opponent. It escapes, indeed, by way of saying something that cannot in any way be tested; but it says no more than this in any case, and thus only exhibits in this unfamiliar field the same peculiarity on which it trades elsewhere. To say that the law can be refuted *here* is to imply that elsewhere it might have been but is not; I have tried to show, however, that nowhere at all does it run the risk of refutation.

Some Questions about Language

6

A Problem about Truth

1. The problem to which this paper[1] is addressed is a quite narrowly limited one: and it can be stated – though not, I think, solved – very briefly indeed. When somebody says something and we say 'That's true', do we therein make some statement about a statement, some assertion about an assertion? Do we say something *about* what he has said? If we do, there may arise the question what the statement or assertion so made may mean: I shall allude to this question too, though only very sketchily.

This problem is one of the matters – there were several others – on which J. L. Austin and P. F. Strawson found themselves in disagreement in their papers in the symposium *Truth in* 1950 (*Proceedings of the Aristotelian Society*, supp. vol. XXIV). It will be convenient to take the relevant parts of that important discussion as a text from which to begin.

I should mention, perhaps, that I shall not discuss the view, which has had distinguished sponsors, that to say that something is true is to make an assertion about a sentence. Both Austin and Strawson took this view to be fairly obviously wrong, at least when the use of a natural language is in question. What can properly be said to be true or false is not a sentence itself, but rather what is, on this occasion or that, asserted, stated, said by one who utters a sentence – not the sentence he utters, but the statement he makes. This is surely correct.

[1] This is a rewritten and somewhat shortened version of a paper which I read first at Princeton in April 1962, and subsequently at several other places. I suspect that I have incorporated in this revised version several points which I owe to discussion with others (and no doubt I ought to have incorporated more): but, memory being both fallible and fragmentary, I cannot now do more than extend a general, though grateful, acknowledgement to those concerned.

From *Truth*, ed. G. W. Pitcher (Prentice-Hall, 1964), © 1964, pp. 54–67. Reprinted by permission of Prentice-Hall, Inc., Englewood Cliffs, NJ.

2. The relevant part of Austin's account – which he took to be, so far as it goes, so obvious as to be practically truistic – was this. Words, we may say generally and doubtless somewhat vaguely, are used among other things in speaking about the world, among other things in making statements about it. For this purpose, and not bringing in more complexities than are needed for the matter in hand, there must be 'two sets of conventions': (a) *descriptive* conventions correlating some words in language with 'types' of situations or states of affairs to be found in the world; and (b) *demonstrative* conventions correlating words as uttered on particular occasions with 'historic' situations or states of affairs to be found, at particular though not necessarily closely circumscribed times and/or places in the world. 'A statement is said to be true when the historic state of affairs to which it is correlated by the demonstrative conventions (the one to which it "refers") is of a type with which the sentence used in making it is correlated by the descriptive conventions.'

Now if the statement that S is true, then the statement that the statement that S is true is certainly itself true, and conversely: but, Austin holds, it is not the case, for this or any other reason, that the predicative phrase 'is true' is, as some have argued, 'logically superfluous', or that to say that a statement is true is not to make any further assertion at all – any assertion, that is, other than that made by the statement itself. For (among other things) the statement that the statement that S is true is, as the statement that S usually will not be, about a statement, and in particular about the statement that S: it is therefore not the same statement as the statement that S, notwithstanding their – of course inevitable – linkage of truth-values and the fact that no doubt, in some sense or other, they convey just the same information about 'the world'. Austin's conclusion, perhaps not quite explicit but I think quite definite, is that the statement that the statement that S is true can be said to state, to mean, that the words uttered (if they were actually uttered) in making the statement that S are correlated by demonstrative conventions with a 'historic' situation or state of affairs which is of the 'type' with which the sentence used (if it was actually used) in making that statement is correlated by descriptive conventions. (The point of the parentheses is to allow for the fact that, for the statement that S to be said to be true, it is not strictly necessary that the statement that S should actually have been made. It may also be noted that this account is quite consistent with the fact that the statement that S may be made at different times and places, by different people, and in different words.) As Austin puts it in conclusion: 'If it is admitted that the rather boring yet satisfactory relation between words and world which has here been discussed does genuinely occur, why should the phrase "is true" not be our way of describing it? And if it is not, what else is?'

To this, that part of Strawson's reply which I wish to discuss runs as follows. Let us allow – though in fact he has substantial reservations of detail – that, when a true statement is made, certain words are in fact related to the world in the ways Austin describes. It is nevertheless completely mistaken, a mistake in principle, to suppose that one who says that a statement is true means, or asserts, that the words are thus related to the world, that he is stating this *about* the statement made. Austin has answered (perhaps and up to a point) the question *when*, in what circumstances or conditions, we use the phrase 'is true'; but he is quite wrong in assuming, as he evidently does, that this answers the question *how* we use it. And in fact, if we consider realistically the question how we use it, we see that we use it in a quite wide variety of ways – in expressing agreement or assent, for instance, in accepting, admitting, corroborating, endorsing, conceding, or confirming what is or might be said. Such a remark as 'That's true' is perhaps, in some bald and uninteresting grammatical sense, 'about' a statement: but its actual use is not significantly different from that of other such agreement-expressing devices as 'Yes', 'I quite agree', 'You're right', or even a nod of the head – none of which, of course, could be supposed for a moment to be employed in making a statement about a statement, or an assertion about the relations of certain words to the world. All these locutions and devices are appropriately used *when* a statement has been made; but it is quite wrong to suppose that any is genuinely used to say something *about* the statement.

3. In his paper, and particularly in this part of his paper, Strawson has been taken by some to be propounding what I have heard called 'the performative theory of truth': but I think it is clear that what he says neither deserves, nor surely claims, any such title. It is indeed by no means perfectly clear what a 'theory of truth' is, what is sought to be achieved by the construction of a theory so-called: but it is sufficiently clear, I believe, that Strawson has not constructed one. For a 'theory of truth' would presumably have to aspire to throw some sort of light on contexts in general in which 'true' or 'truth' might occur, or in which questions of truth or falsehood might arise: whereas Strawson's observations, as they stand, could have application only to occurrences of 'true' as a predicate in indicative sentences whose grammatical subjects refer, in one way or another, to statements. The word 'true' may also occur in, for instance, interrogative or optative or conditional sentences; and whatever its 'per-

formative' function in such settings may be, it can scarcely be that of expressing agreement (etc.). The fact is, I take it, that just as Austin had addressed himself primarily to the particular case in which some statement, what someone says, is (indicatively) said to be true, so Strawson does not attempt to describe quite in general how we use the *word* 'true'; he accepts in effect a similar restriction, to uses of the *phrase* 'is true' as a predicate in indicative sentences. It would in fact be perfectly reasonable to suppose that these uses are fundamental; and in any case, even if such a relatively restricted discussion can scarcely issue in so high-sounding a thing as a 'theory of truth', there is probably no harm in accepting the restriction.

We have to consider, then, these sharply different and seemingly conflicting accounts of such a locution as, for instance, 'That's true.' And first of all it is necessary to raise the question whether they actually are conflicting. It has been, I think, much too easily taken for granted that they are.

With Strawson's view that to say 'That's true' may be, for instance, to express agreement with what someone has said, it is, of course, impossible to disagree: it is quite obvious that that is so, that this is at least one of the ways in which 'is true' is used. But does it follow that to say 'That's true' is not to make a statement *about* what someone has said? Plainly not. For just as I may, say, insult or express hostility to someone by making about him the statement that he is a fool, so surely I might express agreement with what someone has said by making about what he has said the statement that it is true. Agreeing, endorsing, etc., surely do not, any more than criticizing, insulting, etc., exclude the making of a statement: for they may all be done *by* the making of a statement. Again, if someone were to say, correctly, that the phrase 'is a fool' is often used to criticize, belittle, denigrate, or insult the person of whom it is predicated, it is plain that he would not have offered an answer to the question what the phrase 'is a fool' *means*: and similarly, it would seem that one who says, correctly, that 'is true' is often used to indicate the speaker's agreement has offered no answer to the quite different question, what the words 'is true' mean.

Thus, from the fact that Strawson is most undoubtedly correct in saying that the phrase 'is true' is used – as are several other equally handy expressions – to express agreement, to accept, confirm, corroborate, etc., it does not follow *either* that to say 'That's true' is not to make a statement about a statement, *or* that there may not well arise the, as yet quite unanswered, question what the meaning of the phrase 'is true' may be. Thus, for holding that Austin is mistaken 'in principle' in supposing that 'is true' is a predicative phrase commonly employed in making statements about statements, and that its meaning is to be elucidated in terms of some relation between words and world, some quite other ground is required than merely that Strawson is correct in saying that the phrase is used, as are others, in for instance expressing agreement. It is really pretty plain that Austin was not attempting to deny this fact and had not overlooked it, but supposed that it left entirely untouched those different issues with which he himself was primarily concerned: and this supposition looks, on the face of it, entirely reasonable.

4. If then one must find, as I think one obviously must, some other ground for the view that Austin's account is in principle a mistaken one, what other ground might one adduce? I think that what Strawson's argument requires, and what in some measure his paper actually contains, is an attempt to assimilate 'the use' of the locution 'That's true' to the use of such other locutions as 'Yes', 'You're right', 'I quite agree', and so on – an attempt, that is, to show that while the locution 'That's true' has, as it has undeniably, the grammatical air of a statement-making locution, this air is not to be taken seriously as a guide to its 'use.' This might run somewhat as follows:

Suppose that it is raining heavily, and that persons A, B, C, D, and E can see that it is: and suppose that A makes the statement that it's raining heavily. B then says 'Yes': C says 'It is indeed': D says 'I quite agree': and E says 'That's true.' Now certainly the responses of B, C, D, and E are verbally diverse; 'Yes,' I dare say, is not a sentence at all, and the other three sentences have quite different subjects and predicates. But – Strawson might argue – would it not be scholastic and indeed misguided to attach much significance to this verbal diversity? For surely what B, C, D, and E have in mind in responding to A's observation, what they wish to convey, what they are up to, their point, is in each case exactly the same – namely, they wish simply to indicate their agreement with or acceptance of A's remark about the state of the weather. Now it is quite plain that to say 'Yes' or 'It is indeed' or 'I quite agree' is not to make a statement about a statement; and it is no less plain that to say 'That's true' is, in intention and general effect, equivalent to, a mere conversational variant upon, saying 'Yes' or 'It is indeed' or 'I quite agree.' But if so, to hold, as Austin evidently does, that to say 'That's true' is something quite different in character and meaning from saying any of these other things, is surely to attach excessive weight to, and so to be led astray by, mere surface grammar. The *use* of these locutions, which is what really counts, is exactly the same; and there is no more reason seriously to suppose that one who says 'That's true' is making a statement about a statement than there would be to suppose this of one who says 'So it is.' The fact is simply that both, in verbally diverse formulas, would be (for instance) expressing their agreement with what was said.

This, I think, is not unpersuasive. It seems indeed pretty undeniable that one who says conversationally 'That's true' will often mean nothing more than, at any rate in the sense that he has in mind nothing different from, one who may say, for instance, 'I agree.' But here there naturally arises a question: how does it come about, one may well wish to ask, that we should have available for the single purpose of, say, expressing agreement, this rather large number of verbally diverse formulas? If, as the view just outlined evidently implies, their verbal diversity is of no serious significance, does it not seem that we are confronted here with a curious kind of linguistic superabundance, a surprising superfluity of ways of doing just the same thing? How is such linguistic prodigality to be accounted for?

Now surely an explanation of this circumstance comes readily to mind. It must be remembered that although, of course, we speak for the most part with the effortless ease born of years of practice, in fact the making of even a quite simple statement is a performance of some considerable complexity. In saying to me truly, for instance, 'It's raining heavily', you have, intending to comment on current weather conditions in our vicinity, correctly produced exactly that utterance best adapted in our common language to this very purpose: you have not only successfully drawn my attention to the place and time intended, but have also characterized correctly the relevant aspect or feature of what is going on there and then. Now suppose that, on observing your performance, I wish to express no dissent, that I have no criticism to offer of any of the several aspects of your complex undertaking. Well, there is a simple formula available to me, specially designed for letting you know in a single word of my nondissent; I can say 'Yes.' More formally, but just as well, I can indicate my non-dissent in the formula 'I quite agree.' Alternatively, I can as it were commend you for your faultless performance and the correctness of your views; I can say 'You're right.' Or again, concentrating on the point that the state of the weather in our vicinity is indeed just as you say it is, I can respond with 'It is indeed.' But there is yet one further possibility; I can, not directly alluding to you, to your performance, or to the weather, advert to the point that what was said by you in uttering the words you uttered was, as these matters are conventionally understood, such as to designate a particular state of the weather which is further, as these matters are conventionally understood, of just that type for the characterization of which the words used were perfectly appropriate. I can, in short say 'That's true.'

Now are all these verbally diverse responses 'used in the same way'? Well, in a sense no doubt they are. They all have the same general object and serve the same purpose; for they all serve to let you know of my total nondissent. Whichever of these things I choose, or more probably just happen, to come out with, you know that I am with you on the question of what the state of the weather is. Are they then indistinguishable (except trivially, as words)? Surely not. For is it not evident that, notwithstanding their identity of general object, they achieve this single object in quite different ways, by responding to or commenting on different parts, features, or aspects of the whole rather complex performance of stating truly that it's raining heavily? The reason why there are many ways of doing just the same thing, of achieving just the same general object, is that the making of a statement has many sides to it; there are many points at which, and hence many devices by which, our nondissent (or of course our dissent) may be indicated. But if so, does it not seem perfectly evident that what distinguishes 'That's true' from the rest is that it, and it alone, says something *about* what the speaker said, *about* the statement he made? 'Yes' does no such thing, nor yet do 'I agree' and 'You're right': these serve the purpose every bit as well, but not in the same way. Just so I may, say, congratulate an orator by saying 'I congratulate you' or 'That was an excellent speech': and the fact that in either case I congratulate the orator does not imply that these remarks are not significantly distinguishable, or that the second does not differ from the first by being, among other things, *about* the speech that he made.

5. This might be objected to. It might be held, with some justice, that a certain air of artificiality attaches to the above discussion of diverse responses to 'It's raining heavily.' Can it seriously be suggested that, for instance, one who says 'You're right' conceives himself to be, has in mind that he is, saying something about the speaker, as distinguished from one who, in saying 'That's true', says something about what the speaker said, or from one who, in saying 'I agree', says nothing about either? No such distinctions, surely, are in any degree likely to be in such a speaker's mind. What was called the 'general object' of all the responses considered – namely, indication of agreement with what the first speaker said – is likely to be *all* that respondents in such a case have in mind. But if so, what

serious sense can be attached to the claim that one who happens to say
'That's true' is to be *distinguished* as therein making a statement about
what was said?

But this objection, I believe, rests too much weight on the question of
what speakers may have in mind, on what they may consciously conceive
themselves to be doing, and correspondingly too little on what may be
called the mechanism of language itself. Wittgenstein in particular laid
great and justified stress on the idea that the understanding of an expression, the grasp of what (in one sense at least) it means, does not particularly require, and may even be obstructed by, attention to what passes in
the mind of one who uses it when he does so. Similarly, I think, the
question of what a speaker is doing in speaking – a question, we may note,
that in most cases can be taken and answered in several different ways – is
not to be conclusively answered by reference to what he conceives himself
to be doing, or to what he has it in mind to do. One thing that a speaker
does who says 'It's raining heavily' is, for instance, to utter a sentence in
grammatical English, and this may even be essential to his being understood by his hearers: but is it likely that, and does it at all matter whether,
the notion of uttering a sentence in grammatical English was ever actually
in his mind?

Or consider an example somewhat closer to the question now at issue.
In certain circles, in certain parts of the world, agreement with statements
made is not uncommonly expressed in the colloquial formula 'You can say
that again'; and it may well be the case that one who utters these words
will, if this idiom is very familiar to him, have nothing whatever in mind in
uttering them but the intention of indicating his agreement with what has
been said. Nevertheless, it is surely undeniable that what the words
actually mean is that the person addressed has leave, or is at liberty, to
repeat the observation he has just made: and to utter the words is to tell
him that this is so. Could we not hold then, somewhat analogously, that
whereas Strawson probably describes correctly enough what ordinary
users of the words 'That's true' very often, or typically, have in mind in
using them, Austin is not thereby any less entitled to offer his observations
in answer to two quite different questions – first, what the words 'That's
true' actually mean, and second, what speech-act is standardly performed
in uttering those words?

This looks well enough, perhaps; and it has about it a pleasingly
pacificatory air; but it is not yet, I think, quite plain sailing. It might be
urged, for instance, that I have just appealed to a misleading analogy. It is
certainly a feature of the case just cited that, while the words 'You can say

that again' colloquially have, in certain circles, this mere agreement-indicating role, the same words may and no doubt often do occur in quite other contexts. A colleague confides to me, for example, that he made a very gratifying impression in his lectures last term with the remark 'Santayana was the Puccini of philosophy': how, he asks me, can he enjoy a similar success this term? I, knowing perhaps that few people attend my colleague's lectures more than once, might then quite naturally point out the path to another triumph by saying 'You can say that again': and here, while not necessarily endorsing his rather complex assessment of Santayana, I do literally tell him that it is open to him to repeat the dictum in question. But did the plausibility of our distinction between what the speaker has in mind in speaking, and the meaning of his words or the nature of the speech-act performed, not derive perhaps from this un-doubted distinction between colloquial and standard uses of 'You can say that again'? If these words had occurred *only* in their agreement indicating role, it would surely have been scarcely possible to distinguish *from* this the meaning of the words, or what is done by one who utters them. What then of the locution 'That's true'? Is this properly analogous with 'You can say that again'?

Well, the answer seems clearly to be that the analogy is not perfect: but the respect in which it fails tends, I believe, substantially to strengthen Austin's case. The words 'You can say that again', we said, have a *colloquial* role, namely as a mere indication of the speaker's agreement: this is colloquial – or perhaps idiomatic? – in the sense that this role for the words in question is not a mere standard function of their standard meaning, or a standard extention of their standard uses: a foreigner, for instance, well schooled in classical English, would probably not be able straight off to construe their utterance correctly. The locution 'That's true' is certainly not in this position: for it is in no way at all, of course, colloquial or idiomatic. But this is to say – and this begins to seem perfectly obvious – that the use of those words to express agreement (etc.) *is* an entirely standard function of their standard meaning: that, in fact, the reason why one who says 'That's true' can be taken to have expressed his agreement with what was said, is simply that he has said *about* what was said that it is true, and to say this about what was said can be, simply in virtue of what the word 'true' standardly means, to express agreement with it. Whereas, in the case of the words 'You can say that again', we found a (colloquial) agreement-indicating role and *also* a standard use of the words to tell somebody something, we seem to find, in the case of 'That's true', a (noncolloquial) agreement-indicating role *because* of what is meant by the words and done by one who utters them. But if so, some such account of them as Austin offers appears not as an incompatible rival to, but rather as the essential underlying rationale of, such an account as Strawson's. It is precisely *because*, as Austin says, one who says 'That's true' therein makes a certain statement about a statement that, as Strawson says, he thereby expresses (for instance) his agreement with it.

At the same time, it would, no doubt, be most ill-advised to offer 'That's true' as a central or ideal instance of statement-making. For one thing, it has the peculiarity that it will often, perhaps more often than not, be addressed to someone who already knows or believes it, and has indeed, by making the statement referred to, given recent evidence of his knowledge or belief. The statement 'That's true' will only convey to the person to whom it is addressed information about its subject matter if that person either did not make, and did not know to be true, the statement referred to, or – a queer case – made the statement but did not know whether it was true or not. Thus the dialectical function, so to speak, of the utterance 'That's true' is somewhat peculiar: it will not usually be primarily to convey what it actually states, but rather to convey what its making incidentally implies – namely, that the utterer believes, accepts, agrees with (etc.) the statement which his utterance is about. For this same reason it is also the case, no doubt, that one who makes the statement 'That's true' will often not have *particularly* in mind the idea that he is making a statement at all: the point of his statement will be primarily to convey his agreement (etc.), and that he is doing this may well be all that he has in mind. However, although such considerations as these well warrant the conclusion that the utterance 'That's true' is a somewhat unideal specimen of statement-making, they do not seem to me to be adequate grounds for the denial that it is a case of statement-making at all.

6. This conclusion can now be reinforced, I believe, if we reconsider the matter of 'the use' of such verbally diverse locutions as 'Yes', 'I quite agree', 'You're right', 'That's true', and so on. Now it is certainly the case, as Strawson insists, that there are contexts in which any of these could be used indifferently: if, for instance, you have observed to me that it's raining heavily and I wish to let you know of my nondissent, that job will be done perfectly by the utterance of any of these locutions. But is this to say that they are all 'used in the same way'? Plainly not. For – apart from the question whether, even in such a context as this, they may be distinguish-able – the conclusion that they are 'used in the same way' would seem to require, not only that there should be contexts in which they are in-

differently interchangeable but also that there should be no contexts in which they are not. But this latter condition is surely, and significantly, not satisfied.

Let us consider, for instance, the case of agreement. I may, certainly, agree with a statement that someone has made. But not, of course, *only* with statements. I may also agree with a decision he has come to, a policy he has announced, a taste or opinion he has expressed, an appraisal, an estimate, or an assessment he has made. He says, for instance, concluding his argument, '. . . so we must try to get Jones elected instead of Smith', or '. . . on those grounds I judge Higgins to be the more promising man'. Now if I agree with his decision or his assessment, I may of course say 'Yes, I agree': if I believe his decision or assessment to be correct, I may say 'You're right.' But in neither case, surely, would I naturally, or could I properly, say 'That's true.' *This* way of expressing agreement would be quite out of place here. Why? Because, presumably, the speaker with whose words I wish to signify my agreement was not just making a statement, purveying a simple truth (or falsehood), but rather announcing a decision, issuing an appraisal: and though indeed I may agree with him and may express my agreement, the particular form of words 'That's true' seems properly, and so naturally though doubtless not rigorously, to be confined to the particular case in which what is to be agreed with is, or at least is offered and taken as, a statement of fact. Thus, in these and no doubt in vastly many other cases, it appears that our various agreement-expressing locutions are *not* in fact freely interchangeable: though there are cases in which any would do, there are other cases in which one or more will do, while others will not.

But now, of course, the question arises: why should it be the case, as it appears to be, that the locution 'That's true' is naturally, though doubtless neither rigorously nor self-consciously, confined to the case in which what is to be agreed with is a statement of fact? Is this a mere convention of speech, like the use of 'Hear, hear' by way of assent to formal oratory, or of 'Amen' as a mark of subscription to the sentiments of a prayer? It is surely both unplausible and unnecessary to suppose that this is a mere convention. For it seems at this point both natural and quite adequately explanatory to hold that to say 'That's true' is to say, about what someone has said, that it is true; so that *of course* one can express agreement in this particular form of words only if what one is thereby talking about is the kind of thing that *can* be true (or untrue) – that is, is a statement. Thus, the notion that to say 'That's true' is to make a statement about a statement appears not only not to be ruled out by the point that that utterance may serve to express agreement, but actually to be indispensably necessary to understanding of the restrictions on the expression of agreement in that particular form. That – more or less – only statements can be agreed with in this way is explained if the utterance *states, about* what it refers to, that it is true; and I cannot imagine how else that fact is to be explained.

7. One final point. I believe that many people have been inclined to object that, even if one is led by the sort of considerations outlined above to the view that Austin is probably right in holding that one who says 'That's true' makes a statement about a statement, there is still grave difficulty in accepting his implicit view that the statement so made *means* anything so lengthy and elaborate as he says it does. For, one may think, it is surely quite indisputable that those simple and unreflective persons who say 'That's true', quite naturally and effortlessly, dozens of times a day, do not have any such lengthy rigmarole – about demonstrative and descriptive conventions and so on – in mind when they say it. I do not believe, however, that there is much force in this objection. For one thing, there is a high degree of indeterminacy in the notion of meaning (some of it, indeed, perhaps put there by philosophers); so that it is very far from clear what kind of account, how thoroughgoing and far-reaching and how elaborate, of the use or conditions of application of a term can properly be put forward as an account of its meaning. But more generally, there is surely no good reason to believe that a philosophically useful account of 'the meaning' of a term must not be more complex than, or even that it must bear any very close relation to, what ordinary users of the term may have in mind when they use it. It is, after all, a very familiar point that those who habitually use a term quite correctly, and in that sense may be said to know what it means, may be in hopeless difficulties when invited to *say* what it means: and it seems clear that, when an attempt to say what it means is seriously undertaken, the resulting account will very often be of a complexity unsuspected by, and perhaps astonishing to, plain speakers of the language. Thus, whatever objections there may be to Austin's account of what it means to say of a statement that it is true, I do not believe that the undoubted complexity of his account is in itself a ground for the conclusion that it must be incorrect.

My argument, then, can be summed up as follows:

(1) Though it is most undoubtedly the case that, when one says 'That's true', one is often, for instance, agreeing, it does not follow from this that

one is not therein making a statement: for one may express agreement *by* making a statement.

(2) It is certainly the case that, as Strawson says, one may express, say, agreement with somebody's statement more or less indifferently by saying 'That's true', 'So it is', 'I agree', Yes', 'You're right', and so on. But:

(3) It appears *not* to be the case that, as he implies, these verbally diverse responses cannot be significantly and substantially distinguished from one another. For (a) if we bring into view the actual complexity of the business of making even a quite simple statement, it at once seems natural to distinguish these diverse responses as relating to different aspects of or elements in that complex business, notwithstanding the fact that they all achieve the same general object: and the response 'That's true' is naturally seen as differing from the others in being *about* the statement made, what the speaker said. And (b) if we note that the phrases mentioned in (2) above are, though freely interchangeable in some contexts, not so interchangeable in others, we observe that 'That's true' tends to be restricted to contexts in which it is statements of fact that are, say, to be agreed with: and it seems the obvious explanation of this restriction that 'That's true' states, about what its subject-term refers to, that it is true.

(4) It appears in general not outrageous to hold that one who utters certain words therein makes a statement about something, even if he does not clearly and self-consciously conceive himself to be so doing: though

(5) We may well regard saying 'That's true' in the ordinary way as, though in no way deviant or colloquial or idiomatic, yet a somewhat unideal specimen of making a statement.

(6) If we hold, then, with Austin, that to say 'That's true' is to make a statement, albeit perhaps an unideal one, about a statement, we may still feel difficulty in the idea that that statement's meaning can be so complicated as he makes it out. But this is far from conclusive, since there is actually no good reason why a remark, perhaps made very casually, with nothing very complex in mind, should not all the same, when subjected to scrutiny, turn out to have a highly complex meaning, only to be set out in perhaps surprisingly many hard words.

In this paper I have not, of course, done anything whatever to show that Austin's account of *what* is stated about a statement, when one says that it is true, is in detail correct. If I have established anything, it is only that Strawson does not succeed in showing that an account of that kind is in principle wrong – that is, that Austin goes astray in principle in supposing that to say 'That's true' is to make *any* kind of assertion about a statement. I am in fact inclined to believe not only that Strawson does not show this to be wrong in principle, but also that it *is* not wrong in principle: but of course this is not to say that Austin's account is wholly acceptable as it stands,[2] still less that there do not remain far more questions than it answers.

[2] It may be worth pointing out two curious, but not I think very important, slips which Austin's paper contains. First, he says at one point that 'the relation between the statement that S and the world which the statement that the statement that S is true asserts to obtain is a *purely conventional* relation . . .' But this, which Strawson rightly objects to, is not a consequence of Austin's account but actually inconsistent with it. On his own view, all that is 'purely conventional' is that to utter the sentence 'S' is to make the statement that S: whether or not the statement so made is true is of course a matter not of convention, but of fact. Second, he says that 'demonstrative' conventions correlate 'the words (= statements) with the historic situations, etc., to be found in the world'. But again, on his own view, that a particular *statement* relates to a particular 'historic' situation is a matter not of convention, nor in this case of fact, but of logic: for he implies earlier that a statement is identified, in part, by reference to the situation to which it relates. What 'demonstrative conventions' in part determine is not how statements are related to the world, but what statement is made by the utterance of certain words on a particular occasion. It will be noted that I have sought to eliminate this latter slip in my initial brief statement of Austin's view.

7

Truth: or Bristol Revisited

I share Dr C. J. F. Williams's view that the question 'Is truth relational?' is not a perfectly clear question, and that it would probably be more useful to understand why one might be drawn towards, rather than straight-forwardly to settle for, this answer or that. I do not, however, see why, having posed his question, he should proceed as he does immediately to rehearse some of the vexing difficulties confronting the correspondence theory of truth. It is true, of course, that the distinguished symposium of 1950 to which he alludes in the first and last sentences of his paper (and at which I am venerable enough to have been present) was launched by a paper of Austin's in which the – or at any rate a – correspondence theory was propounded, and was continued by a paper of Strawson's in which that theory was pretty warmly repudiated; and it may be that Williams pursues the topic of correspondence simply by way of continuing that particular debate. That would be understandable. Even so, it is not, I think, wholly out of place to observe that his initial question surely does not of itself lead into examination of the correspondence theory in particular; for it seems to me true, and if true not unimportant to the matter in hand, that practically all the traditional, well-thumbed 'theories' of truth imply an affirmative answer to his question, and not only, as he seemingly suggests, the correspondence theory.

This is surely plain enough; the traditional great points of controversy have been concerned, not with the question whether truth is or is not 'relational', but with the question what the relation is, and holding between what terms. The correspondence theory insists, in Austin's words, on 'the trite but central point that truth is a matter of the relation between words and world' (*Philosophical Papers*, 2nd edn (1970), p. 130, n. 1); and he offers an account of what that relation is. I take coherence theories, of one sort or another, to contend that the truth of a given

From *Proceedings of the Aristotelian Society*, supp. vol. XLVII, 1973.

proposition is a matter of its relation to (coherence with) other propositions. Even pragmatist theories also, I suppose, contend that truth is relational; at least Aristotle (cp. Nichomacheon Ethics I vi) places 'the useful' in the category of relation. There are indeed theories of none of these familiar varieties; but it is plain enough that the notion that truth is relational, however lacking in perspicuity, has much wider currency than Williams's way of proceeding would suggest.

This, if true, would bear quite substantially on the matter in hand – taking that matter to be whether truth is relational, or at least why one might incline towards one or the other answer to that question. For it means, of course, that vexing or even insuperable difficulties in stating and defending a correspondence theory of truth should not necessarily incline one towards a negative answer to the question; for even if truth cannot be made out to be a matter of *that* relation, it may very well be a matter of some other. Further, the fact – if I am right in taking it to be a fact – that the notion that truth is relational is not the private property of a particular theory, but is common to several theories of otherwise radically different sorts, strongly suggests that the inclination to answer Williams's question in the affirmative must be more basic, more natural, and so perhaps less perplexing and elusive in motivation, than he takes it for. Why should there be so much agreement?

I believe in fact, perhaps indeed naïvely, that there is nothing particularly mysterious about this. For I should take the unperspicuous but widely shared notion that 'truth is relational' to be a way of giving expression to the profoundly uncontroversial thought that the question whether a proposition (let us say – but 'belief', or 'statement', or 'assertion' would do just as well here) is or is not true is not in general to be determined by mere consideration of what that proposition is, of the proposition itself or of what it 'states'. If you tell me that there are badgers at the bottom of your garden, I may well be absolutely clear as to what it is that you have said; your proposition may be set plainly before me, in all its aspects; I may know exactly what statement you have made, what belief you have expressed. But – the thought is – I do not thereby know, nor am I thereby in a position to determine, whether it (the proposition, *etc*) is true or false. Whether it is true or false turns on, and determination of that question calls for reference to, something else; I shall not get anywhere merely by musing on what the proposition is, since it could, of course, be precisely that proposition, and neverthless be either a true proposition, or a false one. What practically everybody agrees on is, one might say, that the truth or falsehood of propositions is determined by *something* 'outside' the propositions themselves; a false proposition is not necessarily a different proposition from the proposition it would have been had it been true, or vice versa. That truth is a 'relational property' seems a natural way enough of expressing this; for perhaps one thing that a relational property is, is a property such that an item may either possess or lack it without thereby being itself different. If all my nieces and nephews die, I do not (thereby, or necessarily) change, though I cease to be an uncle. If the river changes its course, my last year's map is no longer an accurate map, though it has not changed.

I am not here saying (or denying) that all of this is either ideally lucid or right. My modest suggestion so far is a triple one – first, that the train of thought sketched in the foregoing paragraph could be summed up wholly naturally in the dictum that truth is relational, or is a relational property; second, that the train of thought is either uncontroversial, or at any rate *prima facie* exceedingly persuasive;[1] and third, that that is why, in my submission, that 'truth is relational' should be a notion common to, even unhesitatingly assumed by, very different, if not quite all, theories of truth. It seems to be *after* this point that both major difficulties and major disagreements arise – when one tries to say exactly what the relation is, what it relates to what, just what relational property truth is. I do not really think, then, that Williams need ask, as he does, in a *puzzled* way why 'philosophers . . . insist that *truth* is in some way relational'; I think it is really pretty obvious why they do – and why, furthermore, nearly all of them do, not merely those who look with favour on correspondence theories.

Perhaps, however, Williams will say that this is really too plain and naïve to be much to the purpose. It is not, he may say, particularly interesting to consider what might naturally tempt one, incautiously and uncritically, to embrace the notion that 'truth is relational'; our business is to ask why that notion should tempt a philosopher who has some tolerable grasp of what embracing it would actually involve. A philosopher will reflect that, if he is to stick to the idea that truth is relational, he ought to have something to say as to what the relation in the case is, and what its terms are; he ought to assure himself that it is a 'real' relation; if truth is to be said to be a relational property, he should – even if he holds back from the heady question what it is a property of – be prepared with an 'analysis'

---

[1] It encounters one difficulty at least, in that it seems to cope quite naturally only with the case of contingent propositions: a necessarily true proposition presumably could not have been both that proposition and false. It will be recalled that Austin was inclined to think 'true' not properly applicable in such cases.

to show what the property is, and that it is relational. Williams's suggestion is, I think, that correspondence theorists fail to make much of these requirements, and hence that, even if it may be pre-critically natural to feel that truth is somehow relational, it is a puzzle why those theorists should continue to feel that. Accordingly – pausing only to repeat that truth-as-relational is a notion not actually peculiar to correspondence theories – I had better turn to the consideration of at least some of his offered reasons for thinking that a 'real' relation is, at best, elusive. Here I have considerable difficulty.

'How then,' Williams asks, 'is the notion of *correspondence* to be analysed?' Is it a real relation? I find his treatment of this question remarkably baffling. To start with, he appears, after posing the question, simply never to address himself to it. For he at once cites and considers Aristotle's remark that 'to say of what is that it is and of what is not that it is not is true'; and one difficulty[2] that I have with this is that, while it might well be taken, and was doubtless intended, as supplying an 'analysis', or at any rate some sort of limited elucidation, of the notion of *truth*, it does not even appear or purport to say anything about correspondence. The notion of correspondence might possibly, as some would hold, come into an analysis or elucidation or expansion of Aristotle's remark; but Aristotle's remark certainly offers no analysis of *it*, nor tries to. Similarly with what Williams goes on to, namely, 'Strawson's paraphrase'; for this is a paraphrase of '*A*'s statement is true', not of any sentence in which 'corresponds' or 'correspondence' occurs. And my bafflement on this point persists to the end of Williams's paper; for what he actually considers, from here on in, seems to be a variety of purported analyses of '. . . is true'; the question of how the notion of *correspondence*, as that might occur *in* a certain proposed analysis of '. . . is true', should itself be analysed, seems wholly to drop out of sight, to be not even discussed, let alone answered. If so, then how can it be that he offers reasons for concluding that correspondence is not a 'real' relation? He seems not to tell us anything about correspondence at all, either to its discredit as a putative relation or otherwise.

---

[2] My other difficulty is that Aristotle's remark is so very peculiar; it seems to express the very odd idea that what is (typically, centrally) true is *to say* something. 'To say' is not, indeed, anyway in English, an absolutely impossible subject of the predicate 'true'; for we certainly have the expression (idiom?) 'it is true to say . . .'. However, 'to say' looks pretty superfluous in that expression; it is true *to say* that snow is white because it is true that snow is white; and that's being true does not require or involve anyone's saying anything. It is surely not *to say* something that, in Austin's phrase, is 'at bottom' what is true.

One route out of this perplexity would be to suppose that Williams, though he asks how the notion of correspondence is to be analysed, is not really interested in answering that question at all; he is interested, all along, in the question how *truth* is to be analysed; and his object is, not really to consider what 'corresponds' might mean *in* such an analysis, but rather to show that that expression need not come into the analysis at all. If it can be made out that, in saying that *p* is true, one is not saying that anything 'corresponds', in any sense, to anything, then perhaps we shall have learned, scarcely indeed what the analysis of the notion of correspondence is, but rather that we need not trouble our heads about that notion. We need not analyse *it*, nor even eliminate it; for it need never rear its head. This might even work, in a back-handed sort of way, as an argument that 'correspondence is not a real relation'; for if we can find grounds for thinking that truth is not 'relational' at all, then – without offering any explicit analysis of 'corresponds' – we can perhaps say that, even if 'corresponds' should (as it need not) crop up in an analysis of '. . . is true', it cannot in that context really be designating a relation. It would indeed be queer to offer such an argument as providing an 'analysis of *correspondence*'; but it would perhaps be unfair to say that it told us absolutely nothing about the notion of correspondence at all.

We are really back, then, if I have kept my footing so far, with the question whether truth is, in any good sense, a 'relational property'. If an affirmative answer should seem reasonable, then it would be at least possible that correspondence should be the relation in question (of course there might be other candidates to be considered); and it would then be worth considering exactly what the relation so designated might be. If, however, a negative answer should seem to carry the day, then at least correspondence, however analysed, could not be both a 'real' relation and a proper component of an analysis of '. . . is true' (nor, of course, could any other notion). If so, then the way to take the later pages of Williams's paper would be to read them, not really as seeking an analysis of the notion of correspondence (his question notwithstanding), but as suggesting that '. . . is true' is in no clear or good sense 'relational', and *therefore* that 'corresponds', if let in at all, would not designate a 'real' relation. How cogent are those later pages, then, read in this way?

I believe – though with diffidence, since I have had a hard time with these pages – that they are not cogent; indeed, they seem to me to lead quite naturally to the very conclusion which Williams does not want to reach. He observes at one point that the friends of truth-as-relational have no interest in contending for a relation between propositions and what propositions 'state'; for, he says, 'what these people want is a relation between what a proposition states and how things are'. The fact is, as it seems to me and as I shall now try to show, that his own account, if one presses it just a little futher and harder than he does, provides 'these people' with just such a relation.

First, a trial run. Consider the sentence 'He is as you have described.' Is there, we ask, anything 'relational' in the offing here? Williams, I think, would say that there is not; for though, as he says, it would be colloquially tolerable to say 'He is like you have described', and 'like', being a preposition, expresses a relation, nevertheless 'He is like you have described' is, by purer standards, ungrammatical; and the 'as' in the more scrupulous version is not a preposition at all. This has to be conceded. But is there not more to be said? For what if we now press on a little with the question, what it *means* to say that he is as you have described? One explicatory route that one might take here might be to say that this means: the way that you have described him is the way he is. At first sight this does not look very relational either; for in this sentence we have two substantival expressions connected merely with an 'is'. This 'is', however, can scarcely import identity. For, one may reflect, 'the way that you have described him' really refers to a description, namely the description of him that you gave; 'the way he is', however, does not refer to a description, but rather to his actual state, condition, character or what not. More explicitly, then, we have really the two distinct substantival expressions, 'the description of him that you gave', and 'the way that he is'. The full form of our explicatory sentence will evidently be, then, 'The description of him that you gave . . . the way he is'. What is to occupy the blank? Well, does not 'corresponds to' fit in there very naturally? If this is all right, then perhaps we have reason for concluding that, while the sentence 'He is as you have described' itself contains no relational word, nevertheless, if we set out more fully what that sentence means, if we seek its 'analysis', we find that it does in fact assert that a relation hold between two items. The two items are a certain description, and the way a certain person is; and the sentence says that these are related by correspondence. We might then go on to the question, very difficult no doubt but at least quite real, of what exactly that relation is.

So what about *truth*? If I read Williams rightly, among 'paraphrases' or 'analyses' of 'The statement that p is true', his preferred candidate – at any rate among the non-formal contenders – is 'Things are as the-statement-that-p states'; he has some notion how some, for example J. L. Mackie, might be led to think that some relation was involved here, but himself holds that no relation is involved – 'as' is not a preposition. But here too it seems reasonable to hold that there is more to be said, that we ought to press on beyond this rather quick and bald conclusion. So let us try out one or two manipulations. First – since we are primarily interested in understanding the *predicate* in the sentence 'The statement that *p* is true' – it might be tidy to seek a version of the paraphrase which does not transpose or otherwise interfere with that sentence's subject – that is, which predicates something or other of the very same thing, the statement that *p*. We start our paraphrase, then, with 'The statement that *p* . . .'. What next? Well, the statement that *p* states something (at any rate in the slightly strained but allowable sense, given countenance by Williams, in which statements do state things). So let us try this: 'The statement that *p* states something which . . .'; and we may then round off our sentence with '. . . is as things are.' But that, we may think, is still a bit cryptic and obscure (as well as ungainly); surely what we are really saying here, more explicitly set out, is that the statement that *p* represents (I am tempted by 'constates') things in a certain way, *which is* the way things are. But now, what about that 'which is'? Surely what the statement that *p* offers, or propounds, is what one might call a representation of the way things are; and that, being a representation, cannot literally *be* the way things are. So the full form of our explicatory paraphrase might go thus: 'The statement that *p* offers (or propounds) a representation of the way things are which . . . the way things are.' What is to occupy the blank? Does not 'corresponds to' fit in there very naturally? If that is all right, then perhaps we have reason for concluding that, while the sentence 'Things are as the statement that *p* states' itself contains no relational word, nevertheless, if we seek a more expansive 'analysis' of that sentence, we find that it does in fact assert that a relation holds between two items – on the one hand, a certain propositional representation of the way things are, and on the other hand the way things are. This relation is called, obscurely enough to be sure, 'correspondence': and we are left with the problem of elucidating what that relation is – and also, of course, if we are dashingly mixing the drinks, of elucidating what the terms are between which it holds. My suggestion is that Williams does not so much show that this question does not arise, or that there is 'really' no relation in the case, as simply stop short of the point at which it does arise, and at which the lurking relation looms clearly into view. The paraphrases he employs may be very good paraphrases, genuine 'equivalents'; they may answer some questions; but it is not to be supposed that no questions can arise about *them*, or that they are not themselves a proper topic for further analysis. I suggest that, if one does subject them to a bit more analysis, one confronts soon enough the skeleton that Williams is trying to keep in the cupboard.

So where are we? Not, of course, very far on. The sort of thing that I have just been saying really does no more, at best, than to retain a semblance of respectability for what I mentioned earlier as the thought at the back of the minds of those who intuitively feel, or assume, that 'truth is relational' – the thought that the question whether or not a proposition is true is quite a different question from, and is in general left quite open by answers to, the question what the proposition *is*. The feeling is, one might say, that one has first to get hold, on the one hand, of the way propositions represent things as being; then one has to get hold, on the other hand, if one can, of the way things are; and then, if you like to say so (and why not?), you compare the two. Certainly there is nothing tremendously useful in saying this; for it is, if I was right in what I hazarded earlier, nothing more than the pretty amorphous common ground between (almost) every 'theory' of truth in the field. Still, it does, as it seems to me, and as it seemed to Austin in 1950, have the important merit of at least pointing towards, even if it does not take us at all close to, the root of the matter; and perhaps it is in the present context worth maintaining – since the tenor of Williams's paper seems to be towards denying – that this cloudy line of thought does merit attempted elucidation; it is not a mere *ab initio* misunderstanding, to be merely cleared away by more sophisticated 'analysis'. The feeling that truth involves a 'relation' is, if I am right, far from utterly misconceived, so that there *is* the problem – to which, of course, I in this paper have contributed absolutely nothing – of making out what it is, and what its terms are. I side with those many who have always supposed this to be so.

In conclusion, I ought in conscience at least to allude to a methodological worry which I have, so far, rather weakly shied away from; I have, in fact, had, and have been rather culpably trying to repress, the feeling that it may be *the* thing that needs clearing up. What do we mean, anyway, by 'an *analysis*' of '... is true'? What does Williams mean by it? What, and how much, is an analysis required to do for us? I have been following Williams in using the term 'analysis' pretty freely; but I am actually far from sure that I know what I mean by it, or that either I or he knows what he means by it. It looks to me as if Williams is inclined not to go along with the notion that truth is 'relational' just for the reason that he *can* – as of course he can – produce a paraphrase, a formal or informal 'equivalent', of predications of '... is true' in which no overtly relational expression, or two-place predicate, occurs. This leads him to think that the putative, problematic 'relation' can be made to disappear; if no relational expression shows up in 'the analysis', we conclude that 'really' there is no relation around, however much we may at first have been tempted to think there was. But why should his chosen analyses – paraphrases – have this sort of authority? When does a paraphrase, an equivalent, *count* as an 'analysis'? We surely cannot say that it always does; for that would imply that equivalent paraphrases could always be taken, at will, as analyses of each other, which seems absurd. I suggested above that a relation does come into the picture for the reason that 'Things are as the statement that *p* states' could be analysed into the ungainly form of 'The statement that *p* propounds a certain representation of the way things are which corresponds to the way things are'; could Williams argue – would he wish to argue – that a relation does not (really) come into the picture for the reason that the former neat formulation could be an analysis of the latter ungainly one? Could one say that, *simply* on the ground that they were (if they are) equivalent? The problem is a tricky one. I have been tempted for my part to think that Williams evades, refuses to confront or recognize, the problem for the theory of truth of what *correspondence* is, merely by resorting to ingenious paraphrases of '. . . is true' in which that problematic expression does not actually occur. What problem does that solve? One might ask, on the other hand, why would that be an evasion? Are his paraphrases *not* analyses? For surely one sometimes can legitimately alleviate perplexities generated by a certain form of words, simply by showing that the very same thing can be said and well understood in some paraphrase in which that form of words does not occur. When is that procedure good enough, and when is it not? Apart, however, from the vague idea that an *analysis* should be, not merely equivalent to, but more complex and explicit than, what it is offered as an analysis of – and should genuinely elucidate, not merely circumvent or conceal, whatever troublesome locution is the occasion of the search *for* an analysis – I have nothing much to the purpose to say on this subject. Perhaps, as P. F. Strawson has said (*Logico-Linguistic Papers* (1971), pp. 232–3) how much or how little we choose to pack into an account of 'the meaning' of '. . . is true' is an optional affair. How many of the very numerous things that truth 'is a matter of' should get into an *analysis* of '. . . is true', into 'a theory' of truth? It depends what one wants, perhaps, or what one is up to.

8

Words and Sentences

Gilbert Ryle has written often, wittily, and well about meaning. From what he has written on that subject I want to pick out for further scrutiny one particular topic – namely, that of the relations, or some of them, between the notions of *words, sentences, use,* and *meaning.* On this topic, on which Ryle has written more than once,[1] he seems to me, though battling on the side of the angels, to have gone wrong in some respects; and I believe he has gone wrong through seeking, as one might put it, to cut a longish story too short. If that is right, then there is more to be said, and not only in the sense in which there always is.

The issues I shall consider are these. First, Ryle remarks that, while we talk perfectly smoothly and intelligibly of 'using' words, expressions, phrases, there is by contrast something jarring about, perhaps even wrong with talking, as nevertheless some philosophers do, of 'using' sentences. Second, and consequentially, he maintains that, whereas knowing what a word means can usefully be said to be a matter of knowing 'how to use' that word, knowing what a sentence means cannot be said to be a matter of knowing how to use that sentence. And third, he seeks to explain this alleged linguistic asymmetry by reference to what words and sentences respectively are. I shall look at these matters in the reverse order. I shall try to show that Ryle goes wrong about what words and sentences are, and in consequence does not properly explain, and even does not quite correctly present, the linguistic data to which he calls attention.

[1] I shall refer to 'Ordinary Language', in *Philosophy and Ordinary Language,* ed. C. E. Caton (1963) – hereafter 'OL'; and also to 'Use, Usage, and Meaning' *Proceedings of the Aristotelian Society,* supp. vol. XXXV (1961) – hereafter 'UUM'. 'Ordinary Language' appeared originally in the *Philosophical Review* in 1953, but I shall refer to pages of the Caton volume.

Ryle's account of the difference between words and sentences presents it as a very radical difference indeed. He says, for example: 'Words, constructions, etc., are the atoms of a language; sentences are the units of Speech. Words, constructions, etc., are what we have to learn in mastering a language; sentences are what we produce when we say things' (UUM, p. 224). Now this looks well enough at first. Ryle seems to be making merely the correct points (1) that to know a language is to have acquired (at any rate a good deal of) its vocabulary and grammar, and so (some) ability to construct and construe sentences in which that vocabulary is employed, whereas (2) to say something in a language, it is normally necessary actually to produce, not just some words, but a sentence.[2] But it emerges that Ryle wants to hold that 'sentences are the units of Speech' in a much stronger sense than this; for a sentence, he goes on to say, is not merely what I have to produce in saying something; it actually *is* my saying it, or (sometimes) it *is* 'what I say'. (See, e.g., UUM, p. 229, and OL, p. 120.) This puts things badly wrong, as soon appears.

'In daily life,' Ryle continues (UUM, p. 225), 'we do not often mention as such the sentences that people produce. We speak instead of their allegations, complaints, promises, verdicts, requests, witticisms, confessions, and commands.' No doubt this is true. Sentences are something of a special interest – of, Ryle says, 'people like grammarians, compositors, translators, amanuenses, and editors'. But what these people do, he says, is to 'refer to the things that people say as "sentences" ' – 'what they are interested in are instances of someone, actual or imagined, alleging, complaining, warning, joking, etc., though their special concern is with the punctuation of them and not with their humorousness; with their length and not with their truth; with their moods and tenses and not with their relevance or rudeness'. But this last bit is surely wrong, and wrong in more than one way. For one thing, 'people like' grammarians, etc., are actually interested in very different things – grammarians in syntax, compositors in spaced strings of letters, translators in style and meaning, amanuenses and editors in lots of other matters. But more importantly, reference to sentences is only very misleadingly indeed to be described as reference 'to what people say as "sentences" '. Consider the sentence 'That dog won't eat bananas.' In what sense, if any, is this 'something that people say?' Perhaps no one has ever said of any dog that it won't eat bananas; further, if anyone ever had said of some dog that it wouldn't eat bananas, someone else might have said something else, viz., that some

---

[2] We can of course sometimes say something in a single word. You ask me 'Are you going to London today or tomorrow?', and I say 'Tomorrow.' We need not dwell on this.

other dog wouldn't eat bananas, by uttering the very same sentence. The sentence, then, is 'something that people say' only in the very unnatural sense that it is a grammatical and meaningful sequence of words of English, which accordingly a competent speaker of English *might* utter. But, 'What sentence did he utter?' is not usually what is meant by 'What did he say?' The sentence itself is not, in the usual sense, 'what someone says', only referred to in a rather specialized way; it is a certain grammatically structured sequence of words, in the utterance of which something, perhaps many different things, *could* be said, whether they ever *are* said or not.

Nor is a sentence an 'instance' of 'someone, actual or imagined, alleging, complaining' etc. You allege that Smith's dog won't eat bananas, I complain that my dog won't eat bananas; what we do, and say, is different, but the sentence that we utter may be the same; and if one wishes to talk simply about the sentence, there is no need to bring in anybody's allegations or complaints, whether actual or imagined – though indeed one might have occasion to mention that, of course, one who uttered that sentence *could* therein be alleging, complaining, etc. Again, a sentence is a grammatical item that can have moods and tenses; but *it* cannot have relevance or rudeness (except perhaps in the interesting special case of its containing a 'rude word') – though, in uttering that sentence, something relevant or rude might be said from time to time. Conversely, a joke does not have punctuation, though the sentences may have in which a joke is told.

Things stay very similarly awry in Ryle's next paragraph. Mentioning the well-known dictum attributed to Julius Caesar, he observes, rightly, that there is something queer about the question 'Is "vici" a word or a sentence?'; but then he seems to misidentify what is queer about it. There is, he says, firstly, the word 'vici', a word in the Latin language; then there was Caesar's boast, 'Vici', in giving his self-consciously laconic account of his dealings with Britain; and there perhaps was, on some other occasion, the nervous gladiator's query 'Vici?', as his concussion wore off. That is, there is the word, and there are various speech-episodes, cases of boasting, inquiring, etc., in which that word is used. But there is nothing that could be one of these *or* the other, any more than there is anything which could be a cricket-bat *or* a cover-drive, a gibbet *or* an execution. These simply are not permissible disjunctions. But here one must object that there are not enough pieces on the board. By distinguishing *only* the word from episodes of its utterance, Ryle gives, and gets, the impression that sentences *are* speech-episodes. 'The boast "vici" ', he writes, 'was a different sentence from the question "vici?" . . .'; well, two sentences perhaps, but not, as he implies, because the episode of Caesar's boasting was a different episode from that of the gladiator's enquiring. For a sentence could not *be* a boast, though it might be uttered in boasting; and a sentence could not *be* a question, though it might be interrogative, i.e., such that its utterance would standardly be the asking of a question. If 'vici' and 'vici?' are different sentences, this is not because boasting is different from enquiring, still less because Caesar's boasting was a different episode from someone else's enquiring. Boasting, after all, is different from not boasting, but if I say boastfully, and you say modestly, 'Vici', we have certainly each uttered the very same sentence. 'Vici' and 'Vici?' perhaps are different sentences, but if they are, the reason must be that they are syntactically distinguishable, as 'Vici', said boastfully, and 'Vici', said modestly, are not. Thus, what is queer about 'Is "vici" a word or a sentence?' is nothing so extreme as what is wrong with 'Is that a bat or a cover-drive?' The trouble is that it is not answerable in the simple manner that the form of the question invites, since 'vici', in Latin, *may* occur simply as an element, a word, in some larger linguistic structure, but may *also* occur by itself as a one-word sentence. To say which it is, we need a syntactic setting. The cause of the trouble, then, is the syntactic versatility of 'vici', not the relatively harmless disjunction 'word or sentence'. After all we can say readily and properly enough that 'Dogs bark' is a sentence, not a word, and that 'sky' is a word, not a sentence; also that 'Bark dogs but' is not a sentence, though it is a series of words, whereas 'Dogs sometimes bark' is not simply a series of words, it is a sentence. And listening bemusedly to a highly polysyllabic language like German, I might quite naturally ask, after listening for quite a long time, 'Was that a sentence?', and be given the dispiriting but intelligible answer 'No, that was just the first word.'

Finally (on this point) Ryle says (UUM, p. 229): 'My last sentence but three, say, is not something with which I once learned how to say things. It *is* my saying something.' But surely not; the sentence is neither his saying something, nor for that matter, in the most natural sense, what he says. It is what he uttered – in this case, wrote – *in* saying something, to the effect (if I've counted right) that philosophers wrongly assimilate words and sentences through neglecting the distinction between language and speech. Someone else's saying of this would be a different saying, not the same 'episode', even if he happened to come out with the very same sentence; and also, of course, he (or Ryle) might have come out with a different sentence, and yet said the same thing. It is true that the sentence in question is not something with which Ryle once learned how to say things; it is something that he was able to compose, and write down in saying what he wished to say, because of something else that he once learned, namely, English. Nevertheless, the sentence that he wrote down, and which was subsequently printed, is not to be identified (in the most natural sense) with what he said in doing so, or (in any sense) with his saying it. His saying it, which took place in 1961, was, as I happen to think, ill-judged; but the sentence itself could not be said to be ill-judged, nor to have taken place at that date or any other.

Can anything be said about how Ryle was led to mis-characterize sentences in this way, or in these ways? Two things, I think. First, having remarked to start with that some of the things we say smoothly and intelligibly enough about words 'do not go', as he puts it (OL, p. 119), when we seek to say the same things about sentences, he looks, rightly no doubt, for the relevant difference between words and sentences; but I suspect that he had a preconceived idea of what this relevant difference would be like. At least it would not be surprising if he had anticipated that it would be a *difference of category*, so that the dicta that 'do not go' would be specimens of that philosophically interesting species, *category-mistakes*. I take no stand here on what sort of difference a difference of category is; but at least one feels that it ought to be a good, big difference, really clear and radical, like that between an implement and what one does with it, a bat and a cover drive, a coin and a purchase, a gibbet and an execution. So, if words, phrases, expressions are things used, and if sentences are to go into another *category*, what sort of things must sentences be? Surely they must be, not items used, but *usings*, i.e., speech-acts, episodes of saying. This is one of the answers Ryle gives – partly at least, I believe, just because it was the answer which his very Rylean proforma of a solution temptingly left room for.

Second, in his later discussion (UUM) of much the same issue, I think that his philosophical movements were hampered by his initial introduction of Sir Alan Gardiner's distinction between language and speech.[3] Not that there is anything essentially wrong with this distinction; there clearly is a distinction to be made between languages, Latin, French, English, and so on, and 'the activity or rather the clan of activities of saying things, saying them in French, it may be, or English or some other language' (UUM, p. 223). But in fact, when one comes to talk about sentences in particular, preoccupation with this distinction is inevitably

[3] Alan H. Gardiner, *The Theory of Speech and Language* (1932).

liable to confuse the issue. What happens, I suspect, in Ryle's case is that, finding that sentences cannot happily be located on one side of this distinction, he concludes that they must belong on the other side. Since learning French is a matter of acquiring the words, the syntax and semantics of French, and not of learning all, or most, or even any French sentences, sentences do not go on the 'language' side; so they must go on the 'speech' side, that is, must *be* the sayings of things in (e.g.) French. But this is a case of false alternatives; the language–speech distinction, as so far set out, has not put all the requisite pieces on the board, and in particular not enough for the proper location of sentences. If one does try to fit sentences, without distortion, into this distinction, one finds them, in a sense, recalcitrantly hovering on both sides of it. They hover on the language side, since, while it is indeed true that learning a language does not consist in learning a list, or stock, or repertoire of sentences, it does consist precisely in acquiring, by way of mastering a vocabulary and a 'grammar', the (some) *ability* to construct and construe sentences of that language; but then sentences seem to hover also on the speech side, for the reason that (roughly, by and large) the activity of saying things essentially involves the utterance of sentences, and conversely the utterance of a sentence is (typically, usually) an instance of saying something. A sentence perhaps is not 'part of' a language;[4] but nor is it an act of saying something in a language. It is, more complicatedly than this distinction allows for, something which (a) one who has fully acquired the relevant language has (therein) acquired the ability to construct and construe, and which (b) one who says something (whatever it may be) *in* that language must, or at least may, utter in doing so. We need, to repeat, more pieces on the board – words, sentences, what sentences mean, acts of uttering sentences, 'what is said' when such acts are done, 'what is done' when such acts are done, doubtless other things too. Words and 'speech-episodes' are not enough to get on with.

So now we must look again at our use of the verb 'use'. For if there is something amiss with talk about 'using' sentences, that cannot be so for the large, knock-down reason that Ryle has suggested; it is not that sentences are *usings*, sc. of words, and thus categorially cannot themselves be used. So should we look for some other reason? I think we should not,

---

[4] Though some linguists in fact define a language as a 'set of sentences', not of course that set which one learns in learning the language, but the ideal set, perhaps infinite, 'generated' from its vocabulary by its grammar. This seems a bit artificial perhaps, but unobjectionable.

since I submit that, as a matter of fact, talk – some talk – of using sentences is in no way objectionable. For example, I might, in rendering one of Kant's arguments into English, use five sentences where Kant used only two: Hemingway was fond of using very short sentences, without connectives, to create an effect, one may suppose, of non-literary toughness: interrogative sentences are often, perhaps usually, used in asking questions. And so on. There should surely be nothing surprising about this. For, omitting complications, a sentence is a certain kind of verbal structure, a syntactically ordered sequence of words of some language; and we do not in general concoct such sequences idly, just for fun. Usually, we want to do something with them, we produce them for a purpose, indeed, often, for several purposes at once; and what is this but to say that we do not just compose them, we *use* them? One of Ryle's own examples might here be turned against him. He compares (OL, p. 119) the composer of a sentence with a cook; somewhat as a cook uses ingredients, and also uses kitchen utensils, in making a pie, so I may use certain words in composing a sentence. But then, a cook is unlikely to make a pie for no reason, purely for the sake of making it; having made it, her idea is probably to use it for something, perhaps as an item in the evening meal, or conceivably as a missile in a music-hall routine. Rather similarly, I am unlikely to compose my sentence just for fun; the likelihood is that I shall make some use of it, will use it in saying – and doing – something or other. Ryle's text in fact betrays some uneasiness here; for, after observing that the cook uses her ingredients and utensils, he says cautiously that she does not *in this way* use the pie – that the speaker who uses certain words in composing a sentence does not *in this way* use the sentence. That may be so; but it may be, too, that the cook does use the pie she has made, and the speaker the sentence he composes.[5] No doubt it is true that, as Ryle insists, cooks keep the ingredients they need to use 'in stock', and not what they make from time to time out of those ingredients; similarly words are, so to speak, the 'stock' of a language, in a way in which sentences are not – there are no dictionaries of sentences. But then it will obviously not do to suggest that only items 'in stock', there, beforehand, ready for use, are ever used; I may construct something out of such items, and proceed to use *that*. Bat-makers use pieces of wood in making bats; and the bats they make are used by cricketers. Machines are often used in making other machines.

It is probably true that we do not often *have occasion* to speak of people as

[5] Not, usually, *after* he has composed it; we usually compose and utter, as it were, in one breath.

'using sentences'. In fact the examples I gave of that locution suggest this, since each suggested a rather special interest in language, an interest of a sort that we perhaps do not often take in what people say. That Kant used only two sentences in stating some argument is something that, perhaps, only a translator would have occasion to remark upon. That Hemingway used a lot of short, bald sentences is of interest from the rather special angle of stylistic criticism. Normally, that someone in some way asked a question will be of more interest than that he did, or perhaps did not, use an interrogative sentence in doing so.

But if so, it is not of course at all surprising that philosophers should speak of using sentences more frequently than people usually do; for philosophers in their own way, as translators and critics and grammarians in theirs, have a special interest, not only – sometimes even not at all – in what people say, but in the manner and means and minutiae of saying it. One might add that, even given such special interests, occasions for speaking of using sentences may still be relatively few; for an interest in language will often be an interest in the *words*, and not particularly, perhaps not at all, in the sentential structures in which those words are syntactically embedded. Perhaps, then, talk of people using sentences is somewhat unusual, something we don't often have occasion for; but it seems to me wholly natural, indeed unavoidable, when we do have occasion for it. There is here, then, no genuine linguistic jarring to be accounted for.

But the case is somewhat different with Ryle's other, and perhaps his major, concern. 'We talk about the meanings of sentences, seemingly just as we talk of the meanings of the words in it; so, if knowing the meaning of a word is knowing how to use it, we might have expected that knowing the meaning of a sentence was knowing how to use the sentence. Yet this glaringly does not go' (OL, p. 119). Now this indeed does *not* go, at least not smoothly; so we have to ask why.

Well, first, does this way of speaking really go all that smoothly, even in the instance to which Ryle, here, does not object? '*If* knowing the meaning of a word is knowing how to use it . . .' – but *is* it? It seems to me that, in many cases, this should be recognized as at the very least a very strange thing to say. For it seems to me that, philosophical habits apart, 'knowing the meaning of' and 'knowing how to use' would more naturally be *contrasted* – or if that is too strong, at any rate not thus identified. It seems to me that the sort of word we 'know how to use' (or don't) is typically the sort of word that plays a specific part in what might be called the tactics of

discourse, and which in *that* sense has a special function. The Greek
particles would be an excellent example of what I have in mind. What one
knows about that famous pair 'μέν' and 'δέ', for instance, is exactly how to
use them, partly where to put them in the sentence, but also what they *do*
in the sentence, what their special point is; but I can think of no straight
answer to the question, what they mean.[6] Rather similarly: what does 'but'
mean? Or 'however', or 'nevertheless'? What one knows about 'but' is
again, I think, how to use it – that is, as a conjunctive device, the special
point, or effect, of which is to imply (to put it very inaccurately, no doubt)
that the conjunction, though it holds, might not have been expected. ('We
were in Oxford during August, but it didn't rain.') 'However', similarly,
seems to have a role in discourse, rather than 'a meaning'; I know how to
use it, but I should not find it easy to say what it means. But now, with lots
of other words, it seems the other way around. I know what the words
'trombone', say, and 'emigrate' mean; but I should be puzzled by the
question whether I know how to use them. After all, unlike 'but' and
'however' and 'δήπου', they just are *not* used in any special way; we have
here a quite ordinary sort of noun and an intransitive verb, used just as
other such nouns and verbs are, that is, in all sorts of ways, whenever what
they mean makes such use appropriate.

Ryle says that understanding a word is 'knowing how to use it, i.e., make
it perform its role in a wide range of sentences'. Now 'but', it seems to me,
clearly does have 'its role' in sentences, as does 'δήπου'; and 'understanding' those words is, in that pretty clear sense, knowing how to use them.
But does 'trombone' have 'its role' in sentences? At least it is not at all
clear what this would mean. Surely it does not function in the same way in
every sentence – in 'The trombone is a brass instrument', 'Promise not to
play your trombone!', 'Is that a trombone?' Or does it? Is there perhaps
always *something* that is the same? Perhaps there is; but then that would be
its *meaning*; and if so, in this very common sort of case 'knowing how to use
the word' would not elucidate, but would itself need to be elucidated by,
the notion of knowing what it means. 'Do you know how to use the word
"trombone"?' – 'Well, I know what it means, *if that's the question you're
asking.*'

Of course it is not, I suppose, untrue to say that I do know how to use the
word 'trombone'. I know that it is a pretty ordinary sort of noun, and I
know what it means, so that, whenever it happens to be word that I want, I
have no difficulty in bringing it out. I sometimes use the word, and all goes

---

[6] I note, for what it is worth, that Liddell and Scott conclude that they 'must often be left
untranslated'.

smoothly when I do, so presumably it's true that I know how to use it. But that I know how to use it is nevertheless, it seems to me, a strange thing to say, and particularly so when there is the further suggestion that my knowing what it means is *a matter of* my knowing how to use it. For the fact seems to be that 'trombone', like a lot of other words, just isn't the sort of word of which we would naturally speak in this way. Since there isn't any particular 'way of using' such a word, except of course to mean whatever it is that it does mean, to speak of knowing what it means seems natural, and of knowing how to use it, by contrast, strange; and the other way around, it seems to me, for 'but', '*δή*', 'donc', and words (I say vaguely enough) of that sort. But let me make quite clear what I am, and am not, maintaining here. I am *not* maintaining that to equate 'knowing the meaning of' with 'knowing how to use' is *wrong*; I am *not* denying that to do this might be a legitimate and valuable, though in itself cryptic, introduction to an illuminating account of meaning and understanding. Nothing so ambitious as that. What I *am* maintaining is that to propound this equation is, on the face of it at least and until something further is said, to say something *strange*; and this is pertinent to our present topic, since, if we are to consider an alleged oddity in the locution 'knowing how to use the sentence . . .', we ought not to contrast this suspect locution with 'knowing how to use the word . . .' on the supposition that in the latter there is no whiff of oddity at all. To do this is to allow our philosophical habits to dull the sharpness of our ears for ordinary English, and thus to present our linguistic data in too black-and-white a guise.

So what about 'knowing how to use the sentence . . .'? Having suggested that 'knowing how to use the word . . .' is, at least in some cases, a less smooth, unsurprising idiom than Ryle implies, should we go on to suggest that the substitution of 'sentence' for 'word' is correspondingly less offensive? Well, yes, I think so; but only up to a point. The notion of knowing how to use a sentence does not seem to me so *glaringly* outrageous as Ryle says it is – in particular it seems to me not categorially wrong, not a case of speaking of using what categorially cannot be used. Even so, there is perhaps not much to be said for it, and something fairly serious to be said against.

I would suggest first that, very much as in the case of words, there is a sense in which it is presumably, but uninterestingly, true that people do know how to use sentences. If, in response to your asking me what time it is, I, wishing to inform you that it's nearly half past six, come out with the sentence 'It's nearly half past six', then I have not just uttered that sentence idly but used that sentence, viz., used it in answering your question. Whether or not my answer is right, the sentence is perfectly intelligible to you as an answer, and conveys furthermore just the answer that I intended to give. So all has gone smoothly in my use of that sentence; and presumably it is thereby shown to be true, or at least not untrue, that I know how to use it. Nevertheless, that I know how to use the sentence does not seem a very *pointful* thing to say – it certainly does not even begin to make clear what exactly it is that one knows, in knowing what the sentence means, or what this knowing consists in. It is also, certainly, a pretty *strange* thing to say; very much as in the case of (some) words, if I were asked whether I know how to use the sentence 'It's nearly half past six', I should find the question a puzzling one, and, in trying to construe it, would take it perhaps to be just a queer way of asking whether I know what it means.

But in this case surely there is more to be said, and in saying it we must go along with Ryle, even if not quite so far. One might say that, in talk of knowing how to use words, and of knowing what they mean as a matter of knowing how to use them, there is, even if such talk is in itself a little strange, at least a valuable *suggestio veri*; there are important truths (I shan't here say what they are) about what it is to understand discourse, and to discourse meaningfully, which can quite naturally be introduced in this way, even if (as is obvious) the truths are really a good deal too complex to be adequately summed up in those dicta without further explanation. By contrast, even if we do know how to use sentences, and even if talk of knowing how to use them could be construed as a queer way of talking about knowing what they mean, there is in *this* way of talking an undoubted *suggestio falsi* – the suggestion, namely, that to understand a language is to be able to operate with some finite stock or set of sentences, the uses of which one has individually learned. Linguists, very properly, are never tired of insisting that a conspicuous feature of mastery of a language, the feature most crucially to be accounted for by any theory, is the ability of speakers to construct and construe sentences which they have never encountered before, and which may very well never have been uttered before. My vocabulary, like everyone else's vocabulary, is limited; and if I have never come across some word before, I cannot know, though perhaps I may guess, what that word means.[7] By crucial contrast, the

---

[7] This is really too brisk and sweeping. I can get to the sense of 'eating' or 'eatable' from that of 'eat'; if I know what 'communist' and 'anti-semitic' mean, I shall not be puzzled by 'anti-communist'; and if I knew a bit about Italian, I might work my way from 'trumpet' to 'trombone'. It is obvious, however, that there is not *in general* any principle or set of principles by which the sense of one word is derivable from that of another.

number of sentences I could construct and construe is (theoretically, doubtless not actually) unlimited; and my ability to understand sentences is wholly independent of the question whether I have ever heard, read, written, or spoken those sentences before. In so far as talk of knowing how to use sentences, as a way of saying, or even beginning to say, what it is to know what sentences mean, does tend, as it very well might, to draw off our attention from this crucial contrast, then certainly such talk is very greatly to be deprecated. If it is not quite so radically wrong as Ryle suggested, nor wrong for at any rate all the reasons he offers, he was surely quite right here in scenting danger as he did. The way of speaking he objected to could indeed be dangerously, disastrously misleading; and that makes a good enough case for not speaking in that way.

9

Some Types of Performative Utterance

I believe that the notion, so paradigmatically Austin's, of performative utterances, has proved fertile – as philosophical notions sometimes do – at least in part because of its provoking instability. It has shown a persistent tendency, as of course Austin himself found, both to wobble and to ramify when subjected to close scrutiny, and thus can fruitfully lead one into, not just one topic, but several. I think also, however, that this tendency to waver has, not at all surprisingly, bred certain confusions (in myself among others); and if these are not to become chronic, distinctions should be attempted. In this paper I offer some distinctions and kindred considerations, by no means all of them novel.

I

Let us begin with what was, I suppose, quite clearly the basic thought that gave rise to the notion of performative utterances – namely, the thought, simple enough in formulation though less so in content, that sometimes to *say* something is to *do* something. Two points at once call for attention here.

First, it is to be noticed that this basic thought is – and, historically, was – that *sometimes* saying is doing. It is clear enough that Austin, however his thoughts may have gone at later stages, had at first the idea that performative utterances were to be a special case; the term was meant to pick out some sub-class of utterances, which were then to be contrasted with others which were not performative. We have to consider, then, first, whether, and if so when and why, to say something is to do something, in a sense, if there is one, in which to say something is not necessarily, or

From *Essays on J. L. Austin,* ed. I. Berlin *et al.* (Oxford University Press, 1973).

absolutely always, or even normally, to do something, but is so only sometimes, in special cases.

Second, it is to be noticed that, in this basic thought, no particular restriction is indicated on the *kinds* of doings that sayings sometimes are – except, of course, that they are to be kinds of doings which can be done by saying something. There is, in particular and importantly, no restriction here to the kind or kinds of doings which came later to be called, vaguely enough, 'speech acts'. It seems in fact to be a plain consequence of the foregoing point that this must be so; for if, as came later to be held by many, to issue an utterance is always, even perhaps necessarily, to perform some speech act or acts, we are obviously not going to pick out, by reference to doings of *that* sort, a *sub-class* of utterances to issue which is to do something. In any case it seems clear from Austin's own early examples that he was not at first thinking particularly, or even at all, of (as one might say, Searlean) *linguistic* acts;[1] some of his early examples are, for instance, of legal doings, such as getting married or bequeathing property; he also mentioned at an early stage such performances as betting, naming ships, and baptizing people or penguins. In all this he was clearly thinking in fact, or was perfectly prepared to think, of any sorts of doings at all in the doing of which certain utterances figured as what he at times called, borrowing from lawyers, the 'operative' element.[2]

The question is, then, at this stage, how utterances are sometimes 'operative' – how it is, as one might put it, that one who issues an utterance thereby sometimes does something, *over and above* whatever it may be (and we are not yet going into this) that he necessarily does just as a speaker of the language, merely in saying whatever it is that he says. Well, the answer that Austin first gave to this question is one that indeed very naturally suggests itself; namely, sometimes there exist rules, or legal provisions, or more or less commonly or officially recognized practices – let us say broadly, as he usually did, *conventions* – which provide that saying something or other is to be, is to constitute or count as, doing whatever it may be.[3] There is, familiarly enough, a large class of doings, well exemplified by but of course not confined to legal doings or certain doings in the playing of games, which could be said essentially to *consist in* the exploitation or following or invoking of certain conventions; in a sub-class of such

[1] The allusion is, of course, to John Searle's *Speech Acts* (1969).

[2] E.g. in 'Performative Utterances', *Philosophical Papers* (1961), p. 223; (2nd edn, 1970,) p. 236.

[3] E.g. *How to Do Things with Words* (1962), p. 14; 'Performative Utterances', p. 224; 2nd edn, p. 237.

cases, exploiting or following or invoking the relevant conventions involves, sometimes mandatorily, the saying of certain words; and in those cases, saying the words is, counts as, in virtue of the convention, doing the thing. This seems to me pretty clearly to be the most conspicuous idea discernible in Austin's earlier remarks on this topic – the idea, that is, of utterances which are performative, to issue which is to do something, in virtue of *conventions* to the effect that to say those things counts as, or constitutes, doing whatever it may be: as to say 'Three no trumps', for example, can constitute bidding, an operation defined (as one might say) by the rules of bridge. Four comments on this.

First, it seems clear that, whatever Austin himself or others may subsequently have come to think, there is nothing whatever wrong with this idea. No doubt, like many other ideas, it is a bit fuzzy at the edges. (Austin was well aware of that.) When we have said that we are concerned here with conventions in virtue of which to say so-and-so constitutes doing such-and-such, we shall certainly find, for instance, that we are not always quite sure what is, or whether there is, a convention in the appropriate sense; we shall sometimes ask, for instance, and be perplexed in answering, the question whether there is a *convention* that to say *X counts as* doing *Y*, or whether perhaps it is merely *customary*, or usual, that one who says *X* would *be taken* to be doing *Y*. The notion of a convention, that is, is not absolutely hard-edged, especially perhaps in the slightly stretched sense that the term is here being given. Also, and importantly, as already hinted, if *this* notion of performative utterance is to identify a *sub-class* of utterances, we shall of course have to rope off the conventions we are concerned with at this stage from those which (as some would say) essentially enter into all linguistic utterance merely as such; for if conventions are exploited in simply saying anything at all, it will have to be in virtue of conventions of sorts distinguishable from those that to say is only *sometimes* to do. But these snags are not fatal. There are clear cases, though also penumbral ones, of conventions; there are conventions which, while involving utterance, are clearly not *linguistic* conventions – not, as one might put it, parts of the *language*; and if so, there is an at any rate decently discriminable species of utterances such that, in virtue of conventions that are not linguistic, to issue such utterances is, counts as, constitutes, doing this or that.

Second, if one has *this* notion of performative utterance, it is clearly reasonable and right to investigate, as Austin did early and extensively, the topic of what he called 'infelicity'. For if it is to be by convention that to say *X* constitutes doing *Y*, it will be illuminating to consider why, and in how many sorts of ways, saying X sometimes doesn't quite, or even at all, amount to doing Y – why, and in how many sorts of ways, the purported doing may not happily 'come off'. What is involved in doing it properly will be illuminated by considering how things may go wrong. For of course, in these cases, doing is never *just* saying: it is saying 'happily' – saying, that is, in the absence of the sorts of things that Austin called misfires and abuses – misapplications, flaws, hitches, insincerities, and what not. Where there is a convention that to do (e.g. say) X counts as doing Y, Y will only actually get done if X is done (e.g. said) by the right person, at the right time and place, in the right way, and so on.

Third, it is again clearly right to say here, as Austin did, that one who issues a performative utterance in *this* sense does not commonly, in his utterance, state *that* he is doing what he is therein doing. In saying 'Three no trumps' I bid, but I do not state that I am bidding; in saying 'How's that?' (in cricket) I appeal, but I do not state that I am appealing; and so on. Austin held, I think, that one who, in saying X, does Y in fact *never* therein states that he is doing Y; this is highly arguable, and I argue it later; but it is certainly true and even obvious that he doesn't necessarily.

Fourth, if, as we have said, there is at this point no particular restriction on the kinds of doings that sayings sometimes are – except, of course, that they should be capable of being done, in virtue of suitable conventions, by saying something – it is equally clear, though far more commonly overlooked, that there can be at this point no restriction either on the kinds of sayings that can be doings. If our idea is, as I think it clear that Austin's idea originally was, that of sayings which, in virtue of conventions, constitute doings, it should be perfectly clear that sayings of any linguistic form or sort at all could figure in this role; it is simply a matter of laying down, or of there being, the relevant conventions. Like 'Three no trumps', such sayings need not be sentences; they need not even consist of (in any *other* connection) meaningful words of any language; but where sentences are uttered, they may be indicative, interrogative, imperative, active or passive, and so on and so on. Two points in particular. A saying which, by convention, counts as doing something could perfectly well be the saying of something true or false (though indeed, in such a case, truth or falsehood might not be the point mainly at issue) – so that the happy–unhappy distinction does not in any way *exclude* the true–false distinction (though of course it differs from it);[4] and secondly, while Austin's own

---

[4] Austin says at first that performative utterances are 'not true or false' (e.g. 'Performative Utterances', p. 222; 2nd edn, p. 235; and *How to Do Things with Words*, p. 5), and even seems at times to take that as a partial criterion of performativeness. He qualifies this later –

early examples happened to be mostly of the 'I *X*' form – in the non-continuous present tense, first person indicative active – there is actually no reason why performative utterances, in this sense, *should* be in, or even be capable of being put into, that form in particular. There is, as we shall see, something special about that form, but not in this connection; for it is really obvious that any sort of saying whatever – even an otherwise perfectly senseless one – could in principle, were there to exist the appropriate convention, count as or constitute doing something. For of course what distinguishes performative utterances in *this* sense is not that, grammatically or whatever, they are a special sort of saying, but that, whatever sort of saying they may be, there are conventions in virtue of which that saying counts as doing. The distinguishing feature is extra-linguistic. It is accordingly not surprising that, when Austin raised the question of a 'grammatical' criterion for performativeness,[5] he found that there was not one; what needs explaining is why he should even have toyed with the idea that there might be, and that I shall return to.

To sum up this first section, then: it seems to me that we have here a notion of performative utterance that is, or at least would be capable of being made, quite decently clear. We assume the existence of languages that people speak, in which all sorts of things, on all sorts of topics, can be said. We observe that there are, in law and in games but in many other cases too, things that people do that essentially consist in, or are constituted by, the exploitation or invocation of certain conventions (other than those, if they are such, involved in merely speaking the language); and we observe further that, in some of these cases, exploiting or invoking the relevant conventions crucially consists in, or includes, the uttering of certain words. We can then say with clear sense that, in such cases, one who issues the relevant utterance not merely *says* something (as in any standard instance of speaking the language), but further, in virtue of the applicable convention, thereby (of course if things otherwise go happily) *does* something; and we call the sub-class of utterances of which this is true *performative* utterances. What we have thus got is not, we observe, a special sort of sentences, or anything in any way distinguishable on purely linguistic grounds; what we have is a class of utterances, linguistically quite heterogeneous, which have in common that, in virtue of non-

'Considerations of the type of truth and falsity may infect performatives (or some performatives)' (*How to Do Things with Words*, p. 55) – not, however, as a glance at his text will show, for anything like the reason I have in mind here.

[5] *How to Do Things with Words*, pp. 55ff.

linguistic conventions, to issue them (happily) *counts as doing* this or that. As such they are, of course, a sub-class not only of utterances, but also of what might be called conventionally-significant doings, many of which will differ in not involving utterance at all.

II

To launch our second stage, let us bring up again the basic thought that sometimes to *say* something is to *do* something. We have considered and sketched one way in which this might be taken – in which it would be true that some utterances, but not all, are 'performative'; namely, some utterances sometimes play a crucial, indeed 'operative' role in the execution of convention-constituted doings or procedures. But of course one might move from that basic thought in a very different direction. For surely, one might say, to say something is, not sometimes, but absolutely always, to do something; and this, I take it, though as vague as could be, is undoubtedly in some sense true. There is a sense, then, one might wish to say, in which *all* utterances are performative; that is, whenever anyone says anything, there is always *something* that he therein does. And thus there comes in the whole topic of what came to be called 'speech acts' – of those things that are done, not now just sometimes, but standardly, even always, even necessarily perhaps, in standardly issuing any utterance in a language at all.

Now this topic of speech acts – which is indeed, if not inexhaustible, at any rate very, very far from being exhausted – is not one that I mean to embark upon on this occasion. I want to say in this connection only four brief things.

The first is that, if it is true, as I presume it is, that to say something is always, in a considerable diversity of ways and senses, to do something – so that in that sense, if we choose to say so, all utterance is performative – it obviously does not follow that we were wrong before; it does not follow that the previously-sketched class of what we might call Mark I performative utterances was in any way a bogus class, or that there was anything amiss in our distinction of those utterances from others. There is nothing that this new thought, so to speak, requires us to give up; we are simply moving on to something else. For no doubt it is the case that to say, for instance, 'What's the date today?' or 'The train leaves at three', is to do something – various things indeed; but to say those things is not, ordinarily anyway, to do something in virtue of, or as an element in, some non-linguistic conventional procedure, in at all the way in which to say 'Three no trumps', in playing bridge, is to make a bid. Thus to observe that there is, and to embark on the investigation of, the general topic of the things speakers standardly do in speaking has no tendency at all to show that the foregoing attempt to isolate a *sub-class* of performative utterances has 'broken down';[6] we may think we have moved on from that to something more general and interesting, but we have also moved on to something quite different; for even if all speaking is – in one way or another – doing, it will still be only sometimes that to say is – in virtue of special, non-linguistic conventions – to do.

The second point is this. When we switch our attention from the first idea of a special sub-class of performative utterances to the investigation of what is done in speaking merely as such, we should be careful not to carry over to this latter topic notions that are valid only for the former one. Austin, I think, went a bit wrong here. It was a feature – it was, in fact, the defining feature – of performative utterances in the first sense that it was *by convention* that, in those cases, to say was to do; to say 'Three no trumps' was to bid because, and only because, there was a rule (convention) of the game being played in virtue of which such an utterance counted in appropriate circumstances as bidding. Austin, I believe, was apt to take for granted that the same was to be said of his later interest, speech acts in general – these also were to be, in general, conventional or convention-constituted acts.[7] But this surely is not true in general. It may be that one who issues the utterance 'The train leaves at three' therein says that the train leaves at three because, and only because, there are conventions of English which assign that sense to that sentence (it *may* be); but if, in saying 'The train leaves at three', I am warning you not to dilly-dally over your lunch, there is no *convention* which *makes* my utterance an act of warning, or of issuing *that* warning; it is an act of warning if I spoke with the intention of alerting you to some putative peril, in this case the possible peril of missing your train. This is true, I think, in general, though not without exception, of illocutionary forces; they are not in general convention-constituted – which is perhaps exactly why they can and

[6] Austin himself says at times that 'in its original form' the distinction 'breaks down' (e.g. 'Performative Utterances', p. 238; 2nd edn, p. 251; see also *How to Do Things with Words*, p. 149). He had in mind here both that 'stating' is in a way doing, and that 'something like' truth and falsity can 'infect' performatives. However, if the 'original' distinction is made to rest on the presence or absence of *conventions* in virtue of which certain utterances *count as* doing this or that, it does not break down at all, for those or any other reasons.

[7] E.g. *How to Do Things with Words*, p. 105, and several other passages also.

should be, for most utterances, distinguished from *meanings*. The idea that linguistic doings are somehow *all* 'conventional' is an improper hangover, I think, from the original idea of the Mark I kind of (by definition) convention-dependent performative utterance.[8]

My third and fourth points are almost too obvious to be worth mentioning, but let me not shrink from mentioning them all the same. They are that, if we move on to consider ways and senses in which to say is standardly, even always, to do, and if in that sense we see fit to say that all utterance is performative, it will be even more obvious than it was before that performative utterance does not stand in contrast with or exclude – for of course it will often simply *be* – the saying of something true or false; and it will also be even more obvious than it was before that one who, in speaking, does such-and-such does not necessarily, or even normally, state *that* he is doing it *in* what he says. If to speak is, in general, to perform speech acts, then obviously to say, truly or falsely, 'This train stops at Reading' is to perform speech acts; and if, in saying 'This train stops at Reading', I am, say, giving you information, I do not therein state *that* I am doing so, or *that* I am doing anything else either.

III

I come now to my third stage, which is less drably uncontroversial and, I hope, more interesting. We have just said, fearlessly stating the obvious, that, it being presumably true in some sense that a speaker who says anything at all therein does *something*, it is not necessarily true, or even often so, that in what he says he says *that* he is doing what he is doing (I can warn or advise or rebuke you, and so on, without saying *that* I do); and we may now add to this the observation that, when speakers speak, there will often be, not only no explicit *statement*, but nothing at all in the words themselves, which explicitly signals what speakers are doing in saying them – or it might be better to put that the other way round: when speakers speak, there will normally be at any rate some things they therein do the doing of which is not explicitly signalled in any way in the words they utter. But then our eye may be caught by another special case here – the case of what Austin came to call *explicit* performatives. Well, how do these fit in?

[8] Cf. Strawson, 'Intention and Convention in Speech Acts', first published in *Philosophical Review*, October 1964, pp. 439–60, also in his *Logico-Linguistic Paper* (1971), pp. 149–69.

Now the particular case that I want to say something about here is that common and quite familiar one in which the word for what (or rather, for one thing which) the speaker could be said to be doing in speaking actually enters as the main verb in the sentence he utters – where, in promising, he says 'I promise', in advising, 'I advise you to . . .', and so on. This is not, of course, as Austin often reminds us, the only way in which what the speaker is up to can be explicitly indicated in what he says; for – stretching 'speaker' and 'says' a little – we have for instance the cases of the notice reading 'Please keep car windows closed' with WARNING above, or of the sentence, 'Gas-capes will be worn' on a sheet of paper headed 'Part II Orders'; where it is, I suppose, made explicit that those sentences, respectively imperative and future-tense indicative, are to be taken respectively as issuings of a warning and an order. However, the case in which the word for what the speaker is doing appears, in the first person, as the verb in the sentence he utters has features of special interest, and that is the case that I want to go on about.

The first issue is this. We have here a special class of utterances – the special case in which, as does not usually occur, the speaker explicitly indicates something that he is doing in speaking by incorporating the word *for* what he is doing *in* what he says. Now, is this the *same* special case as that of Mark I performative utterance – the case of 'operative' utterance as roughed out in my first section above? I regret to say that something of this sort has certainly, very sloppily, been supposed; it has been thought, that is, that, starting out with the basic idea that to say is sometimes to do, and going on to reflect that to say, after all, is always to do *something*, we can then be led back, so to speak, to our original notion of a *special* case by observing that there really is that special case in which what is done is explicitly indicated *in* the utterance. Though it pains me to mention this, I myself once wrote as follows:

Austin supposed at first that such [i.e. performative] utterances were a special case – that these cases, in which to say something was to do something, to 'perform an act', could be contrasted with more ordinary cases of simple saying. But later, in the course of trying to make this contrast clearer and sharper, he came to realize that, while his original performative utterances were indeed a special case, they were not special quite in the way that he had supposed. It was not that, in those cases, to say something was to do something, for this, he now held, was true of every case . . . The difference is that, in the cases he had at first considered, it is made *explicit* in the utterance what speech act it is that the speaker is performing. This indeed is a special feature of certain utterances . . .[9]

[9] *English Philosophy since 1900* (2nd edn, 1969), p. 104.

I regret to say, however, that this, though it seems to run quite smoothly and would be, historically, pleasingly neat if it were correct, is actually completely wrong; the train of thought sketched, that is, is a muddled and mistaken one.

It is really perfectly obvious that this is so; we have here two quite different special cases, in no sense one and the same one. For one thing, while the examples with which Austin introduced the notion of performative utterance were mostly (which I suppose is what misleads one) of the explicit performative kind, it is just not true that all were – he cites, for instance, the 'operative' words in the ceremony of marriage, which, whatever they may be, are certainly not 'I marry . . .'. Again, there is really, as I have noted above, no suggestion at that early stage that the doings that sayings sometimes are are to be '*speech* acts'. But above all what Austin says at that stage *about* performative utterances plainly does not require that they *should* be of the explicit performative form, even if it so happened that a lot of his examples were – for if the Mark I idea is, as I think it clearly was, that of utterance which, in virtue of some appropriate convention, counts as or constitutes doing such-and-such, then there is, as we have noted, plainly no restriction whatever on what shape or form such utterances might have, and in particular no reason why they *should* be of the form 'I X', where 'X-ing' is the word for what the speaker does. The idea of saying something which, by convention, counts as doing such-and-such, and the idea of saying something in which the *words* make explicit in a particular way *what* one is doing, are really completely different ideas; the classes of utterances they pick out are not even extensionally equivalent; and therefore I was, of course, completely wrong in representing the notion of the explicit performative formula as some kind of reinstatement, or more sophisticated version, of the original notion. But if I got this point wrong, I do not think Austin himself was perfectly clear about it; for he raises at an early stage, as I have already mentioned, the question whether there is a reliable formal, or as he puts it 'grammatical', way of identifying Mark I performative utterances; and although he comes correctly to the conclusion that there is not, he does not say explicitly, as I think he could and should have done, that there is absolutely no reason to think that there might have been. The notion he thought at any rate worth examining – that performative utterances might be those that were either already in, or could readily be put into, the 'I X' form, in saying which the speaker X-es – is one that, I think, would not have struck him as even plausible if he had quite clearly seen that what he later called explicit performatives were *quite* different creatures from the Mark I variety, 'operative' utterances in convention-constituted procedures.[10] For whereas it is of course the distinctive 'formal' mark of these explicit performatives that the word for what the speaker is doing puts in a special sort of appearance in the sentence he utters, there is absolutely no reason why the operative words in some conventional procedure *should* include the *word for* what is, by convention, done in their (felicitous) utterance. There is no reason why the conventional formulae for bidding (in bridge) should have to incorporate the word 'bid', or for appealing (in cricket) to incorporate the word 'appeal'; such formulae can, as we have seen, be of any verbal form at all, and there could not possibly be a *formal* way of picking them out.

Next, I want to put forward the proposition that latter-day explicit performatives are, not only not identical or co-extensive with Mark I performative utterances, but actually far more unlike them, and far more like what we may vaguely call 'ordinary' utterances, than has, to my knowledge, been supposed hitherto.[11] Consider the Mark I performative utterance 'Three no trumps', as issued appropriately by a speaker engaged in playing bridge. We can agree, I take it, that he therein bids; that it is in virtue of a rule or convention of the game being played that he therein bids; but that, though he bids, he does not in what he says say *that* he bids, or (in this case) say anything at all that is true or false. Now much of this was held by Austin, and has been held more or less unquestioningly by many others, to be true also of explicit performatives, of the 'I *X*' species of utterance in issuing which the speaker *X*-es. This is why Austin said that such utterances were 'masqueraders';[12] being in the first person present indicative active, they look like, one might almost say they pose as,

---

[10] What makes the task of the historical disentangler a rather difficult one here is that Austin in fact – and in *How to Do Things with Words*, fully overtly – introduced the idea of performatives in a 'provisional' way, but did not subsequently consider in any great detail how much of the provisional account was to be conceived of as surviving. It was thus possible to think, as I did, that the 'provisional' performative turned out to survive, after refinement, *as* the *explicit* performative; and it is not, I think, certain that Austin did not think so too, though I hope he did not.

[11] When I first wrote what follows, in 1970, I had the feeling of going riskily out on an otherwise unoccupied limb. I had come across something close to what I wished to say in Stephen Schiffer's thesis *Meaning* (then unpublished); but he, perhaps rightly of course, did not go quite so far. Later, however, David Wiggins brought to my notice his own claim that explicit performatives can be taken as 'straightforward statements', in a then unpublished piece called 'On sentence-sense, word-sense and difference of word-sense', which was to appear in *Semantics*, ed. L. A. Jacobovits and D. D. Steinberg (1971); and he mentioned other allies. See also a tentative footnote in my *The Object of Morality* (1971), p. 107.

[12] E.g. *How to Do Things with Words*, p. 4.

autobiographical *statements* by the speaker about himself, whereas in fact, he held, one who says, for example, 'I promise' does not say *that* he promises, or anything else that could be true or false – he just *promises*, and he does so, moreover, in virtue of a convention. But I now want to suggest that there is actually no need to look at it in this way at all – that explicit performative utterances are *not* masqueraders, that they are to be construed exactly as their form or 'grammar' suggests that they should be, and that conventions do not (necessarily anyway) come in at all here. Austin was at pains to distinguish making it explicit that one is doing something, from saying that one does it; in explicitly performative utterance, he held, the speaker does not say *that* he, for instance, advises, but merely makes it explicitly clear that he does so. I want to suggest that this is not so – that in saying, for example, 'I advise you to resign', I do indeed make it explicitly clear that I am offering you advice, but that I do so just by saying, truly or falsely, that I do. It seems clear that this suggestion, if one can make it stand up, would be theoretically to be much welcomed, as much simplifying any general doctrine of the indicative mood. The class of explicit performatives, that is, would not have to appear as an exception, or anomaly, to the tidy principle that one who says 'I *X*' therein says that he *X*-es, but as a perfectly regular, standard use of the first person present indicative active. For that reason, one would *like* what I am about to propound to be correct; but is it?

Well, some, I dare say, will think it just *obvious* that it is wrong; they may find it just obvious, as apparently Austin did, and as I myself did for years and years, that 'I promise', said in promising, is not true or false, and in particular that one who so says 'I promise' does not say that he promises. But what arguments are there, in fact, against the contrary view?

One, I suppose, might go like this. What I am suggesting is, in effect, that explicit performatives are to be construed as perfectly *ordinary* first person present indicatives. Now one who produces an undoubted sentence of that sort, the sentence, for instance, 'I smoke', undoubtedly says therein that he smokes; and what he so says of himself is either true or false; but of course for him to say that he smokes, and even to say truly that he smokes, is not for him to smoke. So what about, say, 'I promise'? If the case is analogous, then to say 'I promise', however fully felicitously, while it is to say that I promise, will not be to promise. But surely it is agreed on all hands that that is just what it is.

But this argument fails, I think. It relies on the general principle that to say that one does something is not, and cannot be, to do it – from which, of course, it would follow that promising cannot be saying (however felicitously) *that* one promises, or vice versa. But is this principle true? Very obviously it is true in those many cases, such as that of smoking, where *what* one says that one does, and the question whether or not one does it, is wholly independent of, detachable from one's saying that, or indeed saying anything at all; but of course, in the case of explicit performatives, we are dealing precisely with things that people do *in* saying things, their doing of which (or not) is therefore *not* independent of what they say. And may it not be precisely here that the principle of the above argument fails, and indeed should be expected to fail? For if to promise, unlike to smoke, is essentially to *say* something, why should it *not* be to say *that* one promises? Consider a different but obviously kindred case. The notice reads 'Customers are warned not to leave valuables in the cloak-room.' By that notice, customers are warned. But what does the notice *say*? Surely, *it says that they are.* I can see no fissure here between it being said that they are, and their actually being so. Of course, if the notice had read (surprisingly) 'Customers are badly treated here', it would have remained an open question whether or not they were; but that is because the question whether or not they are badly treated, unlike the question whether or not they are warned, is quite independent of what the notice says. Can we not say, in the warning case, that what the notice says – namely, *that* customers are warned – is in effect *made true* by the fact that the notice says it, and hence that saying that customers are warned *is* warning the customers? That the text of the notice sets out, so to speak, to make itself true, and *can* make itself true, is shown, I think, by the fact, noted of course by Austin, that in such a case one can stick in the word 'hereby'; the notice says that customers are warned, not by something or someone *else* who might actually fall down on the job, but hereby, by itself, by this notice, by the very one whose text *says* that customers are warned. 'Hereby' is an indication that the utterance *itself* is doing the job that it says is done.

One might object, more trivially, that while one may indeed, in saying 'I promise', say that one promises, that case is precisely the one in which one does not promise. 'What do you do when your wife complains of your habitual indolence?' – 'I promise to work harder.' This, however, is just what we may call the other use of the present tense; and from the fact that if, in saying 'I promise', I mean that I habitually promise, I do not there and then promise, it cannot follow that I do not there and then promise when, in saying ' I promise', I mean that I there and then do. Once again, 'hereby' might come in here as a disambiguating device. If, in saying 'I promise' I think that it might be supposed that I am therein alluding to what I do on some *other* occasions, I could put 'hereby' into my utterance, and thus make it clear that the promising I say that I do is done in this utterance itself, in what I here and now say.

But, an objector might continue, when speaking of what we here and now do, surely we use in English the *continuous* present; when I play cricket, I state what I then do, if I have occasion to do so, in the form 'I am playing cricket.' So if, say in promising, my utterance were to be statementally about what I there and then do, should it not be, as it is not and cannot be, in the form 'I am promising'? But there is not much in this. Explicit performatives, as a matter of fact, occasionally *are* in the continuous present – 'I'm warning you' is every bit as common as 'I warn you.' But it is actually not hard to see why, usually, they are not. The continuous present, after all, is most at home with doings one is engaged in which extend, so to speak, beyond the temporal boundaries of one's saying, if one happens to do so, that one is doing them; but with explicit performatives, one's doing the thing coincides with, does *not* temporally overspread, one's saying that one does it. And in such a case – the case of, so to speak, temporal concurrence of word and deed – in other instances too, it is the non-continuous present tense that one naturally resorts to. Severing the jugular vein of the patient in the operating theatre, I say concurrently and explanatorily to the assembled students 'I sever the jugular vein . . .'. Thus, if I am to say *that* I here and now promise, that I should say 'I promise' is exactly what one would expect.

But another snag now awaits us. It was first objected that to say *that* one does something cannot be to do it; I replied that I did not see why that should be so, in the case in which what one does, and says that one does, is itself a piece of *saying*. But, it may then be objected, if that is so, saying for instance, 'I promise' could not be, even if it were saying that one promises, saying so *truly or falsely*. For if I promise *in* saying that I do, what I say would substantiate itself and *could* not be false. (We said just above that the notice 'makes itself true'.) But can that be said to be even true, which could not be said falsely? Now one might, in principle, bluntly counter this move by saying: why not? If my saying that *p* were a fully sufficient condition of its being the case that *p*, then indeed I could not falsely say that *p*; but *that p* could perfectly well be either true or false – true, of course, *ex hypothesi*, if it happens to be said that *p* by me, but perhaps false otherwise (cf. 'I exist', 'I am alive', perhaps 'I am awake'). But in fact we do not need, I believe, that line of defence here; for one can well hold, I think, that one *can* say falsely that one promises (and likewise *mutatis mutandis* for other explicit performatives). For promising is, as we earlier platitudinously remarked, not *just* saying that one does so, just producing that dictum. For it to be the case that one promises, there must (very roughly) be some envisaged commitment, asked for by, or offered to, some second party, which in one's utterance one formally undertakes. If I say here and now 'I promise', out of the blue, I have not – other necessary circumstances being absent in this case – therein promised; so that in such a case, maybe, I say that I promise, but falsely – I do not. (Of course I don't make a false promise – that's a different matter.) This is only to say, I think, that, on this present view as on any other, we must take due account of Austinian infelicities. On any view, I do not promise in saying 'I promise' if the circumstances in which I speak are wrong for the purpose; so that, on my view, it seems it can quite well be held that, in unhappy circumstances, one may say that one promises falsely, when actually one does not. And if it were further objected, as it might well be, that in saying 'I promise', just out of the blue, one cannot be supposed really even to have said that one promised, then I could reply *either* that there are less grossly infelicitous cases in which, though I do seriously say that I promise, it is still not true that I do – *or* that, if it is to be held that one really *says that* one promises when and only when one's utterance is fully felicitous and therefore one promises, I must adopt the blunt fall-back position mentioned above – of maintaining, that is, that there is nothing in principle vicious in the idea of a proposition which, while it can be true or false, can't be falsely asserted, or rather, can't be falsely asserted by a particular person. I do not like that, however, in this present case; it seems to me better to say that, since just saying 'I promise' is not, on any view, the sole and sufficient element in promising, it is possible to say that one promises when one does not, just as – or anyway, somewhat as – it is possible to say that one smokes when one does not. (I repeat that this is not, obviously, the case of a false promise, in which case one does promise, not intending to perform.) In all this, of course, I must not be taken as denying that explicit performative utterances are any sort of special case at all. Obviously, in a way, they are – for they have the peculiarity that, since in these cases what the speaker says that he does is something that is done in speaking, and indeed is in fact done by him (if all goes well) in saying the very thing that he says, the truth-value of what he says is involved (let us say vaguely) in a decidedly unusual way with the fact that he says it. But one can quite well concede, as clearly one must, that explicit performative utterances are a rather peculiar lot in *this* way, without holding that they are peculiar in not having truth-values at all, or in being anomalous, masquerading exceptions to the comfortable principle that one who says something of the form 'I X' therein says that he X-es.

I want now to turn from thinking up arguments *against* the idea that explicit performatives are not 'masqueraders', and instead to draw attention to one of its significant implications. It would follow, I think, terminologically most inconveniently, that explicit performative utterances are – or at any rate are for the most part – not performative utterances at all, in the original, Mark I sense of that appellation. This is easily seen. It will be recalled that the class of Mark I performative utterances consisted of those which, in virtue of some not simply linguistic convention, counted as, when happily issued, *doing* this or that – as saying, in playing bridge. 'Three no trumps' constitutes *bidding*. But now, if the suggestion I have been putting forward is correct, most (anyway) explicit performatives are not like this at all. For it is surely the position, if I am right, that what makes it the case that, in saying (happily) 'I promise' or 'I advise you to . . .', I promise or advise is, not a convention in virtue of which to speak so counts as or constitutes promising or advising, but simply the standard, normal *meaning* of the words that I utter. I have already suggested that, if I warn you in saying 'The train leaves at three', it is not a convention, but certain facts about the situation, which make it the case that in so speaking I warn you; what I now want to say is that if I warn you *explicitly*, by saying, for instance, 'I warn you that the train leaves at three', it is again no special convention that makes it the case that in so speaking I warn you, but in this case, straightforwardly, the standard meaning of what I say. You will not grasp what I do in saying 'Three no trumps' if, though you understand English, you are unfamiliar with the rules, or with the relevant rule, of bridge; but I suggest that, in order to grasp what I do in saying 'I warn you that . . .', you need no equipment beyond the understanding of English. If that is so, then explicit performatives, for the most part anyway, are not by *convention* operative utterances, to issue which conventionally counts as doing this or that; there are no special conventions; they are indeed utterances in issuing which (happily) this or that is done, but *what* is done is done simply in virtue of what they mean. If that is so, then they are for the most part not Mark I performatives at all. The qualifications are to allow for the fact that they sometimes might be. Where we have, in some game, for instance, some convention-constituted performance X-ing, then indeed it might be, though of course it need not be, *by convention* an essential constituent in X-ing that the appropriate person is formally to say 'I X'. In cricket, for instance, to declare an innings closed, it might have been required by rule that the captain of the batting side should shout '*Basta!*', or wave his arms at the umpires in some particular manner; but equally it might have been required (though I do not believe it is) that he should formally say 'I declare the innings closed.' Well, *if* the latter had been the case, then the explicit performative 'I declare the innings closed' would not merely have meant that he declared the innings closed, but would also have been *by convention* 'operative' in his actually doing so. The classes, then, of Mark I performatives and of explicit performatives, though they are not the same, could have, quite contingently of course, some members in common.

I can sum up what I have been arguing for in this paper, putting things in a rather different order, as follows:

(1) There is, I suppose, if one chooses to say so, a tolerable sense in which all utterance is, or normally is, performative; whenever anyone speaks there are things – many things of many sorts – that he could be said therein to do; so that we have a general topic, as yet unexhausted nor even very well defined, that we could call the topic of 'speech acts'. We note here that it is not necessarily, though it may be sometimes, in virtue of a *convention* (other than those conventions, if they are such, which give sentences their senses) that to issue a certain utterance is to perform a certain speech act; not all speech acts are 'conventional', though doubtless some are. It will depend mostly, of course, on what species of speech act one is talking about.

(2) The fact that, if we choose to say so, all utterance is in that sense performative does not imply that there is not, and never was, a legitimate *sub-class* of utterances called 'performative', to issue which is in a *special* way to do something; and there seem in fact to be at least two such special sub-classes, very different from each other though having some members in common.

(*a*) First, there is that sub-class of utterances the issuing of which *by convention* (over and above what, if anything, the words uttered conventionally mean) is 'operative' in the doing of this or that; put otherwise, there is a class of conventional acts which can be, or normally are, or even necessarily are, done *by* the utterance of certain conventionally prescribed words; in such cases, the utterance is 'operative' in a *special* way, and can be said in a *special* sense to be a performative utterance. There is, however, no special verbal form that such utterances have to take; there is no reason why they should not sometimes take the form of saying something which is true or false; the word *for* what is done in issuing them *may*, by convention, be required to figure in the utterance, possibly in the first person present indicative active, but there is no particular reason why that should be so, and very often it is not so. Finally, one who does something by issuing an utterance of this sort does not necessarily, or even usually, say *in* his utterance that he does the thing in question.

(*b*) Then there is another sub-class of utterances, identifiable by the purely formal special feature that, being in the first person present indicative active (I omit, merely for brevity, the familiar passive form), they have as main verb the *word for* what (one thing which) a speaker would be said to do in issuing them. This sub-class is importantly distinct from the former one in two major respects – first, that its members, unlike those of the former one, are all by definition of a certain verbal form; and second, that it is not, as in the former case it was, necessarily, or even often, *by convention* that to issue the utterance is to do the thing. At any rate in my submission, we can quite well hold here that the speaker, in his utterance, says *that* he does the thing in question – so that, first, such utterances can be construed as perfectly regular, non-anomalous, un-exceptional, non-masquerading uses of the first person present indicative active, and second, *what* the speaker does is usually a function, not of any special convention, but simply of the standard meaning of what he says. There may, however, occur the special case in which saying that one does something does happen to be, by convention, an essential 'operative' element in actually doing it; and in that case, members of this second sub-class will also be members of the former one.

Well, perhaps that all seems very obvious, and indeed I hope it does. Historically, what has I think tended to obscure the issue is (1) that Austin, from the beginning, introduced *simultaneously* the above two sub-classes – conventionally 'operative' utterances, and explicit performative utter-ances – without explicitly saying, and without perhaps always or wholly clearly seeing, that he had got in the hand two birds of very different feather, not one bird; and (2) that, when he moved on from *special* ways of being performative to consider those many ways in which all utterance could, if one likes, be called performative, he certainly sometimes gave, and it is hard not to think that he also sometimes got, the mistaken impression that the special ways of being performative had turned out to be somehow illusory, that in some way or other the 'original' distinction had, as he sometimes said himself and as others have said too, 'broken down'. Once we have firmly made what I hope are some decently clear and defensible distinctions here, we might perhaps be further assisted by some new terminology; perhaps the *word* 'performative' really has rather broken down, under the strain of being given too many different jobs to do, and might usefully in future be relieved of some of its duties. But I have no particular terminological innovations to suggest.

10

Imperatives and Meaning

I believe that the question of imperatives retains some interest – and even, if I am right, some power to surprise. I am not thinking, primarily anyway, of the large and heterogeneous class of utterances that could be said to function in an imperative way, but of the grammatically identifiable class of actual sentences in the imperative mood. One reasonably has, I think, the initial feeling that occurrences, in the use of natural languages, of sentences of this class are peculiar, perhaps problematic, in being more than usually intimately involved (vaguely) with particular speakers, addressees, and linguistic performances. That one speaker is addressing another person, or other persons, or just conceivably himself, seems in this case somehow to get into the sense of the sentence itself; and questions seem also insistently to arise as to what is going on between the parties, what the speaker is doing in speaking – imperatives seem 'practical' – and all this is connected no doubt with their inflexibility in the matter of persons and tenses. Considerations of this general kind form the main ground, I believe, of the uneasiness which philosophers have often felt about the notion of 'imperative logic'. I believe that this uneasiness is well founded; and in this paper, after sketching (for the record) some of the rather inconclusive, quite familiar perplexities about imperatives, I shall try to bring out what seems to me to be the basic awkwardness in the case. This looks paradoxical, but I think is quite literally sustainable: it is not possible to say what imperative sentences mean.

If there is to be such a thing as imperative logic, there has to be something for it to be the logic of. Presumably that would have to be 'imperative argument', or 'imperative inference'. It is not, however, by any means clear straight off what those would be. Take, for example, one of the little sequences apt to occur in discussions of this topic, 'Do A or B',

From *Contemporary British Philosophy*, ed. H. D. Lewis (Allen and Unwin, 1976).

'Do not do A', 'Do B' – in which the third item is suggested to follow, to be a conclusion, from the other two. One would like this, I take it, to be understandable as a succinct representation of some possible process of discourse or thought; but what process of discourse or thought, and by whom? Are we to envisage someone reflecting 'I tell X to do A or B, and not to do A; so . . .' – but so *what?* So X is to do B? The speaker is entitled, nay required, to *tell* X to do B? Or is it that he has – 'in effect', 'implicitly', though not actually – already done so? Why, in any case, should any speaker tell any addressee to do one or other of two things, *and not* to do one of them? Perhaps he might first issue the disjunctive imperative, and later, on further reflection perhaps, or in the light of new facts, the non-disjunctive negative one; but if so, is it important, and would we want it to be important, in imperative logic in what order imperative 'premises' are set out? With premises, it would not ordinarily occur to us that that could matter. Or are we to look at the matter from the addressee's point of view – to consider, perhaps, how someone, to whom has been addressed some set or sequence of imperatives, might try to work out what, taken collectively, they 'tell' him to do? If so, there seems liable to break in the very awkward question, by whom the imperatives were issued in the first place. A colonel's order 'overrides' a corporal's; but is it a tolerable thought that it should be a matter of logic that that is so? Alternatively, are we to make the general stipulation that imperative 'premises' are always to be taken as issued by one and the same speaker? But that looks pretty curious also, as a matter of logic; for we do not usually, in considering what follows from this or that, need to ask who said it.

It is perhaps only another way of saying the same thing to remind ourselves that imperative sentences do not as such fit syntactically into what one might call the apparatus of argument. Propositions can be argumentatively concatenated by *if* or *since, therefore* or *then*; but to follow *if* or *since*, imperatives must be transformed, and the question arises how that is to be done. 'If I tell you to . . .'? 'If you are told to . . .'? 'If I am told to. . .'? 'If I am to . . .', perhaps? Without transformation, imperative sentences stand, as it were, rigidly in mere adjacency to one another, so that, as I have said, what process of thought is intended does not luminously emerge; but exactly what transformations is one supposed to be allowed to make?

Further, imperative logic seems not well-defined, in that its scope cannot, it appears, be intelligibly limited to imperative sentences. 'Shut the door' is perhaps not in *logical* conflict with 'The door is shut' – in such a case it may be that one should speak rather of 'presupposition'; but 'Shut the door' at least appears to be flatly, directly contradicted by 'You may leave the door open', which latter is, of course, not an imperative at all. But if imperative logic does not treat only of imperatives, how are we to make the extent of its subject-matter tidily clear?

These are all pretty familiar points, and they may well be manageable more or less. If, for example, it is conceded that it is not *clear* what process of thought, what progression of argument, is supposed to be represented by such a string as 'Do A or B', 'Do not do A', 'Do B', it might be said that what is called for is not despair, nor even clarification, but rather stipulation. Perhaps it can simply be laid down that, for this purpose, sets of imperatives are to be appraised in the light of the question 'when given a command, what other commands must necessarily be fulfilled if we are to fulfil the first command' (R. M. Hare, *Practical Inferences* (1971), p. 42); or alternatively, and differently, in the light of the question 'what other things we are, implicitly, commanding when we give a certain command' (ibid., p. 43). Perhaps it is just a matter of making up our own minds as between various possibilities available to us. I do not quite see that all the snags can be negotiated in this way – what, for instance, of the question of logical *liaisons* with sentences that are not imperatives at all? – but perhaps many can be, and in any case, if I am right, there are less tractable difficulties yet to be mentioned.

There is, I believe, a difficulty at least *prima facie* with the notion, in this context, of inconsistency. It is obvious enough that, if we are to be in a position to apply any terms of logical appraisal to imperatives, we shall need to know what 'inconsistent' is to mean here; but it is not of course clear straight off what 'inconsistent' *could* mean here, since of course we cannot define it with direct reference to truth. We cannot say that imperatives are inconsistent if they cannot both be true, since it makes no sense to call such things, or what is 'said' when such things are uttered, either true or false.

I believe that this has usually been regarded, however, as a minor, even an unreal, perplexity, on the ground that a usable sense of 'inconsistent' for imperatives is quite readily derivable from that of what we may call ordinary inconsistency. Somewhat as, we may say, propositions are inconsistent if they cannot both (or all) be true, imperatives may be said to be inconsistent if they cannot both (or all) be 'fulfilled'; and this looks like an intelligible derivative from ordinary inconsistency, since it amounts to saying that imperatives are inconsistent if it would be ordinarily inconsistent to affirm all those things actually to be done which they require should be done. 'Do X' would be thus inconsistent with 'Do Y', if the proposition that A does X is inconsistent with the proposition that A does Y. Imperatives are, in general, inconsistent if their conjunction amounts to requiring that to be done, the actual doing of which cannot be consistently described; the notion of contradictory imperatives is derivable from that of self-contradictory tasks, or performances.

But this manoeuvre, satisfactory so far as it goes, does not go far enough to leave the picture perfectly clear. It has been correctly pointed out by Bernard Williams (*Proceedings of the Aristotelian Society*, supp. vol. XL, 1966) that there remains a certain asymmetry between indicative and imperative inconsistency in that, whereas there is equally something wrong both in making inconsistent assertions and in silently accepting inconsistent beliefs, it appears that there is something wrong only in actually issuing inconsistent imperatives. It is not at all clear, in fact, what the silent analogue of that locutionary performance would be; but if it were, say, *wanting* someone to do inconsistent things, that state of mind may be an unfortunate one, but it is not of course impossible, nor does it involve any 'wrongness' or error – there is nothing in it to merit the professional censure of the logician.

I believe that this is correct; but there seems also something more to be said. There is, from a logical point of view, nothing 'wrong' in being, say, silently inclined to issue imperatives that would be inconsistent in the sense explained; but is it yet clear what would be wrong in actually issuing them? It is extremely important for this topic, I believe, not to be too quickly satisfied with an easy answer to this question.

One's immediate thought is, no doubt, that it must be wrong to tell someone to do something that it is actually – indeed, logically – not possible that he should do; one might want to say, indeed, that if the putative specification of what is to be done is itself self-contradictory, in such a case one has not really 'told' him to do anything at all – that one has in a sense, much as in the case of ordinary self-contradiction, said nothing, nothing that the addressee could even *try* to comply with. But there is a lurking over-simplification here. Presumably if I intend that you should do, and (say) order or purport to order you to do, everything that I say, then I have made a mess of it if that is not logically possible, if my orders are contradictory. But imperatives, of course, are neither necessarily nor exclusively used in giving orders – so that what is wrong with giving someone contradictory *orders* does not tell us in general what is wrong, or whether anything is, with issuing inconsistent imperatives. It may be objected that it *must* be wrong to 'tell' someone to do logically impossible, inconsistent things; but may it not be that, in that objection, 'tell' is liable to be tacitly construed as 'order', so that the remark is still really about orders, rather than imperatives?

Consider the following cases. The commandant of the prisoner-of-war camp, on the losing side in a war that will foreseeably end very soon, receives the desperate instruction from higher authority that all his prisoners are to be shot. He receives this gloomily, not unmindful of possible indictments of the defeated before war-crimes tribunals. He sends for his subordinate officer currently on duty, outlines his warm regard for military duty and his ardent patriotism, and mentions also the foreseeable hazards that in these days may threaten the defeated. He says in conclusion 'So my order is: shoot all the prisoners. My advice is: don't.'

Second, consulted perhaps in my capacity as your broker, attentive as such to your financial interests but acutely conscious also of my own, I advise you to withdraw the money I now hold on your behalf ('Withdraw the money') and go on to implore you not to ('Please don't withdraw it').

What is the right view to take of such cases as these? The commandant in the first case is not in the (I dare say) logically culpable position of having given his subordinate contradictory orders; for he has given him only one order, a perfectly coherent though no doubt ethically objection-able one, and he is, in general, entitled to give him orders. As your broker, in the second case, I do not give you inconsistent advice; for my advice to you is perfectly clear and intelligible, even though I go on to implore you, as a friend perhaps, not to take it. It might be said of course that the com-mandant has not unequivocally 'told' his subordinate to do things which, taken together and all round, it is actually possible that he should do – that, on the contrary, he has been 'told' to do something logically impossible. But it is quite clear that 'told' here simply conceals the problem. The subordinate was ordered to do one thing, and advised to do another; the commandant spoke first as a loyal officer, then as a prudent fellow; is *that* 'inconsistent'? It is even, one might think, quite clear what a subordinate so addressed is actually to do, even though what was said to him contained 'inconsistent' imperatives; having been given an order, and a piece of sagacious advice, he is to consider for himself whether to follow the advice or obey the order. In the second case the broker's proceedings might be thought not only intelligible but positively admirable. I cannot properly, as your financial counsellor, *advise* you to take a certain course of action just because, or mainly because, that would suit my book; my advice must be based on assessment of your financial interests, not mine. But there seems no reason why, after scrupulously giving you advice on that basis, I should not go on to implore you not to follow it. And again, is it at all unclear, really, what you are to do? You are to weigh my professional advice against my non-professional pleas, and make up your mind what you will actually do.

It may be said – and said, indeed, with obvious justice – that there is *something* a bit rum, unideal, about these cases. It may be true that in the normal, neat case of giving (say) an order, he who gives it is unperplexedly of a mind that the addressee should actually do the thing in question. It may be true (though it is not, in fact, at all clear why, even as a rule, it should be) that one who offers advice should want the person advised to act as he is advised to. But what if these tidy conditions do not hold? It is really quite clear that I may be positively obliged to give you an order to do something which I also think you would be most ill advised to do; or that your interests may lead me to give you advice of a sort that my interests make me fervently want you not to follow. It is true that in such cases one is scarcely likely to say baldly 'Do it; and don't'; but one still might, in the course of a not much longer slice of discourse, actually say both.

Are such cases perhaps to be brought under the rubric 'unhappy'? Well, no doubt they could be. But it is again not perfectly clear what we are to make of that. Could it be held that, if I advise you not to do something, there is some sense in which I cannot also have ('really') ordered you to do it? That seems more than dubious. To be given an order and advised not to obey it may indeed be perplexing, but it seems that that *is* what is perplexing – to be actually given both the order and the advice. Both, though no doubt in odd circumstances, really are given; or at least it is not at all clear that that cannot be so.

The source of the uncertainty one feels about these cases is, as it appears to me, the fact that they are cases in which imperatives occur in what one might call different performative modes. It seems plain enough that there has to be something wrong with self-contradictory orders, self-contradictory instructions, self-contradictory advice, or prayers, or pleas; for in such cases, one might say, there ought to be, is supposed to be, some single upshot – what the addressee is, all-in, ordered, instructed, advised, implored to do – and things must be wrong if that one supposed upshot comes out in an incoherent, unintelligible form. But the case of an order-issuing imperative 'contradicted' by an advice-offering imperative is not bad in exactly that way; for in that case there is not in the same sense any purported, single, composite upshot – or if there is, it might be the *non*-contradictory one that the addressee is to weigh up his predicament and make up his own mind. So it is at least not clear that we have here a case of discourse that is logically reprehensible at all – so that either the imperatives in the case are, formal appearances notwithstanding, not 'really' inconsistent, or – which looks even stranger – inconsistency in imperative discourse is not necessarily logically reprehensible. If that were so, the prospect for logic would be indeed unpromising.

A line of thought here temptingly offers itself. Have we not, it may be said, been allowing the picture to become confused and unsatisfactory in consequence of involvement with considerations that, from a *logical* point of view, should be disregarded? For surely, from a logical point of view, it should not be held to matter what particular speakers might be doing in speaking. That all men are mortal, for instance, might be said in warning, by way of a reminder, as an objection, as consolation, purely informatively, and in many other styles, but one need not as a logician become confused by that consideration; one can simply ignore it. For the logical *liaisons* and incompatibilities of the proposition – that all men are mortal – are independent of who says it, why, in what circumstances, in doing what, and indeed of whether anyone has occasion to say it at all. 'All men are mortal' is inconsistent with 'Some men are not mortal'; and that is just so, whoever (if anyone) says either, or whatever he or they may be up to in saying so. So should we not, in order to clarify the logical consistencies and inconsistencies of imperatives, similarly abstract *what is said* – as it were the imperative 'proposition' – from these extraneous issues of illocutionary force? If we do this, it may be possible even in problematic cases to say that what is said, or what certain imperative sentences actually mean, constitutes a clear case of (say) inconsistency; and even if, for other purposes, there may remain a lot more to be said about speech acts and so forth, this may be enough to enable the logician to go professionally to work.

In pursuing this notion further I propose to make exploratory use of some of the things said on meaning and related topics in Stephen Schiffer's *Meaning* (1972). First, on the subject of illocutionary acts. It has often been remarked that, while, as Austin particularly insisted, the species of such acts are very numerous, the fundamental genera may well be much less so. Schiffer suggests (p. 95) that 'the class of kinds of illocutionary acts divides into two jointly exhaustive and mutually exclusive subclasses', which he calls 'the assertive class' and 'the imperative class'. Now this very neat dichotomy is perhaps liable to strike one as too good to be true; and one would certainly like to be able to say something, if there really are just these two fundamental sub-classes, as to why that should be so. There is, however, at the very least a certain plausibility in the suggestion that, fundamentally, there may be two sorts of objects for which speech occurs – to tell people things, or to get people to do things – and, though Schiffer is not of course making a grammatical point here, this suggestion seems to fit quite well with the grammatical phenomena of the indicative and imperative moods. So let us adopt it as the present basis for further discussion.

A speaker S, Schiffer says, performs an act of the assertive kind in uttering x only if, for some p, S means that p by uttering x. Let us leave that on one side for the present. Our present interest is in the other sub-class; and on this Schiffer says that S performs an act of the imperative kind in uttering x only if, for some A and some V, S means that A is to V by uttering x. (Schiffer uses some Greek letters here, but 'V' will do.) Naturally enough, the x that is uttered in this latter case will often, though of course not necessarily or always, be a sentence in the imperative; and this is the case with which we are particularly concerned.

There is a possible objection to this account of which Schiffer takes brief notice at an earlier point (p. 60). The class of 'acts of the imperative kind' is clearly meant to be pretty wide and comprehensive; indeed, he himself instances, as examples of acts of this kind, the rather widely differing cases of ordering, requesting, entreating, and asking, and, later, advising; and one might add, for instance, suggesting. But if so, is not the phrase 'is to' (in 'A is to V') much too strong? Have we not here a case of the rather common failing, all too pervasive in the literature, of construing all imperatives – or rather, in this case, acts of the imperative kind – on the model of *orders*? If the colonel orders the recruit to get his hair cut, no doubt he does therein mean that A *is to* V – the recruit, the recipient of the order, is to do just that. But if I respectfully advise you to get your hair cut, surely I do not mean that you *are to* – but perhaps rather (as indeed Schiffer tacitly notes, at p. 103, in his sketch of advising) that you *should*; and if I suggest taking the dog for a walk – say to a child at a loose end on a Sunday afternoon – I do not mean that the child *is to* do that thing.

One rather ramshackle way of dealing with this point would be, I suppose, to stipulate that the phrase 'is to', in the general account, is simply not to be understood as having any definite sense, but rather as marking a sort of imperative blank, to be differently filled accordingly as particular utterances from time to time are taken to be cases of ordering, advising, entreating, or whatever. That, however, would be to leave things rather painfully in the air; and it might well be thought more tempting (as Schiffer suggests) to advert to the point that, in the general account, we are given plenty of latitude in our choice of values of V. Perhaps we can represent the difference between, say, ordering and suggesting not as a difference in what S means by 'is to', but as a difference in what he means that A is to do – if, in saying 'Take the dog out', I am giving an order, I mean that A is to take the dog out; if making a suggestion, that he is, say, to *consider* taking the dog out. That does not look unpromising.

However, it does not make much difference to my particular argument which of these options one takes; for either device, we must note, has a certain important consequence – namely, that there is a certain question to which the offered account enables us to give only the misleading appearance of an answer. If in uttering x (a sentence, let us suppose, in the imperative mood) S performs an illocutionary act of the imperative kind, what does S mean by uttering x? The account here provides us with the form of an answer: S means that A is to V. But this, as we can see from the point just made, is not really an answer at all; for if the extent of our information is that A issued the utterance, say, 'Take the dog out', then, in interpreting the phrase 'A is to V', either we have no way of determining the sense of 'is to', or we have no way of determining what value to assign to V. We have, that is to say, no way, on either view, of actually specifying what S means, until it is established whether he was giving an order, making a request or suggestion, offering advice, or what not. Of course that may not seem very surprising; for one may say, for that matter, of acts of the assertive kind as well that, if the question is what the speaker means, it will not in general be enough to be told merely what he says. If he utters x, and by uttering x means that p, then, if x is 'Cats don't eat fruit', it may not be that S means (only) that cats don't eat fruit.

It seems to me, however, that the point becomes a more serious matter when we turn to consider, not what speakers mean, but what sentences mean. This is of course a distinction which cannot be drawn for every utterance, nor even for every sentence. It may be, for example, that on a certain occasion a speaker (collapsing into a deckchair) utters 'Boof!', meaning thereby that he is hot and out of breath. It would not be correct, on the strength of such an occurrence, to say in general that that is what 'Boof!' means; indeed, it would be correct, so far as I know, to say that 'Boof!' does not mean anything, so that the question what *it* means can be given no answer at all. The reason for this is (stating briefly and coarsely considerations to which Schiffer and others have devoted much elegance and ingenuity) that, while a speaker on a certain occasion may by uttering 'Boof!' convey, intend to convey, mean that he is hot and out of breath, 'Boof!' is not in English, in general, a standard (conventional) means of conveying that, or indeed of conveying anything else – as by contrast the sentence 'I am hot and out of breath' would be. Thus we cannot, as it were, detach 'Boof!' from the particular circumstances and occasion of its utterance, and say what *it* means.

Consider by contrast the case of an ordinary indicative sentence, say 'Cats don't eat fruit.' It is true, as we noted above, that when in uttering that sentence a speaker performs an act of the assertive kind, it may well not be the case that by uttering it he means *only* that cats don't eat fruit; he may mean ('objecting' – see Schiffer, p. 97) that the fact that cats don't eat fruit is a reason for abandoning my well-meant suggestion of buying apples for the cat. It seems, however, that in such a case we can distinguish what we may (coarsely) call the conventional and non-conventional components in what the speaker means. There is no convention of the language in virtue of which, in issuing his utterance, the speaker is objecting – means, that is, that in the light of what he says my suggestion should be abandoned, or at any rate modified. That he means *that* (and so does that) is a matter, not of English, but of the particular circumstances in which, and intentions with which, he speaks. There is, however, also something which 'Cats don't eat fruit' is, in English, a standard, conventional means of meaning – namely, that cats don't eat fruit. We are thus in a position to say that, while this particular speaker means that the fact that cats don't eat fruit is a reason for abandoning my suggestion, he also means – and, more importantly for our purpose, 'Cats don't eat fruit' means – that cats don't eat fruit. In saying all this I am, I think and hope, agreeing (in coarse terms) with Schiffer's contention that, while what sentences and expressions mean (and so *in part* what speakers mean) is a matter of convention, the illocutionary force of utterances is, in general, not. For the most part at any rate, it is not in virtue of exploiting conventions of the language that speakers warn, object, remind, agree, and so on.

Turn now to the case of an ordinary imperative sentence. One might think (and Schiffer says, at p. 131 for instance, that he for his part does think) that the picture here would be *'mutatis mutandis* identical'; but in fact it appears to me that there are reasons why that cannot be so.

Take a case in which a speaker, in performing an act of the imperative kind, issues an actual imperative sentence, say 'Stay in London.' Now we know that, in such a case, he means by uttering 'Stay in London' something of the form that A is to V. But, as we saw above, until we know the illocutionary force of his utterance, we *either* do not know how 'is to' is to be understood, *or* we do not know what it is that A is to do. Does S mean that A is to stay in London? To stay in London if he likes? To consider the possibility of staying in London? (Is S ordering, requesting, suggesting?) One is tempted here of course, hopefully pursuing the analogy, to ask what it is that – as distinct from what particular speakers may from time to time be illocutionarily up to – 'Stay in London' is a *conventional means* of doing; but does it not now appear that that must be a question without an answer? One would like to say that to utter 'Stay in London' is, at any rate, a conventional means of meaning (something of the form) that A is to V; but we have already seen that that is not really an answer at all; for we can give no definite sense *on the basis of conventions* to 'is to V' as it occurs in that formula. That formula can be given a sense only when the illocutionary force of the utterance is identified; and we do not do that on the basis of conventions of English, but rather of the circumstances in which, and intentions with which, particular speakers speak. If we seriously said that to utter 'Stay in London' is a conventional means of meaning that some person therein addressed *is to* stay in London, we should merely be making what seems to be the sheer mistake of claiming that it is a matter of English usage that imperative sentences are used to give orders. This mistake is indeed, in varying degrees of explicitness, very frequently made, but it is none the better for that.

It is worth observing that I am not suggesting that imperative sentences are as such *ambiguous*; ambiguity is a quite different phenomenon. 'The cat is in the cupboard' is (as quite possibly most sentences, and many imperative sentences, are) an ambiguous sentence, in that what we are coarsely calling the conventions of English enable us to assign to it at least two distinct senses (or 'readings') – one concerning the whereabouts of a familiar kind of domestic animal, the other of a kind of instrument of corporal chastisement. What the sentence means in this or that particular occurrence is a question of *which* conventions are applicable, or are exploited, in particular cases. As distinct from this, my suggestion about imperative sentences is that the conventions of English do not suffice for us to assign to them readings *at all*, even numerous readings; we can indeed mention various things which, in the utterance of a given imperative sentence, a speaker might well mean by uttering it, but in no case would reference to conventions of English alone enable us to assign a determinate meaning to the sentence.

What it comes to is, in a nutshell, this. If we approve Schiffer's suggestion that, when a speaker in uttering x means that A is to V, the sense (or 'value') of 'is to V' depends upon the particular illocutionary force of his utterance; and if, further, we approve Schiffer's suggestion that illocutionary forces (except perhaps in the case of the fully explicit performative) are not constituted or determined by conventions; then, if we further agree that the assigning of meanings to words, phrases, and sentences *is* founded in conventions, we reach the conclusion that, while of course speakers mean something by uttering imperatives and we are normally able to grasp well enough what they mean, there is in general no answer to the question what *what they say* means. And thus the odd-looking thesis stated at the end of my first paragraph appears to come out true: it is not possible to say what imperative sentences mean.

Would it be proper to conclude that the notion of 'imperative logic' should be finally abandoned? It rather looks as if we are in a position to apply terms of logical appraisal to commands, pleas, requests, pieces of advice, and so on – specimens or tracts of discourse in which, *ex hypothesi*, the pertinent illocutionary forces are determinate – but not to imperatives, a class whose bond of union is nothing more than grammatical, and whose relations both internal and external are, in just those respects that might appear to be of logical interest, indefeasibly – if all that we have to go on is that they are imperatives – indeterminate. The imperative 'mood' has no determinate force, so that sentences *in* that mood have no determinate sense.

11

A Question about Illocutions

In *Speech Acts* (1969, p. 19) J. R. Searle laid down as a principle that 'whatever can be meant can be said'. In laying down this principle he was not – though of course the words might be read as suggesting this – taking a stand against possible claims to mean ineffable profundities, thoughts alleged to lie too deep for words. He was propounding a certain doctrine about speech acts; and the doctrine was that, although a speaker in issuing an utterance often does not explicitly indicate (or 'express') in what he says what speech act it is that he therein performs, it is always in principle possible that he should do so. In so far as the meaning of his utterance does not itself 'uniquely determine' what speech act he therein performs, he could be said to mean more than he actually says; but though that is often the case with actual utterances, 'it is always in principle possible for him to say exactly what he means'. This amounts to the thesis that, in principle, every speech act could be fully explicitly performed.

It is possible to doubt whether this thesis is interesting. The claim that what does not occur, and is not perhaps possible, in fact is nevertheless possible 'in principle' is seldom very appealing. Furthermore, since even the utterance of a sentence as fully explicit as is 'in principle' possible is said to determine uniquely the performance of a specific speech act only if 'the context' is also appropriate, it may be thought unclear what is actually being claimed; for one might think that an appropriate 'context' could uniquely determine the performance of a specific speech act, even if the utterance in question were highly inexplicit; so what difference is it that this hypothetically possible explicitness is supposed to make? However, the question that I want to raise here is not whether the thesis is interesting, but whether it is true.

Could every speech act, in principle, be fully explicitly performed? Is there, for every speech act, a sentence (actual or possible) utterance of

From *Philosophia*, vol. 10, nos. 3–4, 1979.

which (literally, seriously, and in an appropriate 'context') would constitute fully explicit performance of that speech act? Put the other way round:
is there any speech act which could not, even in principle, be fully
explicitly performed?

A recent writer who takes the thesis to be clearly false is David
Holdcroft (*Words and Deeds* (1978), pp. 61–3) – and Holdcroft, who
knows the literature better than I do, even says that the point 'has often
been noted'. What, he says, about *hinting*? If, in saying 'I've got a busy day
tomorrow', I hint that we ought to leave the party and go home, it is of the
essence of the case that I do not *say* 'We ought to leave the party and go
home'; nor of course could I hint this (without saying it) by such an explicit
utterance as 'I hereby hint that we ought to leave the party and go home.'
When one hints, one is not necessarily inexplicit as to the fact that one is
hinting; on the contrary, as you are trying to guess who it is that has just
become engaged to Jane, I may say 'I'll give you a hint: we met him
yesterday afternoon.' But in hinting, while I may make explicit *that* I am
hinting, I necessarily cannot make explicit *what* I am hinting; for by
definition, something hinted is not explicitly disclosed.

It is perhaps too obvious to be worth saying that of course ('whatever
can be meant can be said') whatever can be hinted can be said; for one
could simply say it, instead of hinting it. But Searle's thesis seems to
require, not that one could speak fully explicitly *instead* of hinting, but that
hinting could itself be fully explicitly done, perhaps in some such formula
as 'I hereby hint that . . .'. And it seems that, even in principle, that could
not be so.

Holdcroft does not discuss in his book what Searle's response to this
apparent counterexample might be; he seems to suggest, in fact, that,
since it *is* a counterexample, there is nothing for it but to conclude that
Searle's 'principle of expressibility' is not true. I think it unlikely, however, that the point would be conceded quite so easily as that. A certain
concession, no doubt, would have to be made. If a speech act is characterized simply, and very broadly, as something that a speaker does in
speaking, then hinting surely has to be regarded as a (some sort of) speech
act; and if so, since fully explicit hinting is in principle not possible, it has
to be conceded that not every speech act without qualification can, even in
principle, be fully explicitly performed. But it could be urged with plausibility that, when Searle speaks of speech acts in this particular connection,
he is really speaking (not fully explicity!) of *illocutionary* acts; and it might
then be said that, while hinting is presumably a speech act of some sort, it
is not an illocutionary act, and so does not really constitute a counter-

example to the thesis which Searle was really concerned to propound. Holdcroft says positively (p. 61) that hinting *is* an illocutionary act; but are there good grounds on which that could be denied?

I think it is true to say that Austin, in introducing his notion of illocutionary force, was inclined to adopt the thesis which Searle propounded later (though not, I also think, to attach very much importance to it) – that is, I think that he was inclined to suppose that, while the illocutionary force of utterances very often was in fact inexplicit, it could always – 'in principle', and if there seemed to be any particular need to do so – be made explicit. So what about cases in which *not* being explicit is of the essence of what is done? It is interesting that Austin seems to have felt intuitively that such cases were not cases of illocutionary acts (see *How to Do Things with Words* (2nd ed 1975), p. 105). Insinuating, he there says – and hinting would have done just as well – is indeed something that we can do in or by issuing some utterance; and we cannot do so explicitly, by saying 'I insinuate . . .'; but, he remarks – with rather frustrating brevity – insinuating seems 'to be a clever effect rather than a mere act'; that is, it is not a true-blue illocutionary act, and so does not run counter to the supposition that illocutionary acts always could (in principle) be fully explicitly performed. But how do we distinguish a 'mere act' from a 'clever effect'?

Strawson has also had something to say on this topic (though, admittedly, only in the course of discussing another). In his paper 'Austin and "Locutionary Meaning" ' (in *Essays on J. L. Austin* (1973), pp. 46–68), he distinguishes 'three progressively richer senses' of the phrase 'the meaning of what was said', as used in application to some utterance made on some occasion. These he calls the linguistic meaning; the linguistic-cum-referential meaning; and the 'complete' meaning. It is the last of these with which we are at present concerned. Strawson distinguishes (at least) two elements in the 'complete' meaning of 'what was said' which may 'go beyond' its meaning in either of the other two senses. First, there is the question of how what was said was meant, how it was intended to be taken or understood – 'as a request, as an entreaty, as a command, as advice, or merely as a piece of conventional politeness'. He adds that 'this is the dimension of meaning studied by Austin under the title of "illocutionary force" '. Then, second, there is, he says, the 'connected but distinguishable' matter of what the speaker may have intended to be taken to be implying, or suggesting, or (we may add) hinting. If, in saying 'The President has expressed the view that the ideal age for such an appointment is fifty' I imply (or hint) that the President has a favoured candidate who happens to be exactly that age, perhaps grasping the *complete* meaning of what I say might include recognition of that implication.

Now, in saying this, Strawson seems to me to be in part dissenting from Searle's doctrine, and in part not. On *one* interpretation of 'whatever can be meant can be said', it seems to me that Strawson dissents; for it seems to be his view that the 'complete meaning of what I said' could include something which I did *not* say (but for instance implied, or hinted) – and which, if I *had* said it, would *ipso facto* have *changed* the meaning of 'what was said'. That is: Strawson seems to countenance, what Searle could be taken to deny, a sense of 'meaning' in which part at least of what is meant is not, and indeed could not be, made fully explicit in what is said (though it could, of course, be made explicit by saying something else). On the other hand, if we take it that Searle is really talking about illocutionary acts – is claiming that illocutionary force could always 'in principle' be made fully explicit – then at least it may be that Strawson agrees with him. For he distinguishes – as 'connected but distinguishable' – this topic, Austin's topic, from that of implying, or suggesting, or (we may add) hinting; presumably holds thereby that (say) hinting is not an illocutionary act; and so could accept with perfect consistency the general thesis that every illocutionary act could, 'in principle' anyway, be fully explicitly performed.

This prompts us to ask, then: what is the distinction? If the topic of, say, hinting or implying is – as Austin also felt – connected with but different from that of illocutionary acts and forces, what is the difference? *Why* is, say, hinting not an illocutionary act?

Here, however, the present trail goes cold – or rather, leads us round in a frustrating circle. Strawson himself ('Austin and "Locutionary Meaning" ', p. 50), in distinguishing illocutionary force from, or within, '*all* that was intended to be taken as understood by the utterance', accounts for the distinction by saying that 'the distictive feature of the grasp of illocutionary force is that the utterance be grasped as a case of "x-ing", where "x" is one of the verbs that qualify for inclusion in Austin's terminal lists'. But this turns out to be no help for the present purpose (as admittedly, it was not meant to be). For, if we turn to Austin's 'terminal lists', we find that the qualification for inclusion is precisely that a verb 'x' should be such as to disclose explicitly, by its appropriate appearance in an uttered sentence, that the speaker is therein 'x-ing'. What Austin sets out to list is precisely, as he says, 'those verbs which make explicit . . . the illocutionary force of an utterance'. But this makes Searle's thesis (as a claim about illocutionary acts) simply true by definition. There cannot be a necessarily inexplicit illocutionary act, for illocutionary acts are, by definition, those which can, in a certain way, be explicitly performed.

That seems unsatisfactory. Holdcroft for instance, who says that hinting is an illocutionary act which cannot be explicitly performed, is now to be told that hinting is *not* an illocutionary act; but if, when he asks why not, the only reason given is that hinting cannot be explicitly performed – all illocutionary acts by definition can be – he is not going to be impressed. We seem to have a mere case of *ignoratio elenchi*.

My feeling is, nevertheless, that Austin and Strawson (and, I imagine, Searle) were in fact right in holding that, for instance, hinting, insinuating, and implying are not to be classed among illocutionary acts – notwithstanding that they are, of course, done in saying things and so presumably must be speech acts of some sort. What is needed is some other reason for saying so. I believe that something, at least, worth saying on this topic may emerge if we ask what it was that Austin may have had in mind in his cryptic remark that insinuating – like he says, implying – 'seems to be a clever effect rather than a mere act'. Why an 'effect', and why not a 'mere act'? I wonder whether he may have had in mind the difference between one thing, and two things: with an effect, we have the effect *and* what produced it, what it was the effect of; with an act, we have the act. But what does this (cryptic) observation come to, in the particular case?

Something like this, perhaps. Let us take two or three (I hope uncontroversial) verbs that may serve as specimens of verbs that do signify illocutionary performance – let us take 'order', 'request', 'concede', and 'promise'. Next let us take some 'primitive' utterances (as Austin sometimes called them) in which the illocutionary force of the utterances is not made explicit: say, 'You will get your hair cut', 'Pass the salt, please', 'He is rather old', and 'I shall be there'. Now in these cases we could say, by way of specifying illocutionary forces, 'In saying "You will get your hair cut", I was giving an order'; 'In saying "Pass the salt, please" I was making a request'; 'In saying "He is rather old", I was making a concession'; and 'In saying "I shall be there", I was giving a promise.' But now, when the general illocutionary force of these utterances is made clear in this way, there do not arise the further questions 'And what order were you giving?', 'What were you requesting?', and so on. The same utterance ' 'He is rather old' – in which I made a concession, itself specifies what the concession was that I was making; the same utterance – 'I shall be there' – in which I gave a promise, itself specifies what I promised. On being given the utterance in which I made a suggestion, you are also apprised of what it was that I suggested.

It seems to me that, in this sort of way, one might fill out the feeling that, where illocutionary performance is in question, we are dealing with *one* thing, a 'mere act'. We have an utterance x; we grasp, or are told, that issuing x is a case of y-ing; but the question 'y-ing what?', as a *further* question, does not arise; for the same utterance x already gives the answer to that question. The question as to the illocutionary force of the utterance is the question how just *that* utterance is to be taken – 'Try the Camembert', if it is a case of making a suggestion, is *of course* a case of suggesting that one try the Camembert. We only need, as it were, one utterance to play around with, to give us *both* 'what is said' *and* what is (as the case may be) suggested, promised, requested, or conceded, and so on.

And here, obviously, insinuating, hinting, implying work quite differently. If, in saying 'We met him yesterday afternoon', I am hinting something, we have (so far) no notion at all of *what* I am hinting – except, negatively, that it cannot be that we met him yesterday afternoon. I may insinuate that bursars are not to be trusted by saying many things, no doubt – but not by saying *that*. In these cases, one might say, two items have to be involved – 'what is said', the utterance in which insinuating, hinting, implying is done, *and*, quite distinct from that (and necessarily distinct), what it is that is insinuated, hinted, implied. And could this lie behind the idea of a 'clever effect'? In hinting that p, I not only have to get my auditor to apprehend my utterance itself as of a certain sort – he has to grasp not only that I am hinting; I have to implant in his mind a quite different proposition, something left unsaid, which is *what* I am hinting.

Perhaps, then, y-ing is not a true illocutionary act, if, when in issuing the utterance x I y, the *further* question arises *what* I y, the utterance x itself not supplying the answer to that question. It is satisfactory for the present purpose that, if this is right, explicitness or otherwise is not the point at issue. It is true that, if I hint, I must not openly say what it is that I hint – if I do, then I am not hinting after all. But if, in saying for instance 'Is our control system really effective?' I imply that bursars are not to be trusted, I could (I believe) with perfect propriety go on to say quite openly 'I imply, of course, that bursars are not to be trusted.' The issue is not whether I do or do not, can or cannot, openly say this; it is that, even if I openly say that this is what I imply, I do not imply it in saying *that*. I imply it in saying 'Is our control system really effective?' (Notice also that, as in this case, there is nothing at all odd in implying that p in, or by, asking a question. It may not be completely impossible, but it would be pretty odd, for an interrogative utterance to have the *illocutionary force* of an assertion.) Even if 'I imply that . . .' – unlike 'I hint that . . .' – can, as I believe it can, be quite properly employed, 'imply' still fails to be a verb of illocutionary force, for even in such a case of explicit utterance what is said in implying does not itself, and cannot, apprise us of (by being identical with) what is implied.

If I am right, then, we do not have, in for instance hinting, a true counterexample to the thesis that 'in principle' any illocutionary act could be fully explicitly performed. For hinting can be held not to be an illocutionary act – and not only, or even at all, on the ground that it cannot be explicitly done. This does not, of course, show that the thesis is true. But it may make it look pretty plausible (not necessarily very interesting). If, on the topic of illocutionary force, we are speaking only of how an utterance itself is to be taken, of what its issuing is a case of – if we are not bringing in any *other* propositions or any 'clever effects' – well, one might ask, why should it not be always possible, in principle, that the illocutionary force of an utterance should be made, in the utterance, explicitly clear? There seems no particular reason to feel doubts about that.

Ethics

12

Ethics and Language

In a broadcast talk delivered in 1956, the late J. L. Austin began by outlining to his listeners his now well-known concept of 'the performative utterance and its infelicities'; and at the end of that first section of his talk he made this comment: 'That equips us, we may suppose, with two shining new tools to crack the crib of reality maybe. It also equips us – it always does – with two shining new skids under our metaphysical feet.'[1] In this essay I intend to illustrate a particular respect in which, in moral philosophy, the partial pessimism of Austin's comment has proved abundantly justified. I shall try to show how in this field one shining new tool has led in fact to the skidding of moral philosophers' feet – how one bright idea (an idea, as it happens, very closely akin to that which Austin himself was discussing) has led some influential theorists off in the wrong direction, and the rest of us back in the end, with rather little gained, to a position not far from that of our predecessors of about a hundred years ago. This dismal story, I should in justice make clear at the outset, is not that of the whole of moral philosophy, not even of moral philosophy in English; I shall be tracing only one out of several concurrent lines of thought, but the line which I shall trace will be, I think, readily recognized as having been, and perhaps as still being, more conspicuous than most.

One way (not the only way) of launching my story is to consider the way in which, some thirty years ago, the moral theory of 'intuitionism' was occasioning well-justified discontent. It was felt, with good reason, that the doctrines of intuitionism made the concepts of morality seem both mysterious and undiscussable. In that doctrine moral judgements, or at any rate the most fundamental moral judgements, were construed as simple assertions of moral fact. Very much as some things, for instance, are pink or blue, some things, it was supposed, are good or obligatory; just

[1] Austin, 'Performative Utterances', in *Philosophical Papers* (1961), p. 228.

From *The Human Agent*, ed. G. N. A. Vesey (Macmillan, 1968).

as we simply see that a thing is pink, we simply intuit that a thing is obligatory. Further, just as a person who can see does not need to have it explained to him what it is to be pink, and does not need to be shown by any argument that pink things are pink, just so there was supposed to be no question of explaining what it is for something to be obligatory, and no question of deploying any reasoning to show that what is said to be obligatory is indeed obligatory. In the one case we simply see; in the other we intuit.[2] That such doctrines should have occasioned discontent is not, of course, surprising. We know what seeing is; but do we really have any idea what 'intuiting' is? To learn that something is pink we need to look at it, not to reason; but is there really no room for reasoning in moral matters? Can it really be that there is practically nothing to be said? Furthermore, in what does the relevance of these supposed moral facts consist? That something is obligatory is supposed to be a reason, indeed a conclusive reason, for doing it; but why should this be so, if its being obligatory is a simple fact about it, like the fact that some flower in my garden is pink? I may know that some flower in my garden is pink, and find in that fact no reason for doing anything in particular; why then should it be the case, if it is the case, that to have knowledge of the fact that something is obligatory is somehow also to be apprised of a reason for doing it? In such doctrines too little is said, too much is left in undiscussable, *sui generis* obscurity.

Acknowledging, and not in the least disputing the justice of, the objection that I have here presented an ignoble caricature of the views of serious men, let me briskly disregard it and proceed to present another. In what respect are we to say that intuitionist doctrine had gone wrong? No doubt there are a good many possibilities here – a good many points at which a theory of such bald simplicity might well be charged with failure to do justice to the state of the case. But there was one particular idea which, some thirty years ago, was very prominently pervasive in the philosophical air – the idea that there are diverse 'uses of language'; and it is to the criticism prompted by this general idea, by this 'shining new tool', that I wish on this occasion to direct attention. It was suggested, then, that perhaps the trouble, or at least part of the trouble, was that the intuitionists had failed to consider, and so had unwittingly misrepresented, that 'use of language' which is actually to be found in discourse on moral matters.

[2] I have in mind here particularly the more extreme views of H. A. Prichard. Not all intuitionists went quite so far as he did, but it would be beside the present point to bring in the several variant forms of intuitionism.

Philosophers, it was suggested, have always been all too ready to assume, too often unconsciously, that there is only one, or only one interesting, use of language – namely, its use in making statements, in describing things, in saying something true or (possibly) false. Now certainly the intuitionists had evidently supposed that items of moral discourse were of this general kind; they had supposed that a grammatically indicative moral utterance simply made some kind of statement, truly or falsely, asserted or purported to assert some moral fact, and had at once become involved in hopeless difficulties as to the nature of these putative facts, and to the way in which they could be known or discovered, and as to their seemingly mysterious relevance to what people should or should not do. But we now see, it was said with a justified sense of enlightenment and liberation, that there are diverse uses of language; it is far from being the case, and a mere superstition to suppose, that the making of statements, the asserting of facts, is the only, or the only interesting, use there is; so why should we not drop the assumption the intuitionists made? Perhaps the 'use' of language, in discourse on moral matters, is not, or not mainly, to assert facts at all. Thus C. L. Stevenson was led to write, in *Mind*, 1937, that the 'major use [of ethical judgments] is not to indicate facts, but to create an influence'; the use of language we actually find here is not 'descriptive', but 'dynamic'; in saying to a hearer that such-and-such is good, or right, or what he ought to do, I am not asserting either truly or falsely any fact at all, whether mysterious or otherwise, but seeking to influence his interests, his feelings, or, broadly, his attitudes. The resulting new theory, under the name of 'emotivism', was viewed by many as a great liberation, a notable advance. It seemed to rest firmly upon the bright (and for that matter perfectly correct) idea that there are various 'uses of language', and thereby to escape most satisfactorily from the mysteries, muddles, and mythology of intuitionism.

This, however, did not last. Ten years or so later it was beginning to be strongly maintained that, while of course there are diverse uses of language, and while very probably the intuitionists had misrepresented the use that is characteristic of moral discourse, yet emotivism itself had skidded in its particular way of undertaking to set matters right. In bringing into moral philosophy, in place of the old 'descriptive' prejudice, the notion of the 'emotive' or 'dynamic' use of language, had it not perhaps got hold of the wrong thing? It need not be doubted that such a use does actually exist; but is it the use that is really characteristic of moral discourse? There are three main grounds on which it was urged that it was not. First, it is perfectly clear that there are quite other regions of discourse in which this 'dynamic' use is clearly exemplified. It is a feature, and probably the essential, most central feature, of advertising slogans, or of propagandist political harangues, that in them language is used to 'create an influence'; the predominant aim here is not to inform, but to sway; words apt for the purpose in hand will be words with 'emotive meaning', and if any facts are alleged, or even truly asserted, this will really be incidental to the 'dynamic' business which is principally in view. It seems, then, that the emotivist theory of ethics either must hold the unappealing, and surely also unplausible, view that moral discourse is essentially no different from advertising or propaganda, or alternatively must concede that there is, in moral discourse, some feature besides its 'dynamic' use, some feature which the theory itself seems not to allow for, by which moral discourse can be distinguished from discourse in those other and less reputable modes. Second, is it actually true that moral discourse is always emotive, or dynamic? If I tell you quite coolly, even diffidently perhaps, that in my opinion your practices of tax-evasion are wrong, am I really, am I necessarily attempting to work on your feelings, or indeed seeking in any way to 'influence your attitude'? 'I think it's wrong' is scarcely an utterance one would think of as emotively charged. Then, third, even when in some moral utterance my end is, as it some-times really may be, 'dynamic' – even when I really am out to exert a bit of influence – is this the most important, the essential, feature of my utterance? Surely it is not. If I deliver, for example, a serious moral talk to some young persons on the evil of trafficking in drugs, it may be that I hope thereby to influence their attitudes; but what my words primarily offer them is, surely, guidance. Primarily, I tell them what line to take in that matter, and only consequentially, if at all, do I influence or move them towards taking that line. I am, so to speak, steering, not pushing.

In this way, then, it came to be felt that attention to the 'dynamic', or 'emotive', use of language did not really constitute the great advance in moral theory that it had once been taken for – by some, perhaps, that that notion had even done positive harm in opening its seductive primrose path to philosophical error. But if moral discourse is not, then, essentially 'emotive', what is it? We will scarcely be tempted to take up again, in these modern days, the old supposition, or supersition, that it is simply descrip-tive; but then of course we need not do so, since we know that there are lots of other uses of language to choose from. In picking the 'dynamic' use the emotivist theory had evidently put its money on the wrong thing, but no doubt we can find some other use that will turn out to be the right one.

The next idea, in fact, can be seen to emerge very naturally from reflection upon the sort of case last mentioned, the case of my serious talk to my group of young persons. I am therein, as we put it, steering, not pushing. I am offering to them advice or guidance, not merely administering some verbal prods. It could in fact be said correctly that, in discoursing as I do on the evils of drug-trafficking, I am essentially telling my audience something – but telling them what? Not (as an intuitionist would quietly have assumed) that something is the case: what I am really telling them, surely, is what to do, what line to take in their conduct, with respect to traffic in drugs. It may be that my discourse against drugs is actually unsolicited; but we may say nevertheless that, had it been the case that these young persons had confessed themselves worried about this business, and had put to me about it the practical question 'What shall we do?', then my discourse would have provided an answer to that question. May we not say, then, that the use of language in moral discourse is essentially such as to answer practical questions? Moral discourse is not indeed unique in this, since imperatives answer practical questions too; a possible answer to the question 'What shall I do?' would be, for example, 'Mow the lawn', or 'Sell all thou hast and give to the poor.' But at any rate a way of answering such a question would be to tell you what you ought to do, what would be the right thing. And thus, in the manner of Professor R. M. Hare, we may conclude that imperatives and moral discourse should be grouped together as species of 'prescriptive' discourse, of discourse the 'function' of which is to 'guide conduct'. The language of morals is not essentially, though it may be incidentally or deviantly, descriptive; nor is it always and essentially, though it may be on occasion, emotive; the best word for what it really is, is the word 'prescriptive'. This is the use of language which the language of morals crucially exemplifies.

Now the resulting moral theory, which is sometimes called nowadays 'prescriptivism', has in recent years been powerfully and persuasively stated, subtly elaborated, and most ingeniously defended against a variety of objections. It has become too large and complex a structure to be satisfactorily surveyed in a couple of paragraphs; and thus, if I say that we have here yet another example of skids under the metaphysical feet, I cannot hope in the space here available to carry much conviction, unless, perhaps, to the already converted. But my point, though doubtless it could be made to stick only (if at all) by rather extensive and ramified argument, is in itself a very simple point: it is that the prescriptivist theory, like the emotivist theory upon which it was supposed to be an improvement, has picked on something which certainly does occur in moral discourse, but which, on the other hand, does not occur in all moral discourse; which, further, does not occur

only in moral discourse; and which, further still, is not interestingly distinctive even of those tracts of moral discourse in which it does occur.

It is not very difficult, I believe, to see that this is so. Certainly it is true
that, just as there may occur in moral discourse utterances which carry
'emotive meaning' and of which the intention or aim is to 'influence' their
addressees, so there may occur in moral discourse utterances having what
we may call 'prescriptive force'. For, sometimes, what is at issue in moral
discourse is indeed some practical question: some person is considering the
question what he should do; and it may then occur that he is offered, by way
of an answer to his question, guidance or advice in some utterance or
utterances carrying 'prescriptive force' – that is, which tell the question-
raiser what he is to do. But it is plain that not all moral discourse is of this
kind; it is not always the case that, when talk on moral matters is going on,
there is one party engaged in considering a practical problem, and another
in prescribing a course of action to him; moral discourse is not always
addressed by one party to another, and about what that other party is
currently, or in the near future, to do. My discourse may be about my own
actions, not yours; about past actions, yours or mine, not present or
prospective ones; about the actions of absent persons who are not parties in
the conversation, or of dead persons for whom, now, it would be somewhat
pointless to prescribe. The paradigm case of prescriptive speech is the case
of advice; but, while of course the giving of moral advice or guidance does
sometimes occur, it is plain that it is not always occurring when moral talk,
or moral thinking, is going on. In talking and thinking on moral matters we
do many other things, depending on what the particular topic may be, and
on how and in what context the topic comes up for consideration. Sometimes what we say has prescriptive force, sometimes not.

Secondly, it is, I believe, even more evident that the occurrence of
utterances having prescriptive force is not in any way peculiar to moral
discourse. When one gives advice, when one tells someone what to do, it is
not always moral advice that one gives; when one person consults another
on a practical problem, it is not always a moral problem that he brings up.
Even if the advice I offer is such as I would offer to any person in the same
situation as my enquirer is, and even if the course of action which I
prescribe to him is one that I myself would unhesitatingly adopt were I in his
shoes, yet my advice may not be moral advice: for quite possibly his practical
question is not a moral one, raises no moral issue. An utterance may well be
prescriptive, even 'universally' prescriptive; it may, for the matter of that, be
emotive as well; yet it may be concerned with no moral matters whatsoever,
and not a specimen of moral discourse at all.

Thirdly, suppose that we have some utterance which is undoubtedly moral, and which does undoubtedly have prescriptive force; we have, let us say, a true specimen of moral advice. How interesting is it that such an utterance has prescriptive force? From the point of view of moral theory, I suggest, not very interesting. If our interest were in the philosophy of language, then indeed it might well be our main concern to consider what it is in such an utterance, or in the circumstances in which it occurs, which gives it prescriptive force – what it is that makes the issuing of that utterance the giving of advice. But it would seem that, if our interest is in moral philosophy, then we shall want to know, not how it is that the utterance is the giving of advice, but how it is that it is the giving of moral advice; and, even more interestingly, how if at all one could determine whether the moral advice so given was good advice or bad. No doubt, if a specimen of advice-giving is what we have got, it will be just as well to be clear that that is so; but this much scarcely impinges upon moral philosophy at all. That some specimen of discourse has prescripive force is scarcely of more interest to a moral philosopher than would be, to a doctor, the information that some pill-shaped object is a chemical compound. He may be glad to know that it is; but for his particular purposes he needs to know more.[3]

Let me now, before turning into the home straight, briefly review the situation. We started from well-justified complaints made against intuitionism, a body of doctrine which evidently supposed that moral judgements are statements, assert moral facts, or that moral discourse is essentially, as many would put it, 'descriptive'. Against this we set the bright (and correct, though vague) idea that there are diverse 'uses of language'; and we have now surveyed two moral theories which have sought to make use of this idea, the first holding that moral discourse is not descriptive but emotive, the second holding that it is neither descriptive nor emotive, but rather prescriptive. In each case we have suggested that the 'bright new tool', the liberating notion of the many uses of language, fulfilled Austin's warning by functioning actually as a skid under metaphysical feet – and doing so, in each case, in a curiously similar way, namely, by sliding moral theorists away from their proper subject-matter. Emotive meaning, the use of emotive language for 'dynamic' purposes, does actually occur and is, in its way, interesting; prescriptive force, the use of language for advising, for giving guidance on practical problems, does also occur and is, in its own

---

[3] Let me say again here that I am fully, even painfully, aware that by some the last few paragraphs will be regarded as grossly unfair, or even as a foolish travesty. I do not (of course) share this view; but I think I understand it, and I believe that I could, given time, undermine its foundations.

way, interesting. But neither topic has very much to do with moral philosophy, for the reason that discourse on moral matters is only sometimes, not
always and not uniquely and never very interestingly, exemplificatory either
of emotive meaning or of prescriptive force. Each of these latter topics is
something else again; and to confuse either with moral philosophy is, at
best, unhelpful.

I come now, and finally, to a more recent and even more curious, though
curiously similar, instance of skidding. It was one of Austin's major
contributions to good order and philosophic discipline that he sought to
introduce some much-needed clarity and distinctness into philosophical
talk about the 'use' or 'uses' of language.[4] He thought rightly that the notion
of 'use', though no doubt it had done good work in its day by, so to speak,
loosening things up and widening the terms of discussion, had come in the
end to breed new confusions by covering indiscriminately too many distinguishable, and too seldom distinguished, cases. The distinctions which
he was mainly concerned to introduce, within the general notion of 'using'
language, were those between, first, the act of saying something with a
certain meaning, for example, the sentence 'You're not allowed to do that';
second, the act of doing something in the saying of those words, as for
example informing, forbidding, warning, or reprimanding; and third, the
act of doing something by the saying of those words, as for example
deterring, alarming, convincing, or offending. There are things besides
these which might well be called 'uses of language', as for example reciting,
making a noise or a joke; but Austin's main concern was with the above
distinctions, with what he called locutionary, illocutionary, and perlocutionary acts. To ask what locutionary act a speaker performs is to raise
one kind of question about his 'use' of language; to ask what illocutionary
act, is to raise another kind; and what perlocutionary act, yet another kind
again.

Here, then, we have an even shinier and sharper new tool; and, predict-
ably enough, there seems some reason to apprehend that it may compass
the downfall, or at least the distraction, of at least some moral philosophers.
There was published in 1966 a book called *The Revolution in Ethical Theory*[5]
which gives some substantial grounds for this apprehension.

The author of that book has, as he says, read Austin with attention, and
has sought to apply his contributions in moral philosophy. Now up to a point
things go well enough. In bald summary the author argues, making use of

[4] Particularly, of course, in his *How to Do Things with Words* (1962).
[5] By George C. Kerner.

Austin's terminology, that recent moral theories, no doubt partly because of the fogginess of the idea of the many 'uses' of language, have sought to illuminate moral discourse by locating the perlocutionary object, or the illocutionary force, of discourse of that kind; they have sought to identify the perlocutionary act ('influencing'), or the illocutionary act ('prescribing') which moral discourse specifically exemplifies. But, as he rightly contends, such efforts have proved abortive, since the objects thus sought for actually do not exist – moral discourse has no one perlocutionary object, it exemplifies no one illocutionary act. In neither sense is there any single 'use' of language which is specially or uniquely characteristic of discourse on moral matters. So what is the remedy? The author's verdict on the position is, in effect, that recent moral theorists have not gone far enough. They have stuck at some one particular linguistic act, perlocutionary or illocutionary, and thus have neglected the very wide variety of other linguistic acts which discourse on moral matters also exemplifies. The remedy is to bring into account the whole breadth of this diversity; in his own words, 'a fully adequate ethical theory would analyse and systematise the whole variety of linguistic performances and commitments that are embedded in the use of moral language'. What is needed is more, much more, of the same.

But no: is it not quite clear, on a little reflection, that this author thus prescribes quite the wrong remedy for the disease – that he urges us, in fact, to go even further and further in the wrong direction? For the trouble is not only, as he suggests, that there is no single illocutionary act, no single perlocutionary object, which is specifically characteristic of moral discourse; it is also the case that if we consider the whole range, the whole and huge diversity, of all the illocutionary and perlocutionary acts, of 'linguistic performances', that actually occur in moral discourse, we find that all this is not distinctive of moral discourse either. For consider what our author says about 'You ought to do *Y*.' Certainly, he rightly says, this form of words may be used in prescribing; but not only in prescribing – 'it is also used for enunciating and subscribing to principles, placing demands, taking sides, licensing, advocating a course of action, transmitting authority, invoking sanctions, overruling, restricting, instructing, etc., etc.' That is true, and worth saying; but then it should also be observed that no item in this list, nor yet the whole list taken together, has any particular connection with moral discourse – each, no doubt, is to be found there, but each and all may be found in many other settings as well. One could in fact talk minutely, even exhaustively perhaps, about every one of these 'linguistic performances' without even touching on morals at any point; analysis, that is, and system-atization of these might very well involve no mention of morals whatever, and might accordingly yield no ethical theory at all, let alone a 'fully adequate' ethical theory. It is particularly clear in this case, I think, what has gone wrong. Our author, understandably and indeed properly impressed by the bright new tool which Austin had forged for him, is resolved to put this tool to some philosophical use: there are, as Austin has now enabled us clearly to see, dozens and dozens of interestingly distinguishable speech-acts, of linguistic performances; so let our task be the analysis and system-atization of these. Well, let it be, by all means; but if so, let it also be recognized that what we shall be engaged in is the philosophy of language, and not in moral philosophy or anything like it. Advances on this front may, of course, prove serviceable for moral philosophy; but they will not be advances in moral philosophy, whose particular concerns might quite well remain wholly unmentioned in our arduous researches.

But, you may protest, can this really be correct? Consider again the form of words 'You ought to do Y'; and let us suppose these words to occur in discourse (not forgetting that they can play other roles) in such a way as to constitute the giving of advice, and specifically the giving of moral advice. Now if we exhaustively analyse and anatomize such a case, may we not hope to come up with – doubtless among other things – some interesting conclusions as to what moral advice is, what qualifies or entitles a person to be a moral adviser, even, perhaps, what it is for moral advice to be good advice or bad? If so, then it could not possibly be suggested that such study would not be contributory to moral philosophy; for what could be more vitally relevant to moral theory than, say, the ground of distinction between good and bad moral advice? This objection, however, is not at all to the purpose. For in so far as the particular bit of enquiry suggested might yield conclusions of some interest in moral philosophy, it is exactly not an enquiry into the 'linguistic performance'. The linguistic performance is simply the giving of advice; and the analysis of that, as a linguistic performance, will tell us, we may hope, what giving advice is, and how giving advice is to be distinguished from doing other things. But the giving of moral advice is not, or at any rate is not in any sense envisaged by Austin, a different 'linguistic performance' from the giving of advice in any other context or connection; and the giving of bad advice is, regrettably perhaps, the very same 'linguistic performance' as giving good. To raise these further questions is, accord-ingly, to abandon, to go beyond, the analysis of the linguistic performance as such; it is, furthermore, to raise questions whose answers, were we able to find them, would have little to do with any linguistic performance in particular. For is it not to be anticipated that what makes moral advice moral will probably turn out to be exactly the same as what makes criticism, for instance, moral criticism, exhortation moral exhortation, a decision a moral decision, and so on? Expressions of advice, criticism, exhortation, and decision no doubt differ as linguistic performances, and their differences in that respect are of interest in the philosophy of language; but it is quite possible that what makes them, when they are, elements in moral discourse will be some respect in which they do not differ at all, and to which their differences as 'speech-acts' or as linguistic performances are totally irrelevant. Rather similarly, if I take a certain moral decision, advise you that you should also act as I have decided to do, and subsequently judge you unfavourably for failing to do so, it seems clear that what, if anything, makes my moral decision the right decision will be exactly the same thing as makes good advice my advice to you, and subsequently, makes well-founded my unfavourable moral judgement of your failure to take it. What is of interest to moral philosophy is what, in such a case, the decision, the advice, and the critical judgement have in common; how they differ as linguistic performances is neither here nor there.

Thus I suggest, in conclusion, that our author of last year has drawn exactly the reverse of the correct conclusion from his enquiries. He has observed correctly that there is no single 'use of language', understanding thereby no single linguistic performance, which is specific to and characteristic of moral discourse. He has observed correctly that some influential recent theories have fatally erred in alleging that there is. He has further observed, again correctly, at Austin's prompting, that we find in moral discourse an immense diversity of linguistic performances – and, he might have observed, in fact exactly the same diversity as is to be found in discourse that is not moral discourse at all. But the conclusion to be properly drawn from these observations is exactly the reverse of the conclusion which he actually draws; it is that the analysis of linguistic performances has nothing in particular to contribute to moral philosophy. Such an analysis is an exercise in the philosophy of language – doubtless of absorbing interest, but what it will illuminate can only be respects in which moral discourse does not differ from discourse in general. What is of concern in moral philosophy is not to enquire how advice, say, is to be distinguished from exhortation; it is, in fact, exactly the reverse of this – to enquire, that, is, what moral advice and moral exhortation, and for that matter moral judgement, criticism, resolution, or regret, have in common, what it is that makes them all instances of moral talking or thinking. What then may it be that all these things have in common? Surely what they all have in common is a certain kind of grounds. And thus we are led back again, sadder and perhaps a little wiser, to regard as the central question of moral philosophy that question which, among others, J. S. Mill set before us rather more than a century ago – the question, as he put it, 'concerning the foundation of morality'. If we have recently made no striking progress in answering this question, part of the explanation may lie in the fact that some of our most influential and able moral philosophers have attached their shiny new philosophical tools to their feet, and then unwittingly have skated away into another subject.

13

Comments on Frankena's
Three Questions

Professor W. K. Frankena mentions me as one of the participants in what he calls the Movement in moral philosophy, and I think he is right; I was so moving, or being moved along among others, ten years or so ago, and I think I find myself still inclined to so move, while recognizing with regret, when I come to look back at it, that, as he courteously observes, 'what such writers say is not as clear as one would like'. I embark on commenting upon his lectures with considerable trepidation, however, for the reason that, while his own writing surely is as clear as one could reasonably hope for, I have had great difficulty in figuring out what exactly it is in the Movement (or View) that he substantially dissents from, and have the lurking suspicion that there may be something that I have just failed to see. Tentatively, though, I tend to think that the root of my difficulty has been that he offers, in opposition to the Movement, an account of these matters that is really, in the end, not intelligible; and my main task in this commentative piece will be to try to explain why I think that.

Philosophers of the Movement, Frankena says, 'all think of Morality as having a function, job, point, purpose or object, or as being *for* something'. Let me first have one more try at sketching out why I think that, or at least what it is that I think. Take something that we should, I suppose, all agree to be a moral virtue – for example, truthfulness (recognizing of course, but for present purposes disregarding, that we might differ a bit about what exactly that is, and rather more about what, in this particular case or that, its exercise would require). Now it seems clear to me that, whether or not one is seriously inclined to question whether truthfulness really is a moral virtue, it makes perfectly good sense, and is indeed perfectly natural, to raise the question *why* it is. (Two questions, indeed: why is it a *virtue*, and why is it a *moral* virtue? But I shall say nothing here about the second

From *The Monist*, vol. 63, 1980, copyright © 1980, *The Monist*, La Salle, Illinois. Reprinted by permission.

question.) We say that people should cultivate and exercise the disposition to be truth-tellers; why should they? (Not 'why *do* they?', which is an interesting enough but different question.) Well, why should they? One might say that the goodness of truth-telling is just self-evident; but actually it is not, so we need not spend more time on that. One might say that its goodness is evident 'from the moral point of view'; but that is not much of an answer, since, though indeed not false, I suppose, it merely restates what prompted our question in the first place. One might say that truth-telling always works to the truth-teller's advantage in some way; but for one thing that is rather obviously not true, and for another, even if true it would not explain very well why it was a moral virtue. It seems to me that one needs to say, if one's answer is to be both pertinent and plausible, something like this. Speaking mendaciously, deliberately saying or giving to be understood what one believes not to be true, is something that, quite early in the lives of most of us, we find to be both quite easy and often rather tempting; it may often in some way not suit one's book that the truth should be known, and in such cases the inclination may very intelligibly arise to give to be understood something other than what one believes to be the truth. So what is there to be said against indulging that natural inclination? It seems to me that the *main* thing – doubtless not the only thing, and making a long story short – is that, if people were to freely indulge that natural inclination, there would plainly be an end or at least a severe diminution of trust. People would have to be, because they would have very good reason to be, more suspicious of one another, more wary of one another's words, more cautious, circumspect, calculating, and no doubt in many circumstances more fearful and apprehensive. There would probably be all sorts of cooperative undertakings upon which, mistrusting one another, they would be unable – being all very reasonably unwilling – to embark. And so on. And that would be a bad thing. We all know that for a person to be (as we all sometimes are) suspicious, mistrustful, fearful and apprehensive is a bad, uncomfortable thing. Now, in saying that, do I mean bad 'from the moral point of view'? No – just bad, bad from *any* point of view, disagreeable and disabling. So, in reverse, things will be better for people (not morally better, just better) if they are (usually, mostly) able and willing to trust, and in particular to trust the words of, their fellow men; and that is in essence why the somewhat counternatural dispositon to be a truth-teller is a good disposition for people to cultivate and exercise, a virtue. (Why it is specifically a *moral* virtue is a slightly different matter.)

Put more generally: there are ways for people to be and to feel, ways for them to act and to be able to act whether separately or together, circumstances for them to be in, which – because of what people are and their situation is – are good. Not morally good, just good; better than, preferable and almost universally preferred to, alternative predicaments which people might quite easily be in and (if it comes to that) quite often are in. Let us call these good, or at any rate better, situations, lumping them all together for present purposes – let us call them O. I would submit, then, that what is good in the moral virtues, what makes it reasonable to take them so seriously as some of us do, what makes them desirable dispositions both to preach and to practice, is that their cultivation and exercise to a rather large extent actually does – and to a far greater extent would, if their cultivation and exercise were more effective and general – tend to promote O. 'Moral distinctions' rest ultimately upon, call for explanation in terms of, are reasonably defensible only because of the existence of, nonmoral distinctions. Why is it morally good to give food to a starving man? Because – there is more to be said, but at least this *must* be said – it is simply better that the man should not be starving. And, that I submit, is not a *moral* judgement; to see that starving to death is a bad thing, I do not have to be a morally good man, or even a nice man – I have only to be a sane man. Even, if being very nasty, I watch with relish his starving to death, I am not unaware that starving to death is a bad thing. On the contrary, its being so, and its happening to him, is just what I take pleasure in.

(A few related but different questions. Does everybody want O? No, unfortunately; many people do not very much care how other people are getting along, though of course the situation would be likely to be better, albeit not necessarily for them, if they did. If I do not care a straw for O, ought I to be moral? Yes, obviously, because O-promotion is good, whether or not you personally care a straw for it. But *will* I be moral? Quite possibly, with luck and if you have been well brought up – but also, alas, very possibly not. Are good people good out of the desire for O? Probably, in part, if they happen to think of it, but many no doubt never do; and some may recognize that O-promotion is good, even though they do not particularly *want* it. Would morality not be a good thing, if its practice did *not* tend to promote O? The question is not easily intelligible – how could it fail to? Might I think that O itself was not a good thing? Yes, of course, and you would be mistaken.)

So, what is it in this to which Frankena takes essential exception (apart from its being still, no doubt, far from perfectly clear)? I believe that he feels that 'the View' *demeans* morality, makes it out to be something less than, lower than, we wish to think it to be, and indeed than it actually is; and that it does this by representing morality as dependent upon, as needing, or at any rate as being capable of, explanation and justification in terms of something *else*, by reference ultimately at least to standards of some sort, or values, other than its own. Morality, he wants to hold, is not, and does not have to be, *for* anything; what is morally good does not have to be, and is not, good because of anything *else* that is good. It is not 'instrumental'. The 'object' of morality is not to produce anything *else*; its object, if you can call it that, is just moral goodness, rather as the object of poetry-writing is poetry, and, one hopes and intends, good poetry. Now, although I understand this line of thought in a sort of way, in a more serious way I do not understand it at all. If material want were not a bad thing, could charity be a virtue? If pain were not horrible, could cruelty be wicked? Is it, to the virtuousness of charity, not *relevant* that material want is a bad thing? There are, in the ways in which people (and, for that matter, animals) live in the world, things by which they are injured or distressed, afflicted, damaged, frustrated – *bad* things. There are, on the other hand, things that are welcome, wanted, needed, by which people are helped or comforted, benefited and sustained – *good* things. It is not *morality* that tells us – indeed, we do not need to be told – that these things are good and bad. Morality enters only when we turn to the question of human *intervention* – intervention by 'rational beings' – in the way the world goes; and what morality then tells us, in a heroic oversimplification of my view, is that it is good (moral) to be disposed so to intervene as to promote good (nonmoral) and to diminish bad (nonmoral), and bad (moral) to fail in doing so or to do the reverse. If it were not for the basic, nonmoral goods and bads, the whole question of intervention by rational agents would have no interest, be of no importance; it would be unintelligible that we should be asked to take it seriously, or to divide ways of intervening (except aesthetically perhaps) into good ways and bad ways. So, of course, *that* sort of discrimination between good and bad (between virtue and vice) is in that sense secondary to, intelligible only by reference to, the other sort – the sort that we made before morality came on the scene at all. The sense of this view (or View) – which of course is not, when you come to work it out, as simple as all that – is to my eye so luminous that I do not find denial of it really intelligible. So now I must try to explain why, as I indicated earlier, I find really not intelligible the view which, against the View, Frankena puts forward. I shall do this by examining the three 'clauses' in which, in his first lecture, he sketches out his own 'conception of morality', and trying to show that they do not constitute a coherent whole. It must be remembered that he says that they sketch his position 'somewhat roughly', but I hope that there will be at least rough justice in proceeding in this way.

1. Morality (that is, a morality or any morality) is or centrally involves the making and uttering of evaluative or normative judgements about rational beings, their actions, character traits, intentions, motives, etc.

Well, no trouble so far; we would all go along with that, only noting perhaps that the rational being who most often and most fittingly comes up for judgement is very likely to be one's self. (Some accounts of moral judgement seem to me to go awry through a sort of assumption that one judges only, or primarily, *other* people.)

2. Such judgements and utterances are moral (as versus nonmoral) only if they have justifying reasons consisting of purported facts about the bearing of these actions, etc. on the goodness or badness of the lives of sentient beings, including the lives of others besides the agent or speaker if others are affected.

I should like to make two comments on this, one fairly trivial (I think), the other less so. First, I imagine we are to take it that the 'purported facts' offered as reasons are not to be brought in just somehow and anyhow, but as having, depending on what facts they are, what one might call a *direction.* Thus, if, for instance, what comes up for judgement is some envisaged action, the purported fact that it would 'bear' upon the life of some sentient being by making it *worse* would presumably tend to justify the judgement that the envisaged action ought *not* to be done, rather than that it ought. I think we would not happily accept as 'a morality' a system of judgements in which making things bad for sentient beings was typically offered as a reason why things ought to be done, and making things better a reason why they ought not.

But observe, second, how large a stride in this clause has been taken, at least, towards embracing the View. We see mention here of facts, or purported facts, about the bearing of actions on the goodness or badness of the lives of sentient beings; and since this mention occurs in, is part of, an offered sketch of what morality is, we are presumably to take it that here 'goodness or badness' imports not *moral* goodness or badness, but that other sort (or sorts) with which we are already and independently familiar. (We take the account, that is, not to be simply circular.) But if moral judgement, as is here said, has to have as its justifying reasons facts of this sort, is this not to say that moral distinctions – those made, that is, in moral judgement – call for explanation in terms of, are reasonably defensible only because of the existence of, nonmoral distinctions? That surely has to be so, for, if we were to make for purposes of argument the admittedly absurd supposition that there were no such nonmoral distinctions to be made, it would follow that moral distinctions could not then be made either; for there would then be no justifying reasons for moral judgement, and therefore – since the account very properly implies, or assumes, that anything seriously to be called 'judgement' must have reasons – no possibility of, no basis for, moral judgement itself. But then, if moral judgement has to have reasons of this sort, is it any more than saying the same thing in a different way to say that morality has a certain 'object?' For if, say, 'affecting for the better the life of sentient beings' has to be a reason for moral judgement – and, as we took for granted a moment ago, for *favourable* moral judgement – is this not to say that the 'point' of moral judgement is, at least ultimately, that the lives of sentient beings should be affected for the better? (A more sonorous way of saying the same thing is 'amelioration of the human predicament'.) It seems to me that one could resist this conclusion only by taking the highly fantastic position that moral judgement is not even meant to be in any way efficacious, that we simply judge for the sake of judging and that is all, nothing being meant consequentially to happen or be done. But if the 'object' of judging, say, that something ought not to be done is even in part that it should not be done, then morality, moral judgement, has the 'object' of actually promoting that which is a ground for favourable moral judgement, and of averting or deterring that which is a ground for the reverse.

However, in saying all this, I *think* I am saying nothing from which Frankena is much concerned to dissent. For he himself says, of his clauses 1 and 2, that 'such a conception has had many recent proponents', and I find myself listed among them. So, unless I have in some way misunderstood his clause 2, and I hope I have not, it is common ground that, so far, we are on common ground. And indeed it is, if I make it out rightly, Frankena's contention that his clause 3 is what the View overlooks, and what needs to be added. So, let us turn to that.

3. Such a system of normative discourse is not inspired by a desire for some (external) O, but by a concern, independent of one's other ends or motivations, for what is right or good on the basis of such considerations as satisfy Clause 2.

Now there is, I think, a sense in which this is surely right – but not, I also think, the sense which Frankena intends, since, so understood, Clause 3 looks not very interesting and has probably never been denied by anyone. One might take it to be a claim about actual human motivation. It might be the claim that, when I raise, say, the question 'Would that be fair?' and conclude perhaps that it would not be fair, it is extremely unlikely that, in so wondering and deciding, I am 'inspired' by the desire for amelioration of the human predicament. Not, I suppose, that I might not be; but it does look extremely unlikely, and certainly not every moral discourser is always 'inspired' to discourse by – let alone *only* by – a desire so diffuse and long-run and generalized as that. It certainly looks more likely that, when we wonder whether it's fair, we are 'moved' just by a concern for whether it's fair. But I doubt whether anyone who has held that morality has 'a function, job, point, purpose, or object' has ever meant to insist that it is a fact about people that the 'object' is that the desire for which, alone and always, inspires people to moral thought or utterance. That, as a claim about the way people think, is really *too* implausible. Certainly the revered Mill did not think that, in every single case of moral thought or utterance, the actual motive was always and only the desire to promote Utility, or even that it ought to be. The general character of the claim surely is, and always was, that 'some (external) O' comes in, not always and immediately as a *motive*, but ultimately, if one cares to think and argue about it, as a *justification*. This, and not the other claim, is what it would be interesting to deny; and I *believe* that it is Frankena's real intention to distance himself from the View, by, in Clause 3, denying it.

But this, then, is what in the end I cannot make sense of. Let us take it, as I anyway am very ready to do, that 'such considerations as satisfy Clause 2' are indeed, speaking generally, the grounds of moral judgement, its 'justifying reasons'. Then indeed it is true that, in moral thought or utterance, one is 'inspired by' – or at any rate that (lowering the psychological temperature) one has – a concern for what is right or good on that basis. In fact that is clearly even better than true, being in fact a tautology; in trying to make (and it is redundant to add 'with reason') a moral judgement, I am therein concerned with reasons for moral judgement. No one, I trust, is going to try to deny that. But is that all that there is to be said? Do we have to insist further that, if I am to be a proper moral judgement-maker, I must not be 'concerned' with anything else, or that, *in* being concerned with moral reasons, I *am* not thereby concerned with anything else? This is not presumably, I repeat, just an argument about actual human mental processes; we are considering not what people do actually think about, but what, in moral judgement, justificatorily comes in. Well, the tautologous answer is, of course, 'moral reasons'. But is that all that there is to be said?

It is not. How could it be? Let us agree that, as a proper moral judgement-maker, I have 'a concern . . . for what is right or good on the basis of such considerations as satisfy Clause 2'. Now, if I am a rational person (as, for this purpose, I am by definition) my concern to judge rightly on the basis of those considerations, taken as in Clause 2 as 'justifying reasons', must imply the supposition (whether or not I do actually raise this question) that considerations of that sort do deserve recognition as reasons. It would not be rational to be concerned to judge rightly on the basis of certain 'purported facts', unless I took it that such facts did indeed constitute reasons for judgement. Now such facts are of the general sort: 'X will tend to make better (or worse) the lives of sentient beings.' And what makes that a reason for favourable (or unfavourable) judgement? It seems that there can only be one answer: betterment (worsening) of the lives of sentient beings is good (bad). And that does *not* here mean 'a morally good (bad) thing to *do*'; on the contrary; deliberately to bring about betterment or worsening of sentient lives is a morally good or bad thing to *do* only because such betterment or worsening *is* good or bad – as of course it would *be*, whether or not there was any question at all of deliberate intervention either way, that is, whether or not any *moral* issue arose.

But now it seems to me that what I am saying is that 'concern . . . for what is right or good on the basis of such considerations as satisfy Clause 2' is something that rationally implies, makes no sense without, concern for 'some (external) O'. For if we look at the considerations that *do* satisfy Clause 2, they have to do with the goodness and badness of sentient lives; and if I have no concern for this as an O, why should I, how rationally could I, be concerned with judging rightly or wrongly on the basis of it? And this O is of course an 'external' O in the sense that, when I judge – or as Frankena interestingly has it, accept the *fact* – that some sentient life is better or worse, it is not a *moral* judgement that I then make. Which is to say that I find it completely impossible to *distinguish*, as Frankena's Clause 3 undertakes to do, between 'desire for some (external) O' and 'concern for what is right or good on the basis of such considerations as satisfy Clause 2'. For when one takes another look at what those considerations are, and why they ever found their way into Clause 2 in the first place, it seems to me to emerge that they constitute an O, concern for which alone makes rational, or even understandable, Clause 3's 'concern'. Or rather: it is not exactly that these things cannot be distinguished, but rather that, so far as I can see, they cannot be separated. It does not make rational sense to try to separate concern for moral right or good, from concern for that which the practices of moral rightness and goodness (tend to) bring about. Clause 3 strikes me as incoherent, in that it purports to do exactly that – to separate the inseparable.

I had better mention, in conclusion, that I have been taking for granted that Frankena does *not* attach enormous importance to the distinction between 'desire' and 'concern'. One could, I suppose, argue that the goodness of sentient lives is not something that moral people do in fact often, consciously, *desire*; and, in the sense that they probably do not very often think of it in that general way, that is probably true, though they might very well agree that they desired it if the question were put to them. And one could, I suppose, argue that a moral person, while necessarily concerned to judge morally rightly, does not necessarily – or necessarily does not? – actually *desire* to. But there would seem to me little point or interest in either argument. I take it that philosophers of the Movement, in arguing that morality has some external O, would not want to make much fuss over whether that is or ought to be an object of 'desire' or an object of 'concern', and I feel fairly sure that nothing much turns on this issue for Frankena either. But – suspecting as I still do that there may be something that I have simply missed – even about that I can feel only *fairly* sure.

14

Morality and Language

Professor Hare contends that philosophy can be brought to bear on practical problems, and in particular that moral philosophy can be brought to bear on the practical problems of moral education. This contention seems to me to be correct, but not for the reason that he gives, or at any rate not for the main reason that he gives. I shall first mention two ways in which it seems to me pretty clear that moral philosophy can have some relevance, even if of rather limited importance, to moral education, and then I shall argue against the main contention which Professor Hare advances.

First, then, I think we can agree with Professor Hare that moral philosophy could be, at least in part, an attempt 'to elucidate the meanings of the moral words'. I would not accept the phrase he actually uses – 'the moral words like "right" and "wrong" ' – for the reason that 'right' and 'wrong' are not moral words. Of course they occur when moral matters are under discussion – moral views, moral decisions, moral acts and so on may of course be right or wrong – but they occur no less characteristically when what is under discussion is, for instance, arithmetic, or rock climbing; the sums that I do, and the way I go about trying to climb a mountain, may also be right or wrong. These are no more 'moral words' than they are mathematical words, or mountaineering words, or horticultural words – nor, of course, are 'good' and 'bad'. However, no doubt there *are* some moral words – for example, the names of moral virtues and vices, or, come to that, the word 'moral' itself; no doubt it is part of the business of moral philosophy to elucidate the meanings of these; and it is hardly deniable that to be clear about the meanings of these words can be of some practical benefit, and could be of some considerable importance in moral education. In two ways, it seems. First, as Professor Hare remarks, if we are to

From *The Domain of Moral Education*, ed. D. B. Cochrane, C. M. Hamm and A. C. Kazepides (Paulist Press and Ontario Institute for Studies in Education, 1979).

think or argue using 'moral words', it is clearly desirable that we should know what we mean by them – and in particular, perhaps, whether other people mean by them the same as we do. Then, secondly, it seems pretty clear that the important business of moral discrimination – of distinguishing cases that differ, and (no less importantly) not distinguishing cases that do not differ – is likely to be considerably advanced by the acquisition of a decently extensive, decently clear moral vocabulary. This is the sort of thing that Aristotle undertook in his examination of the 'virtues' and of (as he claimed) their attendant failings by way of excess and deficiency; and I think he was right in supposing, as he did, that such examination was of practical importance, and not merely of academic, theoretical interest.

Moral philosophy can also have practical bearing in a quite different way. A certain kind of traditional (and not yet dead) moral philosophy consists in the attempt to 'systematize' morality – to exhibit moral views, moral principles, moral phenomena in general as not separate, isolated, piecemeal, but as fitting coherently together under some comprehensive *rationale*, or as resting upon some unifying 'foundation of morality'. But this sort of enterprise (as it is of course not at all original to say) may involve a sort of two-way trade. I may reject some 'theory' of this sort on the ground that it conflicts with some particular moral conviction of mine; or, conceivably, I may abandon or modify my moral conviction on the ground that it is not conformable with the theory. It is doubtful how commonly the latter occurs; but clearly it could occur, and almost certainly it sometimes does; in this way also, then, moral philosophy may, and almost certainly sometimes does, have practical bearing, by actually modifying the moral convictions of those who engage in it, or are, perhaps by way of moral education, exposed to it.

This, so far, is uncontroversial stuff. But this, though I believe that Professor Hare would go along with almost all of it, is by no means what he takes to be of central importance. 'Moral education,' he says, 'is, at least in part, education in the use of a language – that is to say, in the use of the moral language'; and there is, according to him, something else, something hitherto unmentioned, about 'the moral language' which, for moral education, is *the* important thing. I shall now try to show that in this he is wholly mistaken – that the features of 'the moral language' which he puts forward as being really important are, for one thing, not really (in a sense to be explained) features of the moral language at all, and are also, for another thing, not particularly important. The two features of moral judgements upon which Professor Hare particularly insists are, of course, first, that such judgements are 'prescriptive', and second, that they are 'universalizable'. I shall first try to show that, in a sense to be explained, these are not features of 'the moral language' at all.

First, prescriptivity. Professor Hare in his paper does not go into technical detail about this, and I shall follow his example. It is not perfectly clear to me, really, what 'prescriptive' means, or in what sense of that word, if any, it could possibly be true that *all* moral judgements were prescriptive; still less can I make any good sense of the notion of prescriptive *words*, though Professor Hare has sometimes claimed that there are such. But let us on this occasion leave all that on one side, and take it that what Professor Hare means can, in his own words, 'be roughly described by saying that moral judgments are things that you are supposed to act on'. I shall not attempt to disagree with that; nor, since it is admittedly rough, shall I fuss inappropriately about what precisely it means.

Am I then agreeing that moral judgements are prescriptive – are 'things that you are supposed to act on'? Well, yes. But is not prescriptivity, then, a feature of the moral language? Well, no – not particularly. For the fact is that prescriptivity – if this is what it is – is a feature of absolutely every 'language' in which it is said that anybody ought to do anything, or that to do anything would be either right or wrong. Suppose that we are watching a cricket match, in which the batsmen are showing every sign of settling in for a long stand. 'Just consider how strange we should think it if some-body' – let us suppose, the captain of the fielding side – 'came to us and said "I'm very bothered about what I ought to do; can you advise me?" and then it turned out that he did not think that whatever answer he gave to the question had the slightest bearing upon his action . . .' Indeed, we should think it strange. If we said 'I should give that young leg-spinner a try', and he agreed, and then neither did so nor offered any explanation for not doing so, we should certainly, and rightly, be much perplexed. But I do not believe that prescriptivity is an important feature of 'the language of cricket' – nor yet of arithmetic, or mountain climbing, or gardening. That one is 'supposed to act on' acceptance of the conclusion that one ought to do something, or that something would be the right thing to do, is not a fact about morality or 'the moral language', any more than it is a fact about cricket, or long division, or growing runner beans. It is a fact about what 'ought' means, or about what 'the right thing to do' means – and not, incidentally, a very exciting fact, since it is an absolute truism, which one could safely assume to be long familiar to anyone of school age. No child of school age, for instance – to take an example of Professor Hare's – really supposes that 'wrong' means no more than 'forbidden by my parents'; for he will have occasion to say, for example, watching his sister clumsily fixing the new bicycle saddle back to front, 'That's wrong', not meaning thereby 'That's forbidden by my parents', but that one is not supposed to do it like that. If, as may well be the case, there are some things forbidden by his parents as to which he cannot see why, or even that, those things are wrong, it will not be what 'wrong' means that will be giving him trouble, but what reason there is for saying that those things are wrong; he will need to think more about (as it might be) morality, not about what 'wrong' means, or whether, if one agrees that something is wrong, one is supposed not to do it. No one has much trouble with the latter points.

About 'universalizability' I can be brief, since the point that I want to make here is exactly the same. Moral judgements, let us agree, are universalizable; but this is not a fact, let alone an important fact, about 'the moral language', since it is, once again, a quite general truism about 'ought'. 'When I say that I ought . . . to do a certain thing' – for instance, to put a man on the square-leg boundary – 'in my own situation' – confronted, as captain of the fielding side, with a batsman fond of the hook shot – 'I thereby commit myself to the view that if the situation remained exactly similar, except that my own role in it was different' – for instance, I was batting – 'then the person, who in the new situation occupies the role which I now occupy' – that is, is captain of the fielding side – 'ought to act . . . in the same way' – that is, to put a man on the square-leg boundary. Well, of course. But this, as we can see, is a point no more about morality than about cricket (no more relevant to moral education than to physical education). It is a quite general point about any judgement that anything ought to be done, or would be right (or wrong) to do, or would be all right (or not) – and a pretty obvious point as well, though I dare say it would not be easy to state it quite exactly. (In fact, is not the situation rather worse than that – in that what we have here is a point not even about 'ought'-judgements in general, but simply about judgements in general? If 'That is an inkwell' is true in this situation, then it is true in *any* situation exactly similar in the relevant respects.)

But all is not yet over. One might agree – I do not see, in fact, how one could possibly *not* agree – that prescriptivity and universalizability are not peculiar to moral judgement, nor particularly characteristic of 'the moral language'. But one might still wish to argue that these features, even if not peculiar to moral discourse, are nevertheless of great importance *in* moral discourse, and therefore are important also in moral education. I shall now try to show that this is not true either.

First, then, prescriptivity again. Professor Hare's own view about this is not perfectly clear. At one point he seems to agree with the contention that prescriptivity *by itself* does not amount to much, since it leaves us 'free to prescribe or to adopt absolutely any way of life we please'. That, he says, is true – and goes on to claim that it is only in *conjunction* with universalizability that prescriptivity can do much for us. Earlier, however, he cites a couple of respects in which, he thinks, prescriptivity *is* important by itself. So we had better look at those.

The first is that, because of prescriptivity, 'nobody is likely to be much of a success as a moral educator if he is not himself trying sincerely to live up to the principles which he is advocating'. There are two things wrong with this (not that it is untrue). The first – familiar by now – is that this dictum has no unique relevance to moral education; I shall not be much of a success as a prudential educator if, urging the extreme inadvisability of smoking cigarettes, I am seen to make no attempt to give up smoking myself. The other point is that which Professor Hare later makes himself; the importance of the dictum is surely limited by the fact that, by itself, it sets no limits to *what* the moral educator may be trying to put across. It is probably true that, if I am to make a success of inculcating racial prejudice and a generally aggressive, bullying attitude to other people, then in my classroom I had better exhibit racial prejudice and treat my students in an aggressive, bullying style: otherwise, they may think that I don't really mean what I say. But that thought is scarcely an important contribution to moral education.

Another thing one might mention here is that the point is surely too familiar to take rank as an important finding of moral philosophy; and I am thinking there, not only of standard saws about practising what one preaches, but of, for instance, the more revealingly unselfconscious fact that a colloquial synonym for 'You ought . . .' is 'I should . . .'. (See my advice, above, about the young leg-spinner.) This colloquial synonym reveals, I think, rather pleasingly how well we all know that what I say you ought to do is what, in your shoes, I would do. I believe any child of school age knows that already.

Professor Hare's other point is, I think, that, because of prescriptivity, one's attitude to moral teaching and learning cannot be 'detached' – for 'the end of the process of moral education (if it ever ends)' is 'a choice of a way of life', and one could hardly suppose that that was of no great importance. What is wrong with this is that it is not a fact about, nor a consequence of, prescriptivity. It has nothing to do with 'moral language' at all. Agreed, moral judgements are 'things that you are supposed to act on'; but that the moral views I come to hold amount to something so important as adopting 'a way of life' does not follow from that, but only from a quite different thesis, needing to be quite differently and independently argued for, about the inescapability and pervasiveness of moral choice, and about the special importance of at least trying to get it right. For all that prescriptivity tells us *by itself*, morality might be no different from cricket: if I conclude that I ought to put a man on the square-leg boundary, then indeed I am supposed to act on that – but, of course, I might simply decide not to play cricket, and even if I do, it does not really matter very much (at my sort of level) if I sometimes do not bother to do what I recognize I ought to do. In bringing in as he does the notion of 'adopting a way of life', Professor Hare is smuggling in, as if they were facts about 'moral language', two very different and wholly non-linguistic theses – first, that one cannot just decide not to go in for morality (as one might decide not to go in for cricket or fishing, or perhaps even politics); and second, that morality matters very much. Perhaps both of these are true; but they are not contained in, nor do they follow from, prescriptivity.

In any case, as we have seen, Professor Hare later claims little for prescriptivity by itself. 'But when it is combined with the second feature, universalizability, the two together give us all that is essential to hold us in the path of a morality which is sufficient to make life liveable with others in society.' That is why universalizability, in particular, 'is obviously of crucial importance for the practice of moral education'. I shall now show that this claim too is completely preposterous, and is, furthermore, completely unsupported by what is said, in Professor Hare's own text, in its support.

It is really not difficult to see that the claim is preposterous; for it is open, fairly obviously, to precisely the same objection as that which Professor Hare himself admits to be cogent against prescriptivity taken on its own. Prescriptivity, he admits, cannot be all that important by itself, since it 'left us free to prescribe or to adopt absolutely any way of life we pleased': so our pupils might fully learn (if they did not already know) that moral judgements are prescriptive while making, and continuing to make, moral judgements that were perverse, or silly, or horrible, or in other ways not good. Very well. But it is perfectly clear, is it not, that to bring in universalizability at this point makes almost no difference at all? I might indeed 'adopt' any way of life I pleased, however fantastic or horrible; but equally, for all that universalizability tells me, I might prescribe universally, as proper for everyone, any way of life, however fantastic or horrible. If I have attended and duly conned Professor Hare's lessons in 'the moral language', I shall have learned that, if I judge that, say, women should be oppressed, humiliated, and regularly beaten, then first, this, according to me, is supposed to *happen*, and second, *any* woman is to be so treated (including me, in any possible world in which I were a woman). But those lessons do not disclose any *objection* to taking that view as to the proper treatment of women (or of, as it might be, children, or imbeciles, or one's parents); so long as I prescribe, and universalize my prescription, then I am doing all that the Professor has taught me – I am displaying full mastery of 'the moral language'. But how can these two features be of *importance* in moral language, and so in moral education, if full acceptance and comprehension of them could perfectly well coexist with moral views (and deeds) that were perfectly horrible – or, of course, perfectly fatuous, or perfectly inane? So far from taking us the whole way, or even most of the way, towards the state of being morally educated, they rather clearly get us nowhere at all.

So how does Professor Hare contrive not to see this? The answer is very curious. He would not perhaps, in a cool hour, wish to deny that, so far as bare possibility is concerned, it would indeed be possible to prescribe universalizably ways of life of the utmost absurdity, not to say fantasy and horror. But, he reflects, this is not really going to happen. For in the first place, we can try to cut out absurdity and fantasy, in practice, by inculcating 'the ability to discern and discover what the effects of our actions are going to be', and most particularly 'the ability to discern the feelings of others and how our actions will impinge upon them'. But that, though of course it is a very great deal, is not enough; for I might *know* exactly how others feel and how my actions affect them, and yet simply not care, or I might even take pleasure in causing them annoyance and distress; so we must try to inculcate also *love* of our fellow men, so that I shall not want to cause them distress, but on the contrary will positively want to help, and benefit, and please them. But now, if we have people like *that* – people thoroughly clear and well-informed as to what they are doing and the consequences of what they are doing, sensitively perceptive to the feelings and reactions of others, and imbued with love and concern for their fellow men – then *their* universalized prescriptions will be absolutely splendid. For them, prescribing universalizably will be the crowning achievement of moral education.

Well, yes. But, rather obviously, *everything* of importance here has come in, not in the explanation of prescriptivity and universalizability, but in all the other considerations which have to be added if those two features (by themselves) are not to allow ludicrous and morally intolerable implications. To argue as Professor Hare does is rather like an oculist's saying

'For safe driving, the crucially important thing is to have good eyesight' – then adding, *sotto voce* and rather hurriedly, 'assuming of course that you do know how to drive a car, and are neither drunk nor disabled nor suicidal nor murderous towards other people' – and then concluding loudly and triumphantly 'so, as I was saying, in mastering safe driving, good eyesight is the really crucial thing.' His way of proceeding is really very strange. He mentions two features of 'the moral language', namely prescriptivity and universalizability, with the claim that understanding of these is really important in moral education. He then sees (or half-sees) that they cannot really be of importance by themselves, since moral views, *even if* universalizably prescribed, could so far as that goes be wholly ridiculous or otherwise all wrong. So he adds that, if we are to get good results in moral education, we need *also* to make sure that our students become thoroughly well-informed, and imaginatively perceptive of the feelings of others, and that they learn to love others. He then seems to say that; *with that added qualification*, study of 'the moral language' – of prescriptivity and universalizability – *will* be very important in moral education. But here a very small tail is wagging a very big dog. Everything really important, and everything difficult, alike in morality and in moral education, has gone into the qualification, as if it were just incidental to the main business, the study on Harean lines of 'the moral language'. But the true proportions of the pictures are just the reverse of that. Study of 'the moral language' is of scarcely any importance at all: *everything* that matters comes in when we stop talking about language, and set about trying to become as well-informed as we can, as fully aware as we can of how other people feel and are affected by what we do, and – obviously most importantly of all – when we try to cultivate in ourselves, and to inculcate in others, that kind of concern for other people that one can call 'love'. None of that – nothing of what really matters – has anything significantly to do with 'the moral language' as Professor Hare describes it. So far as that goes, then, I have to conclude that Professor Hare has made no case for the practical value of moral philosophy; a little bit of a case could be made, as I earlier indicated – but not in his way, or on his grounds.

Ignorance is not a linguistic failing, nor is crass insensitivity, nor is callous indifference. It is not through the study of language that these things are to be – so far as they ever will be – cured.

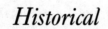

Historical

15

The Primacy of Practical Reason

'Two things fill the mind with ever new and increasing admiration and awe, the oftener and more steadily they are reflected on: the starry heavens above me and the moral law within me.'[1] These words, which occur in the 'Conclusion' of Kant's *Critique of Practical Reason*, are of course very familiar, and have often been respectfully cited as a succinct expression of his intense and highly characteristic feeling for the sublimity of nature and of the moral law. They have, I think, less often been critically considered. That the starry heavens are a proper object of admiration and awe is a proposition which I do not intend to discuss on this occasion, though it is, no doubt, discussable; but about the moral law there are questions, seldom raised, which I think may prove of interest. In a word, my question is this: why was Kant awe-struck? Why did he, in this and other passages of similar tone and topic, present the moral law as preeminently, indeed uniquely, a proper object of reverence, respect, and veneration? I do not particularly wish to suggest that he was wrong to do so, but only to seek to understand why he did.

The interest of this question is by no means purely historical. For in our own day most, if not all, philosophers who discuss the nature of morality appear to agree with Kant in the opinion that, where moral considerations are relevant to some problem of conduct, they must certainly be accorded preponderant weight over all others; but very seldom is anything said as to why this should be so. There are indeed ethical theories which yield the implication that a man's moral views are, simply by definition, those which regularly preponderate in his practical decisions; but if, as I think is clear,

---

[1] This and subsequent quotations from Kant are taken from *The Critique of Practical Reason and Other Writings in Moral Philosophy*, translated and edited by L. W. Beck (1949). The passage here cited is to be found at p. 258 of that volume. Subsequent references to pages of the volume will be given in the text.

From *Proceedings of the British Academy*, vol. LII, 1966. (Offprints are available from Burlington House.)

such theories are mistaken – if, that is, the question what moral considerations are is logically separable from the question what weight they should
carry, or do in fact carry for this person or that – then the question arises
why moral considerations should be accorded the preponderant weight or
authority which, by pretty general consensus, is actually and often tacitly
ascribed to them. It would surely be impossible to go further than Kant
did in insisting upon the overwhelming authority of the demands of duty
on our obedience; it is of particular interest, accordingly, to consider in his
case on what foundation this tremendous authority was supposed to rest.
He, if anyone, might be expected to have clear and definite views on this
matter. I am not primarily raising here the psychological or genetic
question of how or why Kant came to have feelings that he did towards the
moral law; that question, in the answer to which the special character of
his early upbringing, and particularly his religious upbringing, would
doubtless bulk large, is neither unimportant nor irrelevant, but is not here
in issue or really within my competence. I shall in fact have occasion to
allude to it, very briefly, in my conclusion, but my main and prior question
is: does Kant's theoretical account of what the moral law is, taken along
with his views on other related matters, justify, make reasonable or
appropriate, the peculiarly awe-struck attitude towards it which he so
readily adopted and so frequently avowed?

What then did Kant find so tremendous, so uniquely deserving of
respect, in the moral law? One might be inclined to think that in general
there are three, not mutually exclusive, possibilities here. First, it might be
held that the special respect-worthiness of the moral law derives from its
source – for example, as some would hold though Kant of course did not,
its source in the nature or will of a supreme law-giver and creator.
Second, one might seek to derive the 'worth' of the law from some
valuable end which its promulgation and general observance would be
calculated to promote. And third, one might argue that its claim to
peculiar respect rests upon, and can be substantiated by, consideration of
its own nature, of what it itself is. Now it could, I think, be said truly
enough that Kant rests his case on considerations of each of these three
kinds; but then it must be added that, in one way or another, for him all
these seemingly diverse considerations boil down to the same thing. He is
indeed anxious, in certain passages, to insist that the moral law subserves,
and moral action aims at, no end at all – that the worth of moral action, and
the respect-worthiness of the law, do not consist in anything which either
produces, or has as an actual or probable consequence. But in another and
less ordinary sense moral action does have, he holds, an end – namely,

human nature or, more strictly, *rational* nature; that is, that element or capacity in human beings which makes them capable of moral action and proper subjects of moral judgement. 'Rational nature exists as an end in itself', and has in itself 'absolute worth' (p. 87). But then 'rational nature' is taken also to be the source of the moral law; for Kant's celebrated doctrine of the autonomy of the will is exactly the contention that the obligations of morality are (and necessarily are) self-imposed by any rational being in virtue of his rationality; being rational is the condition, both necessay and sufficient, of being a self-legislating member of the 'Kingdom of Ends', bound, equally with all others, by laws of one's own making. And then, finally, it is for Kant another way of saying the same thing to say that the law demands respect simply because of what it is – namely, an imperative categorically pronounced by, and unconditionally binding upon, every rational being in virtue of his rationality, of the instantiation in each such being of 'rational nature'. 'Rational nature' is thus at once the source, and end, and essence of the moral law; and the peculiar respect-worthiness of the law is not so much derived from, as indissolubly united with, the 'absolute worth' of rational nature.

Now these are high words, and words not without their attendant and more or less familiar obscurities. But my concern at the moment is with the content, rather than with the merits or adequacy, of Kantian doctrine – with the question what he is saying, rather than with the question whether what he is saying is right. And what he is saying, I think, is really plain enough. He is saying that there is something in human beings (and possibly, or at any rate conceivably, in other beings too) which itself is, and in virtue of which they are, of preeminent value, of 'absolute worth'; and this is *reason*. But reason necessarily involves – this is his contention – recognition of and subjection to the moral law; such recognition and subjection is in a sense the distinctive characteristic of a rational being; and thus, in revering the demands of the moral law, one is really paying due reverence to that in oneself and others, namely reason, which has, and alone has, value for itself, real and unconditional 'worth', a proper claim to be not merely admired, or liked, but 'respected'.

But why, one may now ask, does Kant see reason in this light? Let us suppose, for the sake at least of the present argument, that he is successful in deriving the moral law from the concept of 'rational nature', and so in attaching to one the awe-striking properties, if any, of the other; but why is 'rational nature', why is reason, so peculiarly to be valued? Why should one be so particularly, and indeed uniquely, struck by it? The answer that Kant offers is sufficiently plain. It is simply that reason is itself unique.

Reason is not valuable, he holds, for any good that it does; that the sedulous employment of reason contributes, for example, to the happiness and well-being of human beings is, he believes, far from certainly the case. Besides, even if that were the case, it would be a purely contingent fact that it was so, and perfectly conceivable that the good produced might have been secured, as effectively or more so, in some different way, for instance by the operation of sheer, blind instinct. That would not make instinct in any way particularly worthy of respect; while by contrast, even if the use of reason were to yield no particular benefits, its worth would thereby not be diminished in any degree. It is what reason *is* that counts – its being, in itself, unique in the universe. In the inanimate world, Kant believed (and believed that he could prove), there can be no occurrence that is not the law-determined resultant of antecedent occurrences and states; in the case of animals, and of men also to the extent that they are animals too, there is a determined, quasi-mechanical succession of 'inclination' and action not essentially different from the operation of physical causes in and on inanimate things. It is only in rational beings that anything different is to be found; and this is precisely the capacity to exercise reason, independently of, and sometimes in opposition to, physical or psychological influences, sensory stimuli, or 'inclinations'. This capacity, in Kant's view, raises 'rational nature' entirely above the natural order; here alone do we find an exception to, and independence of, that natural, law-governed sequence of causes and effects which prevails in all the rest of creation. In this, then, we find what he calls 'the sublimity of our own nature' and, derivatively but inseparably, the sublimity of the moral law which reason, freely and yet necessarily, prescribes for itself.

But at this point a further question very naturally arises. Is there not, one may thing, a puzzling disparity between the argument Kant thus offers and the conclusion he draws? He insists, repeatedly, eloquently, emphatically, upon the uniqueness, the astonishing, awe-inspiring, absolute uniqueness, of reason; he insists correspondingly upon the uniqueness in creation, and so the sublimity and 'absolute worth', of rational nature or, as he sometimes expresses it, of personality. But how, we may ask, does he effect the transition from this – why, indeed, does he seem scarcely aware of making any transition – to his impassioned avowals of respect for the moral law? For surely there is a transition of some magnitude here. Let us suppose, as before, that Kant is wholly successful in his argument that any rational being is, as such, unconditionally bound by the moral law, that *qua* rational he can and must act as duty requires; yet this, plainly, is not all that a rational being can do. Let us grant that there is, employed in moral deliberation and action, what Kant calls 'practical reason'; but then, there is 'theoretical' reason as well, and all its manifold doings. Indeed, on Kant's own insistence, there are not really two faculties of reason, one practical and the other theoretical; if there were, we might have asked why Kant should have regarded the former as somehow more awe-inspiring (almost more unique!) than the other. But rather, as he says himself, 'in the final analysis there can be but one and the same reason which must be differentiated only in application' (p. 54); and if so, then we may well be inclined to ask all the more insistently why Kant should have regarded, as he evidently did, *one* application of reason, namely its application in moral thought and action, as peculiarly respect-worthy. He seems, indeed, quite often to forget about theoretical reason altogether in this connection, and to locate the 'worth' of rational beings in their capacity for practical reasoning alone; or, put otherwise, he seems often to write as if practical reasoning, which for him is identical, at least in its pure form, with moral thinking and decision, were the only kind of reasoning there is.

It is, I think, a pleasing curiosity in the history of philosophy to observe here how closely, for a moment, Kant's course approaches to that of Aristotle, and then how widely, and as yet unexplainedly, they ultimately diverge. Each seems clearly to employ uniqueness as a sign, or even as a proof, of distinctive worth; for each, the question what is distinctively valuable in man is to be answered by finding that respect in which man is unique; and, though Aristotle of course does not share Kant's belief in the strict determinism of nature in general, they agree in the conclusion that reason, 'rational nature', is what really distinguishes men from all other beings – at least from all other terrestrial beings. But at this point Aristotle finds it natural to conclude that theoretical reasoning must be the highest of human activities; for, though reason is indeed employed in practical matters, he thinks it plain that the timeless, incorruptible, non-sensuous objects of theoretical contemplation provide a worthier field for reason's activity than the humdrum situations and predicaments with which practical deliberation has, often inconclusively, to do. But Kant, so far unaccountably, turns the other way; the theoretical employment of reason is by him given scant regard, and is never, I think, spoken of in the exalted, awe-struck tones which he so regularly feels to be appropriate to practical reasoning. But why, we may ask, did Kant not draw Aristotle's conclusion, having reasoned so far as he did along substantially the same line?

It is both true and, as I shall suggest in a moment, highly significant, that this is a question of which Kant was only flickeringly aware. The primacy of pure practical reason, and so of the moral law, impressed him so forcibly that he was conscious only occasionally of any need to account for it; and such accounts as he offers may well be found perfunctory and unconvincing.

There is one passage of the second *Critique* in which Kant addresses himself formally and explicitly to argument for the 'primacy' of practical reason; but before considering that I would like to mention another matter which carried, I believe, some weight with him on this issue. Kant frequently observes, in a manner which implies that the observation is peculiarly striking, that reason in its practical use can 'determine the will'. He regards it, with some justice, as a distinctive feature of moral decision, at least in human beings, that such decisions can be and often are made independently of and often contrary to 'inclination'; and indeed the capacity so to decide seems to be for him just what the possession of a 'will' consists in. Now he is, I think, clearly of the opinion that in the use of theoretical reason no such thing is to be found; there is absent here the peculiarly striking capacity of reason to determine the will, so that, in this respect, practical reason is much the more extraordinary and distinctive phenomenon of the two. I believe, however, that this supposed contrast, by implication so much to the advantage of practical reason, actually vanishes if one examines more closely what it is taken to consist in. We must note that, in the practical employment of reason, it is 'the will' that reason is said to 'determine'; Kant is not saying, and it seems indeed that he could not consistently with his own principles have said, that reason can 'determine' physical happenings, for example, movements of the limbs in human action. We may say, then, that it is the inner, intellectual performance of decision, or of resolution, which is determined by reason; and if so, what Kant is saying is that, in the practical employment of reason, we are able to decide in the light of what we take to be reasons for so doing, and do not merely pass quasi-mechanically from thought to action as would creatures governed solely by 'inclination' or reaction to stimuli. But if so, it seems no longer at all clear in what respect this exercise of reason is to be regarded as essentially different from, and much more striking than, its purely theoretical exercise. For in the exercise of theoretical reason also we are, or at least we are no less inclined to suppose that we are, able to think, to believe, to argue, to conclude, in the light of what we take to be reasons for so doing, and do not merely slide, as it were, from thought to thought in sequences capable only of causal description and explanation. It is true that, outside the context of practical reasoning, we do not naturally, or not often, speak of the will as being involved, but there seems to be nothing in this point that would serve Kant's turn. For one thing, if practical reason determines our decisions rather than our actions, it is not clear in any case that Kant can properly speak of it as determining the will; for one might reasonably hold that, if the notion of a 'will' is to be employed at all, it should be supposed to be employed at the point at which decisions are put into execution, rather than in the process of arriving at decisions; practical reasoning, one may think, terminates in a practical conclusion, and it is only after that point, in the executive rather than the deliberative phase, that 'the will' takes over. Alternatively, if 'the will' is taken to be exercised merely in reasoning independently of, and perhaps contrary to, the influence of 'inclinations', then it would seem pertinent to point out that we may, for reasons, reach non-practical conclusions, just as we may reach practical conclusions, that may run counter to our inclinations. We may be reluctant to believe things no less than to do things. Just as we may find that there are reasons for doing what we would much prefer not to do, we may find that there are reasons for thinking what we would much prefer not to think.

However, Kant's explicit case for the 'primacy' of practical reason is not made to turn on the notion of the will. In a somewhat contorted passage of the second *Critique* which deals with this issue he writes in part as follows:

If practical reason may not assume and think as given anything further than what speculative reason affords from its own insight, the latter has primacy. But suppose that the former has of itself original *a priori* principles with which certain theoretical positions are inseparably bound but which are beyond any possible insight of the speculative reason (although not contradictory to it). Then the question is: Which interest is superior? It is not a question of which must yield, for one does not necessarily conflict with the other.... But if pure reason of itself can be and really is practical, as the consciousness of the moral law shows it to be, it is only one and the same reason which judges *a priori* by principles, whether for theoretical or for practical purposes. Then it is clear that, if its capacity in the former is not sufficient to establish certain propositions positively (which however do not contradict it), it must assume these propositions just as soon as they are sufficiently certified as belonging imprescriptibly to the practical interest of pure reason. (pp. 194–5)

What does this amount to? Kant's argument could fairly be summed up as follows. The power of reason in its speculative employment is, as the whole of the first *Critique* had been directed to establishing, strictly limited. It is not the case indeed, as Hume had contended, that nothing whatever about the world can be established *a priori*. Nevertheless, it can be shown, Kant thinks, that by theoretical arguments nothing whatever can be established about the world except as an object of 'possible experience'; and this implies, as the 'Dialectic' in the first *Critique* seeks to show in detail, that the traditional grand objects of metaphysical ambition are in principle unattainable by speculative reasoning. No valid argument from known premises, set out in intelligible terms, can have as its conclusions that there is a God; that the soul is immortal; that the will is free; or can tell us anything at all of the world as it is 'in itself'. But the case, he holds, is otherwise with the practical employment of reason; here we do find, at least, reason to believe at least some of these speculatively indemonstrable propositions. For some of these propositions are, as he calls them, 'postulates' of pure practical reason; they are not exactly proved by, but nevertheless must be accepted as the basis or condition of, practical reasoning. 'These postulates are those of immortality, of freedom . . . and of the existence of God' (p. 235). Briefly: we must believe that the soul is immortal since we are conscious of the requirement to achieve moral perfection, and have no prospect of doing so in the course of any finite existence; we must believe that the will is free since only on that supposition is morally assessable action, indeed *action* of any kind, a reality; and we must believe that there is a God since the 'highest good', an ideal coincidence of happiness with desert, can be supposed to be attainable only if a beneficent creator has designed that sooner or later it should be attained. But these are propositions which, by the purely speculative exercise of reason, we could find no reason to believe, and which indeed could be shown to be theoretically indemonstrable; if, therefore, in the exercise of practical reason and the implications of that exercise, we do find reason, and indeed the necessity, to believe these propositions, then it must be concluded, in Kant's submission, that practical reason has, in this very crucial respect, the edge. It would not do, indeed, for the postulates of practical reason to conflict with anything that can be theoretically demonstrated; but since these are topics on which speculative reason is necessarily quite silent, we may be sure that that is not the case here.

Such is Kant's central argument for the primacy of practical reason, and hence for the peculiar veneration with which he regards the moral law; and it is fairly evident, I think, that it does not amount to much. It is, for one thing, very far from clear that what he offers as the indispensable 'postulates' of practical reasoning have any very serious claim to be so regarded. That the will is free, at least in some sense or other of that profoundly obscure and perplexing phrase, no doubt is presupposed in our attitudes towards and beliefs about the actions of others and, perhaps most importantly, of ourselves; but the two other supposed 'postulates' would probably be regarded by many as singularly dispensable. It may well be the case that moral perfection, as perhaps for that matter perfect physical health, is not attainable in the course of any finite span of terrestrial existence; but why is it necessary to believe that it is attainable at all? If it is said that its being attainable is implied by the proposition that we ought to attain it, we may reply that that implication is easily avoided by substituting the proposition that we ought to *strive* to attain it, a proposition which seems to have just as good a claim to express the substance of the moral conviction in question. Similarly, it is far from clear that it is necessary to believe that the 'highest good' is actually attainable; and if so, then it is not necessary to believe in any supernatural arrangements for its realization.

But let us suppose, again for the sake of the present argument, that these allegedly necessary 'postulates' really are necessary; even so, I believe that it can quite readily be seen that argument on this basis for the primacy of practical reason is far from conclusive, and may, indeed, be regarded as positively double-edged. Much turns, it seems to me, on the question in exactly what terms the argument is set out. Kant would wish to put it in this way: in the 'practical use' of reason we find grounds for accepting those important propositions which are its postulates, but which speculative reason is demonstrably powerless to establish. This seems to say that practical reason yields, so to speak, a bonus or dividend not procurable by any other means. But some might feel disposed to express the matter in this way: in the 'practical use' of reason, we find ourselves obliged to accept as its preconditions propositions which cannot conceivably be shown to be true, and which otherwise we have no reason whatever to believe. And this seems to say that reason in its practical use lies under the logical disability of leaving, so to speak, intellectual loose ends, of constraining us to accept what we cannot possibly show to be true. What is the real difference between these two ways of expressing the matter? They do not differ structurally, or logically; in each case it is said – and this is the substance of Kant's argument – that certain propositions which cannot be theoretically established play the role of 'postulates' in the employment of reason in practical matters. The difference is that our hypothetical anti-Kantian takes it to be a bad thing to be committed to accepting what cannot be established as true, whereas Kant very evidently regards it as a good thing that at any rate these propositions should be accepted. But why is it a good thing? It seems that his answer would be that acceptance of these propositions is morally and spiritually salutary, and that this 'interest' far outweighs any speculative, rationalistic discontent that might thereby be occasioned. But this, of course, is to assume the conclusion of his own argument – namely that, at any point of divergence between the practical and theoretical uses of reason, it is to its practical use that 'primacy' is to be accorded. It seems clear that, if the argument does not begin with this tacit conviction, it can quite naturally be read as establishing the opposite position – the position, namely, that the theoretical use of reason is more admirable, more impressive, more fully satisfactory than its practical use, since it does not, as the latter does, lie under the dialectical disadvantage of committing its practitioner to mere assumptions for which no support is conceivably forthcoming.

I believe that in fact one must now say, without further beating about the bush, that Kant's convictions on this matter really cannot be adequately supported, or even explained, within the confines of his own theory of morals. It is the fundamental contention of that theory that, to exhibit man as a moral being, nothing further is required than the supposition that man is a *rational* being; the source, and indeed the content, of the moral law is to be located in or extracted from 'concepts of pure reason' alone. It is thus inevitable that sentiments of 'respect', or even of awe, towards the moral law should have to be explained in terms of the peculiar respect-worthiness of reason; and this poses for Kant the difficulty, from which in my submission he does not escape, that while he does not really wish to accord such respect to reason in general, this is actually what his own theory would require him to do. He might have made a case, and indeed does make something of a case, for the idea that the faculty of reason is, when considered in a certain light, peculiarly striking, perhaps quite unique, very crucially distinctive of humans from other (at any rate terrestrial) creatures and objects. It would have been understandable, even, that he should have been somewhat awe-struck by this remarkable and seemingly unique phenomenon. But the fact is that, to beat no further about the bush, this simply is not the conclusion that he wanted to reach; he really wanted to display as the proper object of veneration not reason, but virtue; and the fatal difficulty was that his own theory of morals precluded him in effect from distinguishing relevantly between the two.

It is interesting, but perhaps not surprising, to observe that Kant was apparently not always unmoved by the more general, as it were Aristotelian, respect for reason which was, I have suggested, the natural outcome of his theoretical position. In a note written probably in the 1760s, he says:

'By inclination I am an inquirer. I feel a consuming thirst for knowledge, the unrest which goes with the desire to progress in it, and satisfaction at every advance in it. There was a time when I believed this constituted the honour of humanity, and I despised the people who know nothing.' (p. 7) This attitude – which, discounting a certain romanticism of expression, is indeed sufficiently Aristotelian – is one which, Kant implies even at that relatively early date, he had decisively abandoned. But we find him again, in an essay published some twenty years later, speaking of reason as 'the highest good on earth' – and not, in this context, as being the ground of virtue and the moral law, but rather as being 'the ultimate touchstone of truth' (p. 305). But now, if, as no doubt was natural enough, he was disposed at one time to regard as 'the highest good' reason in its specifically intellectual, non-moral employment, what led him eventually, and with such fervour, to embrace the alternative view – to accord the 'primacy' to *practical* reason, and to consiousness of the moral law as its peculiarly awe-striking expression? Was he in fact moved by the arguments which we have considered, and have found to be, in my submission, by no means adequate to their intended purpose? I believe that it is clear that he was actually not moved by those arguments. In the note of the 1760s which I have just mentioned, he attributes his conversion from the 'blinding prejudice' of veneration for the theoretical intellect to Rousseau; and what he learned from Rousseau, what actually brought about his conversion, was surely not those arguments which he later deployed in the second *Critique*. Rousseau's gospel was of the sanctity of uncorrupted natural feeling, of the holiness of the heart's affections, of man as a sensitive – some would say, sentimental – rather than a rational being. It was, it seems to me clear, from this Romanticist source – combined, no doubt, with the persistent influences of a Pietist upbringing – that Kant's awe-struck veneration for virtue was actually derived; such were the grounds on which (with occasional lapses) he came to abstain from speaking in such reverential terms of reason in general. The trouble is, though, that his later ethical theory is itself unbendingly rationalistic; and thus we find him in search, albeit somewhat perfunctorily in search, of some sort of philosophical grounds for a conviction which it does not occur to him to question, but to which his theory, I believe, can actually offer no support.

Is there anything of more general philosophical interest to be extracted from this brief scrutiny of Kant's dilemmas? I believe that there is something to be learned, if only from the circumstance that, so far as I know, this particular aspect of Kant's moral theory has been so seldom considered. Kant wished to assign to moral virtues a special preeminence among human characteristics, to moral 'imperatives' an authority predominant over any other practical considerations. Though much in his moral theory has been exhaustively and critically examined, this feature of it has, I believe, too often been accepted without any examination at all. But even if one supposes that Kant was obviously right here, should there not be some stateable reason *why* he was right? And if the reasons he offers seem insufficient for the purpose, should one not raise the question whether better reasons are to be found? It is, I think, a just criticism of much recent moral philosophy that from this issue it seems determined positively to avert its gaze.

I would myself be inclined to venture somewhat further than this, and to draw from Kant's example the further supposition that, if the 'worth' of moral virtue is to be effectively argued for, then the argument will surely have to bring in considerations of a type which he was determined to exclude. One will surely have to raise the question: what good does it do? Kant himself, I believe, falls into a not uncommon trap here. When, towards the close of his second *Critique*, he asks 'what pure morality really is', what is 'the distinctive mark of pure virtue', he proceeds at once to describe an extreme example of devotion to duty at a terrible price – specifically, of steadfast refusal to bear false witness, with disastrous consequences to the virtuous man himself and also, along with him, to all his family and friends. In this he presents us, no doubt, with an instance of 'pure virtue'; but do we find here its 'distinctive mark', what pure virtue 'really is'? Is it distinctive of virtue that its practice has disastrous consequences? Is morality 'really' a way of bringing catastrophe upon yourself, your family and your friends? Is this what we are supposed to learn from this dramatic example? Well, of course, it is not; what Kant wishes his example to teach us is that 'pure virtue' is to be valued *without regard* to its consequences. But then it is not clear that the example shows any such thing; for it is by no means impossible, surely, to derive from it the moral that virtue is to be valued even if sometimes the consequences of its practice are disastrous, on the understanding of course that usually they are highly desirable. Kant feels, no doubt rightly, that unswerving devotion to virtue is most admirable, most striking, when the cost to the virtuous man is great; but it is surely fallacious, though perhaps not uncommon, to infer from this that the 'worth' of virtue has *no* connection *ever* with the question what comes of its practice. To take thus, as seems often to be done, as the typical, representative, central case of virtuous action that case in which no good, and perhaps much harm, comes of it, is indeed to limit very severely the grounds on which it can thereafter be urged that the practice of virtue is to be valued above all things. Perhaps our consideration of the case of Kant may further the suggestion that that limitation cannot sensibly be accepted at all. If we eschew the question what good comes of being virtuous, then awe in contemplation of virtue is hard indeed to explain.

16

Liberty

On the topic of liberty Hobbes is best known, I believe, to philosophers at large for what he says in the first three paragraphs of the chapter of *Leviathan* which he devotes to this subject (chapter XXI). His controversy with Archbishop Bramhall is no doubt read by many; nor do I mean to imply that, in *Leviathan*, nobody bothers to read more than those three paragraphs. It is rather that they have been found the most interesting in a general philosophical point of view – and, on the whole, rightly so. His chapter is entitled 'Of the Liberty of Subjects', and its principal theme, as that title indicates and as, of course, one would expect in the second part of *Leviathan*, falls within the bounds of political theory. It is only at the very beginning of his chapter, and very succinctly, that he handles the more general, perhaps more philosophically interesting, and certainly even more philosophically perplexing, problem that we know as that of free will, or the freedom of the will.

In this lecture I shall briefly sketch what Hobbes has to say – himself very briefly – on that problem, but that is not what I want chiefly to discuss (being far from confident that I should have anything useful to say about it). I want to consider mainly his political–theoretical theses on 'the liberty of subjects' – and, in particular, to suggest a reason why he should have prefaced those theses with a few general remarks on free will. For there does seem to be a serious question why he should have done that. The problem of free will, or the freedom of the will, is a topic which one might well think to be, and which indeed has been almost universally treated as if it were, quite distinct from that of political liberty, and only rather deviously, if at all, connected with it. The question in what conditions, or whether actually in any conditions, the will is free seems to have little to do with the question of the nature, of the merits or demerits, of the proper limits if any (and so on) of political liberty. Why then does Hobbes, in setting out to discuss one of these topics, rather puzzlingly begin by

---

Unpublished lecture delivered in Oxford to commemorate Hobbes's tercentenary, 1979.

briefly discussing the other? I am inclined to think that, in proceeding in this way, he was evincing cunning rather than confusion. Hobbes has, I shall suggest, a tactic here, and one of some ingenuity.

Let us first glance briefly, then, at what he has to say about free will. Well, what every schoolboy (or at least every undergraduate) knows, I take it, about Hobbes on this topic is that he was an early exponent of the position that is commonly known nowadays as 'compatibilism' – that determinism is of course true, and also that of course we have free will, or at least that it is entirely possible that both those propositions should be true together. In his words: *'Liberty* and *Necessity* are consistent.' The case for this claim is both simple and familiar – and, for that matter, certainly valid so far as it goes. A man is free, Hobbes says, when he can do what he will – 'A FREE-Man, is he, that in those things, which by his strength and wit he is able to do, is not hindred to doe what he has a will to': somewhat as water flows freely down a channel when its flow is not blocked or impeded, or a bird is free when it is released from a cage. Well, clearly all of us, even the weakest and most witless, are, for most if not all of the time, free men in that sense; there are many things that we have strength and wit to do, which we are not prevented from doing if so inclined. And that that should be so is entirely consistent with 'necessity'; for if I choose to cross the road and do so, then I act freely, even if there are – as Hobbes held to be certainly the case – antecedent causal factors determining, necessitating, that I so chose and acted.

I should like to offer two digressive observations on this, before pressing on. First, Hobbes insists specifically that 'liberty' is consistent with 'fear': if I abstain from going swimming through fear of sharks, there is no derogation from my liberty – I still could have gone swimming, but, whether reasonably or not, chose not to. But he apparently holds also, and as if it were the same point, that I act freely if, with a pistol at my head and in immediate fear of death, I hand over my money to the footpad – for after all I choose to, and am not prevented (certainly not by the footpad). But that is to treat the coercive act of another person as just a causal factor, like any other, determining my choice; and that looks dubious; might one not wish to say that I act freely, not only if I am not 'hindred', but also if I am not forced, or compelled? It might have been a good thing if Hobbes could temporarily have set aside his immense contempt for Aristotle, and considered what Aristotle had to say about 'mixed actions' and kindred matters.

My second observation is simply that, if the exercise of 'liberty' is thus defined, it is evident that it is not a sufficient condition of responsibility (in at least one important sense) for one's actions. For if a person so gravely demented as to be, while not totally witless, yet 'not responsible' should escape from his straitjacket or his cell, he would then be a free man in Hobbes's sense, would exercise liberty, until such time as he was re-captured and reconfined. But since the topic of free will interests us, I suppose, largely because of its pertinence to questions about responsi-bility, that raises the question whether Hobbes says enough on this particular topic to be really interesting.

I return to exposition. The other famous thing that Hobbes says on this subject, in which he was followed perhaps even more famously by Locke, is that the whole issue is apt to be wrongly posed if we pose and press the question whether 'the will' is free. He does not quite say, as Locke did, that to ask whether the will is free is actually senseless – 'it is as in-significant to ask whether man's will be free, as to ask whether his sleep be swift, or his virtue square' (*Essay Concerning Human Understanding*, II, XXI). But he does insist that for the will to be free is, properly understood, neither more nor less than for a man to act freely. If I say that a gift is a free gift, I do not therein ascribe some deep, mysterious, and elusive property to the gift. I mean only that the giver, in giving it, acted freely. Similarly, a free will is not a will with some important, rather inscrutable and elusive property of its own; it is simply what a man can be said to have, and to exercise, when he acts freely. If a person acts freely, then whether the will is free is not a further question. That, Hobbes assures us, is the plain sense of the matter.

Now let us turn to the principal theme of Hobbes's chapter – political liberty, or, as he calls it, the liberty of subjects. The main strategic object of his treatment of this topic is, I think, pretty clear, and, in the light of the general character of his political theory, not at all unexpected. One could say that his main object is to lower the temperature. He is keenly aware that 'Liberty' is an emotive, popular cry, that liberty is and long has been unquestioningly taken to be a great and good thing, a thing that all good men want or at least have good reason to want, and furthermore a thing to which they are apt to take themselves, and to be on all hands rhetorically encouraged to take themselves, to be entitled absolutely and as of right. Men are liable, as he puts it in an unfriendly phrase, to 'clamour' for liberty; and it is a short step, in his view, from clamour to tumult and disorder. Further, he must of course have been also aware that his own political argument would inevitably be, was peculiarly liable to be, abused and denounced in the name of liberty; for his Sovereign is absolute, and absolute rule and liberty are at least rather naturally supposed to sort ill together. His response to such 'clamour' for liberty is deflationary in intent. He does not confront his expected opponent head on, but seeks to make him look ridiculous. He hopes that the cry will be silenced by being made to sound foolish.

Now this he seeks to achieve in a way, or by a repeated pattern of argument, exactly and interestingly similar to that which he has employed, introductorily and prefatorily, on the topic of free will. To the anxious person who insists, or doubts, or wishes, or merely hopes that he has free will, Hobbes's first response is that of course he has it, both certainly and obviously; for it is both certain and obvious that, like all other men, he is usually not physically prevented from doing what he has a mind to. But if the anxious person protests that there is more to it than that – that indeed he and others may be free men in that sense, but that that is not enough to establish that 'the will' is free – Hobbes's second response is that in so protesting he is merely confused, asking for he knows not what. To be unimpeded in doing what one chooses to do is indeed a possible, and doubtless desirable, state of affairs – not, however, one about which to make a great deal of fuss, since actually to be in that state is both very common and very familiar. But to ask for more – to ask, for instance, that one's will, one's choices, should have no determining antecedent conditions – is to be merely confused; for it is actually impossible (Hobbes tells us) that that should be so, nor would it be in the least desirable, even if it were possible, that it should be so. In what way would it add to the felicity or dignity of man that his choices and inclinations to act should be simply inexplicable, causeless, random? Thus, the contention runs, there is nothing to fuss about, no rational occasion for clamour or even concern. On the one hand, in the clear and proper sense of 'free will', it is obvious that we actually have it: and on the other hand, the demand for something more springs from mere confusion, and would never be made by a person who saw clearly what he was about. If you will only think what you mean, you will see that you either have it, or do not really want it.

And this, as I see it, is the pattern of the deflationary programme which Hobbes seeks to follow in his treatment of 'the Liberty of Subjects' also. That expression, as he is keenly and correctly aware, is not univocal; but in whatever sense, he will seek to argue, we may construe it, we shall find that it denotes either something that we uncontroversially have, or, if misunderstood otherwise, something that no reasonable person would clamour or hanker for. Let us see, then, how the programme goes, and how far it may be judged successful for the purpose intended.

What is it that a person wants who says, in a social or political context, that he wants liberty? Of the several possibilities let us take it, first, that he wants freedom from constraint, to be not 'hindred', as Hobbes put it, in doing what he will. Well, Hobbes says first, nearly every man, quite obviously, already has this. 'For if,' he writes, 'wee take Liberty in the proper sense, for corporall Liberty; that is to say, freedome from chains and prison, it were very absurd for men to clamour as they doe, for the Liberty they so mainfestly enjoy.' But, the protester may protest, that is not enough. It may be true that I am not actually restrained by chains and prison, but I may still feel the unwelcome constraint of the prospect of those things if I do not comply with the law – of which Hobbes, indeed, speaks himself as 'Artificial Chains'. But no, Hobbes replies, that does not in fact derogate from your liberty; in the prospect of penalties you may well see a reason for compliance with laws, but if for that reason you decide to comply you do so freely; and you are also free to break laws (as many do) if you so choose. Let us even put the issue as sympathetically as we can: let us take Liberty to consist in the absence *both* of corporal restraint *and* of legal restriction; it is still, he says, manifest that men have liberty.

For seeing there is no Common-wealth in the world, wherein there be Rules enough set down, for the regulating of all the actions, and words of men, (as being a thing impossible;) it followeth necessarily, that in all kinds of actions, by the laws praetermitted, men have the Liberty, of doing what their own reasons shall suggest, for the most profitable to themselves.

What then can it be that you demand, that you do not already have? Can it be that you are asking not merely for what you already have, that is, liberty in all those matters on which the law is silent, but that there should also be no requirement to comply with such laws as there are? But that would be an utterly absurd demand, being merely for 'that Liberty, by which all other men may be masters' of your life. Laws that need not be complied with are no laws at all, and if liberty were taken to mean unconstraint of that sort, then it would be the mere anarchy that no reasonable man would desire.

But perhaps, second, something quite different may be at issue. When, say, the eighteenth-century American colonist demanded liberty, what was it that he sought? Presumably that American territories should be, as a political entity, self-governing, independent of external political interference and control. But if that is what is meant by liberty for Americans, then, although they perhaps did not enjoy it at that time, liberty is again something that most men already have: for mostly they are citizens of states, or 'Common-wealths', that already have the independent political management of their own affairs. In this sense, the subject of an absolute ruler, or any other sort of ruler, of an independent state is already a free man – that is to say, the inhabitant of a free country. May he protest that that is not enough – that he should be a free man not only as being a citizen of a free country, but himself free exactly as his country is free? But that would be an absurdity, born of confusion. If men, Hobbes says, 'for want of Judgement to distinguish, mistake that for their Private Inheritance, and Birthright, which is the right of the Publique only', then once again the liberty they demand 'is the same with that, which every man should have, if there were no Civil Laws, nor Common-wealth at all'. Do I really want to be free to declare war on my neighbour – or that he should be free to declare war on me? The confused demand that particular men should be free exactly as – and not merely in the sense that – their state or nation is free, is once again a demand for that mere anarchy which no reasonable man would desire.

But there is another possibility. The cry for liberty, Hobbes thinks, may sometimes be for a particular kind of constitution, for what are indeed sometimes called 'free institutions'. This he believes to be a complete mistake, and a mistake that he lays, with characteristic ferocity, at the door of the writers of classical antiquity. The business of government, in his view, is to govern; it is to any man's interest, as any reasonable man will perceive, that he and others should be governed; and by comparison it matters not at all, in Hobbes's opinion, what particular institutional forms a government may have, or by what forms and procedures the legitimate governing authority may be identified. That authority may be, for instance, a hereditary monarch, or an elected assembly; in either case its functions and duties, and its relation to those governed, must be exactly the same. No species of constitution can be intrinsically, necessarily, more or less 'free' than any other; there is a job to be done, and the job, and the rights of government is executing the job, must be the same, by whatever mechanisms the sovereign 'representative' is identified as such.

Why has anyone ever supposed otherwise? Because, Hobbes holds, we have been corrupted by miseducation. The Athenians were a 'popular', that is, a democratic state; and to ensure their contentment, he says, they were absurdly instructed by their orators and politicians, and even by philosophers, that only citizens of that sort of state were free, and all other men were slaves. Later, in the Roman republic, after the deposition of

Rome's kings, men of influence had an obvious interest in denigrating monarchy, and taught similarly that 'all that lived under monarchy were slaves'. Such Greek and Roman writers then came to be regarded, in later generations, with uncritical reverence by learned but unthinking persons. And thus, Hobbes says (warming to his work),

> by reading of these Greek, and Latine authors, men from their childhood have gotten a habit (under a false show of Liberty,) of favouring tumults, and of licentious controlling the actions of their Sovereigns; and again of controlling those controllers, with the effusion of so much blood; as I think I may truly say, there was never any thing so dearly bought, as these Western parts have bought the learning of the Greek and Latine tongues.

So: 'If you will only think what you mean, you will see that you either have it, or do not really want it.' Has Hobbes then succeeded in his deflationary undertaking? Are we to agree that, as 'subjects', we (nearly) always actually have liberty, and that 'clamour', or even complaint, always springs from confusion or from folly or perhaps from both? His reader, I believe, is not likely to agree quite so easily. For it is natural to think that there are further 'versions', as we may call them, of political liberty which have not yet been mentioned, and which, contrary to Hobbes's programme, may well be thought desirable, and yet be not necessarily or always possessed, by reasonable men.

The first of these is very simple indeed, and it may well be thought somewhat surprising that Hobbes has nothing to say about it, or, worse, when he approaches the topic seems deliberately and rather disingenuously to look away from it. The very first sense of 'liberty', it will be remembered, that we considered – the liberty 'of subjects', that is, or political liberty – was that of freedom from constraint by laws. In his comment on this Hobbes said, of course, 'you actually have it' – 'in all kinds of actions, by the laws praetermitted, men have the Liberty, of doing what their own reasons shall suggest, for the most profitable to themselves'. And if we are not contented with that answer, Hobbes chooses to suppose – one might well think, less than ingenuously – that we must be hankering, absurdly, to be exempted from the constraint of any laws whatever. But why does he not consider that a man, who is perfectly aware that he has some freedom from legal restriction, may perfectly reasonably wish to have more? May he not intelligibly demand to be *less* constrained by laws, or constrained by *fewer* laws, without having attributed to him the pretty manifest absurdity of asking to be bound by no laws at all? Hobbes says himself, a few pages later:

In cases where the Sovereign has prescribed no rule, there the Subject hath the Liberty to do, or forbeare, according to his own discretion. And therefore such Liberty is in some places more, in other places lesse; and in some times more, in other times lesse . . . .

Why does he not here mention that more liberty may reasonably be thought, and if necessary demanded as, a good thing – particularly since, though in a rather different connection (chapter XV), he has himself observed that 'there are very few so foolish, that had not rather governe themselves, than be governed by others'?

One might think that the explanation of Hobbes's reticence, even deviousness, on this point is simply that the point did not suit his book: if clamourers for liberty were to come out looking always confused, he needed to skate rapidly over a demand for liberty which looks, on the face of it, perfectly sensible. But the case is not quite so bad as that. I take it that Hobbes would have said, and would have been right in saying, that, if you raise this question of degree – *how much* liberty it is desirable that subjects should enjoy under the law – then there is practically nothing that, in general terms, can usefully be said about it. Are you thinking, for example, of peacetime or wartime ('other times . . .')? Of southern England, say, or Northern Ireland ('other places . . .')? It would be absurd to say without qualification that more liberty, less constraint, is always better, and can always reasonably be demanded. And though one might suggest that subjects, in general, should be accorded as extensive liberty as the exigencies and contingencies of particular situations may allow, it might be doubted whether so bland and emollient an observation was really worth making.

But, one may protest, the demand for liberty, in the sense of *more* liberty, may be made not only, and indeed pretty vacuously, in quite general terms. Might a subject not think that, not in general, but in the precise time and place and conditions in which he found himself, he ought to be less constrained by laws, or constrained by fewer laws? And might it not be perfectly sensible for him to say so? But I take it that to this also Hobbes would not have agreed; and we see here, as we shall see again, that in his treatment of this particular topic he must fall back from time to time, no doubt not surprisingly, on other doctrine. It is of course central to his theory of politics that subjects cannot – rightly, he insists, and necessarily cannot – *make* their sovereign governors accord to them more extensive liberty than they choose to do; but he held it also to be in general idle, perhaps even senseless, to aver that this or that ought to be the case, where there was no way, and could be no way, of enforcing that judgement. It would thus follow that for a subject to say, in any circumstances, that he 'ought' to enjoy more liberty must always be idle – and, so far as not merely idle, positively mischievous.

Thus here too Hobbes would have held – drawing on other doctrine – that the demand for *more* liberty, even in quite specific times and places and conditions, should never be made by reasonable men. It is still, however, rather odd that, though he has what he would certainly have regarded as a conclusive rebuttal of the demand made in this sense, in his chapter he neither mentions the demand nor sets out what is wrong with it.

Let us take one more topic, on which Hobbes finds very little to say. There is surely a sense, and, both historically and today a most important sense, in which freedom, or liberty, is regarded as standing in contrast not merely with constraining power, nor even with excessive and oppressive constraining power, but rather with *arbitrary* and *unlimited* power. When, say, the eighteenth-century Englishman congratulated himself upon being a free man, and compared his condition complacently with that of, say, his French or Muscovite contemporary, he did not mean, I think, or did not mean only, that those governments as compared with his own were oppressive to their subjects – he perhaps had no very clear idea whether or not that was so. What he meant, I think, or at least a most important part of what he meant, was that French or Muscovite government, however indulgent to this class or that or even to everybody, was still essentially despotic. However much or little political authority and power might choose to do in fact, there was in principle nothing that it could *not* do; and further it could, even if it did not often, act arbitrarily, from mere whim or *pronunciamento*. When peoples eject dictators and proclaim that they are free, it seems to be arbitrariness, whim, *diktat*, even more than actual oppression, which they believe (often, alas, mistakenly) that they have got rid of. Some might say, of course – his American contemporary would probably have said exactly this – that the eighteenth-century Englishman was actually deceived in this matter – that he had indeed largely freed himself from the despotism of kings and the arbitrariness of the royal prerogative, only by subjecting himself to the despotism of an un-qualifiedly sovereign Parliament, and to the (potentially at any rate) arbitrarily exercised prerogative of ministers and officials. Indeed we hear talk today, for that very reason, of the need, for the defence of freedom, of some sort of explicit schedule of entrenched citizen's rights, a fragment of fundamental law, of written constitution, some area upon which even Parliament and its executive may not, merely by way of ordinary 'due process', entrench. But in any case, whatever may be the historical facts as to its realization or otherwise, that is what the demand – *this* demand – for 'the liberty of subjects' appears to be. It is the demand that legitimate acts of government should not be arbitrary, and that there should be for any subject at least a certain area within which no one at all, not even his government, is entitled to compel or to constrain him.

I think it clear that Hobbes was not simply blind, or indifferent, to this demand; on the contrary, he does the very best that he can to accommodate it. There is indeed, he says, a certain area within which any subject has an absolute right to resist the incursions of his sovereign (or of anyone else); and he even locates here what he calls, with some emphasis, 'the true Liberty of the Subject' – 'the things, which though commanded by the Soveraign, he may nevertheless, without Injustice, refuse to do'. It is true that, in his argument, this area is not very extensive. According to him, a subject has 'true liberty', an absolute right, to refuse to act directly to his own destruction or physical injury, or to allow others to do so; to refuse to accuse or incriminate himself; and (rather pleasingly) to refuse military service, provided that he is able to field an able-bodied substitute in his place. Nevertheless, though not extensive, there is, he says, such an area; any man is absolutely entitled to these refusals, and indeed therein lies, in Hobbes's own phrase, his true liberty.

But then, of course, what Hobbes thus concedes with one hand to the claims of 'true' liberty, he is at once obliged by his general doctrine to take away with the other. One might naturally suppose that, if I have the absolute right to refuse to do something, then no one can have any right to compel me to do it. Not so, says Hobbes; and indeed, in his usage, the term 'right' actually has no such implication. I have the right, in Hobbes's usage, to resist my sovereign if, say, he orders my death; but he also, and at the same time, has an absolute right to kill me if he chooses. If he seeks my death by proceeding under forms of law, then I may do my best under forms of law to frustrate him; but that is not much use, for he may also, brushing law aside, proceed by mere whim, and then also, though still I may resist him, he does no wrong – 'it may, and doth often happen in Commonwealths, that a subject may be put to death, by the command of the Sovereign Power; and yet neither doe the other wrong'.

Thus my true liberty, as Hobbes conceives and concedes it, though indeed it consists in an absolute right that I have to refuse certain coercions, is not an area in which no one has any right to coerce me. There is, Hobbes of course must hold, no such area. For sovereignty essentially is and must be, not necessarily oppressive, but absolutely despotic –

'nothing the Soveraign Representative can doe to a Subject, on what pretence soever, can properly be called Injustice, or Injury'. So if, in demanding liberty, what you demand is not only an area within which you have absolute rights, but an area within which no one else is entitled to interfere with you, the only thing that Hobbes has to say is that you cannot have it.

And what thus becomes clear is that, of course not surprisingly, the particular topic of political liberty cannot be further pursued except by a general engagement along the whole front of Hobbes's political theory. His general strategy in this chapter is, I have suggested, to try to head off, to undermine, any 'clamour' for liberty by the repeated contention that, if we will only see clearly and state accurately what it is that is demanded, we shall see in every case that we either already have it, or would not reasonably seek it. We *are* normally free to do what we elect to do; and though our choices are determined, no reasonable man would think it preferable that they should be random. We *are* free in many things from legal coercion or constraint; and though in some things laws do indeed constrain, no reasonable man would desire that they should not. We *are*, or at least most of us are, inhabitants of 'free' states; and no unconfused man would wish to be, or think that he could be, personally free in the same sense as most states are. And if we say that we wish to be governed under free institutions, it is a mere mistake, begotten by uncritical reverence for the rhetoric of classical antiquity, to suppose that any institutions are necessarily, intrinsically, in any new or any interesting sense, either more or less 'free' than any others.

But then it might appear that Hobbes's programme runs into a difficulty. If it is put to him that there is an important sense in which a free man is, not of course a man at liberty to do whatever he pleases, but a man protected at least within a certain area against the arbitrary incursions of political power – a man so placed that not only, within a certain area, has he the right to do so as he pleases, but also that within that area no one at all has any right to interefere with him – it seems he can say only, flatly and disappointingly, that there can be no such thing. But in fact Hobbes would not admit any 'difficulty' here. For we have here, in his view, not a failure of his strategy, but merely a further instance of its application. For it is not, he would argue, that he is obliged, contrary to his strategy, to admit at this point that there is a species of liberty both not always enjoyed, and yet reasonably regarded as a desirable thing to enjoy. It is of course the whole tenor, a leading theme, of his theory of politics that not only *can* no effective limit be set to the scope of permissible exercise of political power, but also that no reasonable man would desire or demand, even as the purest matter of theory, that there should be such a limit. The essential attribute of a Hobbesian sovereign must be power; and a reasonable man is invited to see that, for the peace of society, such power must be irresistible, and unlimited in its legitimate exercise. Thus here too Hobbes will say, of *this* demand for liberty, not of course that we have it, nor merely that it is not practically possible that we should, but that we do not really want it – it is not a thing that any reasonable, clear-sighted person would regard as desirable. And whether he is justified in so claiming is neither more nor less than the question whether, quite in general, his political theory is well founded and sustainable. This is not the place to begin to go into that.

In a previous lecture in the series in which this paper was originally given Professor H. Bull, having regard to a certain flinty realism, a single-minded concern with power and interests, in Hobbes's view of international relations, hinted that Hobbes might be seen as, on the plane of theory, the Kissinger of the seventeenth century. One might venture another transatlantic comparison: that Hobbes was the B. F. Skinner of the seventeenth century. He was as fully insistent as Skinner upon determinism; he was as convinced a materialist, and equally con-temptuous of those who toy with any fancied alternative; it was a cardinal doctrine of his, as of Skinner's, that while humans are more complicated than, and in that sense different from, pigeons or pineapples, they are as much a part of the natural order, and to be understood in ways that are in principle the same. Now Skinner, a few years ago, wrote a widely acclaimed book called *Beyond Freedom and Dignity*; for him, as that title suggests, freedom is a means, not any sort of end, and a means, further, that is habitually and rhetorically overvalued through lack of under-standing. What is needed, as Skinner puts it, is to 'redesign the environ-ment' so that constraints and controls on human behaviour will produce desired results; and what he calls 'the literature of freedom' strikes him as simply an obstacle here. It leads people foolishly to think it somehow important, not simply that people should act as they ought, but that they should act as they freely choose to do – even worse, that it is somehow a demeaning, disgraceful thing deliberately to manipulate them and their environment so as to ensure that they will reliably make 'proper' choices. But all that is moonshine. The end result, called by Skinner 'preservation of our culture', is important; the means to that end, provided that they are economical and efficacious, are not, and in particular should not be distorted and hamstrung through silly deference to human freedom. What matters is what people do; if they will do it freely, well and good; but if not, they must be brought to do it through appropriate devices and mechanisms of control.

I believe that there is not a word in this from which Hobbes would have dissented (except perhaps that his end result was more individualistically conceived). The plain fact is, and in the end has to be admitted, that he attached no particular *value* to liberty. The end – peace and self-preservation – was the important thing; and the problem was to devise means that would effectively lead to its realization. It is for Hobbes, as for Skinner, a purely technical question how far, and in what circumstances and ways and senses, men, if that end is to be secured, may be left to act freely, and there is nothing intrinsically desirable or valuable in their doing so. Thus, what I think underlies Hobbes's chapter on 'The Liberty of Subjects' is something which he never quite explicitly says. He says that, in this sense or that, men actually have all the liberty that, if they were clear in the head, they would see reason to desire: he does not quite say, though I am quite sure that he believed, that the whole topic in any case does not deserve the excited attention which it is apt to evoke.

I conclude, then, with the fairly unoriginal observation that, at this point as at others, Hobbes emerges as a much more ruthless, whole-hogging Utilitarian than was, for instance, J. S. Mill. One feels that Mill would not really have contemplated with approval a society of Skinnerian human artefacts, however *happily* they inhabited the carefully designed environment which their programmer had invented for them and conditioned them to enjoy. He did not really think it to be a good thing for people to be free agents *only* because , if, and in so far as that conduced to their happiness. But that, I believe, is just what Hobbes really did think. His basic thought, underlying all his distinctions and definitions and ingenuities, was that Liberty, after all, did not really matter very much.

17

Saturday Mornings

During the 1950s, just before each university term or sometimes in the first week, I and others used to receive from Austin a small card about 'Sat. mng. mtgs.' (*sic*) for the coming term. Usually, I think, all that it conveyed was where and when we were to meet; the question of what we were to do – if it was not just carrying on with what we had been doing the previous term – would be settled by agreement at the first meeting. The stated time was 10.30 a.m. Austin and a few others were usually present then; but one could turn up at any time, or if otherwise occupied not turn up at all, without attracting comment; and although the meetings broke up in time for people to get away to lunch at about one o'clock, there was no sort of obligation to stay to the end. During any Sat. mng. there were pretty constant comings and goings. Except for the fact that one could attend only at Austin's express invitation, it was, ahead of its time, a sort of unstructured talk-in; no one had to be there or stay there; no one read a paper and no one replied; deviations from the agreed topic were frequent, and if there was a fairly well-marked tendency to 'address the Chair', it was by nature and not by convention that that came about.

Philosophers in Oxford at that time had no premises of their own; we met, as did other philosophical societies, in various colleges. The room I remember best was a shabbily comfortable, leathery, Victorian common room in the front quad of Balliol, secured for our use by R. M. Hare. Less frequently, a rather similar, but smaller and older room next door in Trinity, arranged by Patrick Nowell-Smith. At least one term, a cold and hideous lecture room, with little desks, also in Balliol. Occasionally, by arrangement with H. P. Grice, we used a rather splendid modern room in St. John's, with a big central table and highly executive chairs, looking like the board room of a prosperous and soberly go-ahead commercial company. Officially anyway this was the room that Austin favoured; he

From *Essays on J. L. Austin*, ed. I. Berlin *et al*. (Oxford University Press, 1973).

claimed to regard armchairs and an informal *mise-en-scène* as philosophically debilitating, preferring deployment round a table and a more upright
posture; somehow, though, it seems usually to have been in the club-like
asymmetry of Balliol that we actually met. The explanation of the cold and
hideous lecture room was that, in that term, a blackboard was necessary;
exceptionally, and with a certain sense of dogged duty, we had agreed to
get ourselves lectured to, on mathematical logic. Marcus Dick, who had
recently returned formidably armed in that line from a year at Harvard,
was specially invited to come and tell us what we ought to know. That
must have been in the very early 1950s.[1]

One recurrent cause of deviation from our agreed term's topic was that
at that time the Philosophical Society met, three times a term, on Friday
nights; most people would have been at those meetings; and it was
common for the public discussion on a Friday evening to be continued the
next morning in our more private gathering. But the discussion, of course,
had not always been interesting enough for that to happen.

There were two main respects, neither perhaps very easy to convey, in
which these meetings were quite unlike any others that I have attended.
The first was a matter of the position of Austin himself. I cannot think of
any comparable instance of personal authority so effortlessly exercised. It
was not that the proceedings were formally disciplined; on the contrary,
they were exceptionally fluid and free, with no formal order at all. Nor
were they solemn; on the contrary, they were continuously enjoyable and
amusing – *funny*, in fact. Quite apart from the fact that he enjoyed
philosophical argument, Austin liked jokes – sometimes really silly jokes,
real farcical fantasy (of which the most representative instances in his
writings are to be found, I think, in his paper 'Pretending'). He did not by
any means resemble Wittgenstein, as Norman Malcolm reports him,[2] in
not liking other people to laugh at what he himself found laughable;
indeed, it is not impossible that Malcolm should have had Austin in mind
in his sharp reference, in the same passage, to the 'facetious tone' that is
'characteristic of philosophical discussion among clever people who have
no serious purpose'. (It is even possible that Austin did not have a 'serious
purpose' *absolutely all the time*.) Even so, these discussions were never just
casual, and not even really relaxed. Austin's contemporaries and younger
colleagues not only felt great respect for the extraordinary freshness and

[1] My wife tells me that, some years later, Charles Taylor, then at All Souls, was similarly
commissioned to instruct us in Merleau-Ponty's *Phenomenology of Perception*. Since my
mind seems blank on this, I incline to think I must have been away.

[2] *Ludwig Wittgenstein: a Memoir* (1958), p. 29.

force of his intellectual gifts; it was also entirely out of the question for them not to treat him personally with respect. It was always just a little as if the headmaster were present; however untrammelled the talk might be and however informal the atmosphere, he was still the headmaster, and there were certain kinds of casualness and unbuttoned disorder that, one knew at once, would not really do. It was plain whose the guiding hand was and where the initiative lay. A recurrent proof of this, by which I never ceased to be both amused and impressed, was the extraordinary way in which the atmosphere would change when, as sometimes happened, Austin himself had to leave our meetings early (when he moved from Magdalen to Corpus Christi as White's Professor, he was sometimes involved in the transaction of that college's business on Saturdays); as the door closed behind him, even though the discussion went on without diversion or interruption, there was an unmistakable sense of people slumping more loosely in their chairs, talking rather more impetuously, laughing – sometimes even giggling – with more abandon. They were now out of range of that formidable magnetic field. I was never quite able to decide what Austin himself felt about this, or even how far he was aware of it. Certainly he preferred a certain formality of manners, or at any rate a strictly limited informality, in relation to people who were not – as most of us were not – his personal friends. I think also that he certainly liked authority, and did not pretend otherwise to himself or to anyone else. But I sometimes thought that he did not always realize how effortlessly his authority was conceded, how unquestioned it was. It is, I suppose, natural enough that his uniqueness, which seemed obvious to us, was not so evident to him. It never crossed our minds, though perhaps it did his, that there might be any other, or rival, Sat. mngs.

The other thing is that these meetings were uniquely free of that combative, gladiatorial style which is so common in philosophical debate, and can be so very wearying. Of course we disagreed a lot; but it was not, so to speak, an axiom that one *had* to disagree, to look out specially for something, in what anyone said, to disagree with. No one was trying to win, no one was conscious of defending a position, there was to be no dialectical victim at the end of the morning, metaphorically stretched on the carpet in humiliating defeat. There were several reasons for this. The most obvious is that, as I mentioned, no one read a paper and no one replied; so that there was not, as so often there is, right at the outset any deliberate taking up of prepared antagonistic positions, thereafter, for the sake of one's credit, to be bristlingly maintained at all hazards (the 'adversary method' of philosophical inquiry, which is not always bad but is not the only possibility). There is the point as well that those who came to the meetings were in any case not predisposed to disagree; some, perhaps all, had at least a natural share of philosophical argumentativeness, but at least there were no standing hostilities, or obvious obstacles in the way of communicative rationality. Austin had, and no doubt knew that he had, critics among philosophers who, for one reason or another, would have had to be described as really hostile, who intensely disliked the sort of thing that he did and his way of doing it (and perhaps him too); not unreasonably, those people were not invited to be present – nor, probably, had they been invited, would they have come. So not only were there no, so to speak, procedural antagonisms set up by the form of the occasions; there were no real antagonisms either. But above all (I shall come back to this) it was taken for granted that the object actually was to reach agreement if possible – not, of course, because agreement is cosy or comforting, but because some point on which, say, a dozen professional arguers reach general agreement stands at least a decent chance of being actually right. Austin once, when asked to state his 'criterion' of philosophical correctness, replied that, well, if you could get a collection of (he said) 'more or less cantankerous colleagues' all to accept something after argument, that, he thought, would be 'a bit of a criterion'. In any case, to get something right, to say something pertinent and true, was what he wanted to do; and this aim, on these occasions at any rate, was generally accepted. We talked in collaboration, not in competition.[3]

Here I must not give a false impression of general sweetness and light, or even of inhumanly unflawed objectivity. Of course Austin did not make the sheer mistake of really believing that we were all equal collaborators; in my view at least, a large part of the point of our being there was that we certainly were not. But also, I think quite often, in bringing up some topic to be talked about, he had already, though he did not at once disclose, a quite definite view as to what should be said about it; and, though sometimes he did not seem to want to show a hand of his own at all, he often knew which way he wanted the talk of the rest of us to be nudged along, and nudged it accordingly. And certainly he did not himself like to be wrong. The capacity to be absolutely unmoved by the fact that a propostion, shown to be untenable, had just been asserted by *oneself* and not somebody else – to say nothing of being positively pleased by that, as Plato says Socrates was – that capacity was not one of Austin's. Not to

---

[3] It is also important that 'Saturday mornings' were not *public* academic occasions. Collaboration with Austin in giving public classes was – as Berlin, Hart, and Grice would testify – an altogether flintier experience.

mind making public mistakes can be an admirable characteristic, not unknown among philosophers though certainly extremely rare; it can also be symptomatic of the less admirable modesty of those who are conscious of having a lot to be modest about – one may just know that, alas, one's being wrong is not particularly interesting. Austin did not feel like that. It mattered to him – and I think he instinctively felt that it just *mattered* – that he should not get things wrong, and it was not at all easy for him to concede, except at his own prompting, that he had. However, since he did not after all very often make mistakes that the rest of us were sharp enough to notice, it was more important in practice that he did not particularly mind being disagreed with. Indeed, he did not mind at all – he rather expected to say things that we should not all easily swallow, at any rate to begin with; that was part of the idea.

So what, on all these successive Saturdays, actually went on? Since Austin is generally regarded – of course not altogether wrongly – as having had very definite and idiosyncratic views about what might be called (he would have hated the phrase, unless perhaps it had struck him as comical) philosophical methodology, it ought to be stressed that what went on was very often not idiosyncratic at all. We were not always sternly applying the procedural precepts of 'A Plea for Excuses'. Very often this was because we were construing an actual text, and not usually anything very recondite either. My impression is that we discussed most regularly passages in Aristotle's *Nicomachean Ethics*. After 1953, Wittgenstein's *Philosophical Investigations* came up almost as often. At least once, probably earlier, we spent a term on Frege's *Foundations of Arithmetic*, of which Austin had done a translation in 1950. (I remember, for no particular reason, Austin's puzzlement at Frege's apparent demand that a definition of 'number' ought to tell us that Julius Caesar is *not* a number. Why should definitions provide answers to silly questions?) There was Merleau-Ponty. Then, in 1959, I anyway heard here for the first time the name of Chomsky; we devoted the autumn term of that year to *Syntactic Structures*. In such cases the aim was the quite unidiosyncratic one of trying to get absolutely clear on what was said in, and meant by, the text before us, and of considering whether we were convinced or not by what it said; and Austin had no particular nostrums for the pursuit of that aim. But perhaps there is one thing that should be mentioned here. Austin's favoured unit of discussion in such cases was the *sentence* – not the paragraph or chapter, still less the book as a whole. Roughly, he seemed inclined to make the assumption that, as books are written, or anyway printed, as an ordered sequence of sentences, they should be read by taking the sentences *one at a time,* thoroughly settling the sense (or hash) of each before proceeding to the next one. This naturally worked out rather slowly, and that was all to the good; but perhaps it did not always work out ideally well. The *Tractatus* (which I think we never did discuss) is indeed, at least prima facie, constructed with a view to that sort of step-by-step reading; but most writers, some more than others, often say things, whether wittingly or not, that are only fully intelligible in the light of other things that they have not yet said. This did not greatly matter in the case of Aristotle, with the whole of whose text Austin was perfectly familiar, and the rest of us decently so. But the *Investigations*, I think, did not come up looking at their best in this relentless light; and in some other cases one felt that texts before us were being subjected to a concentrated pressure at every point which, poor things, they were not in the least fitted to withstand. I suspect that with Chomsky, too, we should have got on better if we had started with more notion of where these highly unfamiliar-looking sentences were headed.

I mention, again for no better reason than that I happen to remember it, that one of the things in the *Investigations* that we discussed at some length was the account given there of such sentences as 'I have toothache', the whole question of 'reports', 'descriptions', 'expressions' of pain. Stuart Hampshire (at least if I remember the incident right, and I apologize to him if I do not) had seemed to be taking inarticulate indications of pain, such as groans and grimaces, as a kind of pain-*behaviour*, as something that people in pain *do*. Austin said 'Well, you'd be a tartar in the wards, Hampshire – "Lights out, *and no groaning!*" '

But of course there were plenty of occasions on which the discussion did take a turn peculiarly characteristic of Austin, though perhaps not always quite in the way one would have expected. Groping through my imperfect recollections, I find, I think, three different sorts of somewhat idiosyncratic occasions, of which the third and perhaps the second may be found a bit surprising; but first for the expected one.

As one would expect, there certainly were some occasions on which we, in effect, made lists of English words and phrases, and tried more or less minutely to discriminate their senses and to learn from the distinctions encapsulated in their ordinary uses. Three such cases come readily to my mind, and I mention them in what I believe, though not confidently, to have been their chronological order. One of them took its start from the use, apparently as something of a technical term, of the word 'disposition'; this word, around 1950, was very much in the philosophical air as a word of virtue, having been put there, of course, by Gilbert Ryle in *The Concept of Mind.* Austin, who believed that philosophers' technical terms, or ordinary terms used in technical ways, were *liable* – though of course not necessarily – to blur preexisting distinctions which sometimes ought – though of course not always – to be preserved or at least noticed, wanted to know what dispositions *really* were; and this led us to compare and contrast the word 'disposition' with, for instance, the words 'trait', 'propensity', 'characteristic', 'habit', 'inclination', 'tendency', and others. I remember that Austin called our attention to the use of 'habit' as a word for certain kinds of, as it were, professional dress, or identifying uniform – monks *wear* habits; and to the botanist's way of speaking of the 'habit' of plants. And I remember that he asked us to try to imagine in detail what, say, a lodger in one's house would probably have been up to (a) if one complained of his 'nasty habits', and (b) if one complained of his 'nasty ways'. We also considered the sentence (Austin's) 'His *susceptibility* to colds renders him unfit to take part in the International Geophysical Year.' Another somewhat similar tract of discussion arose – presumably, though I do not actually remember – from the philosopher's use of 'use' in talking about meaning, perhaps actually from the comparison of words with tools. This went two ways. On the one hand, we tried to think what sort of thing exactly one would expect to be told, under the general heading 'how to use' this or that (would one be told what to use the thing *for*, or merely told about 'the way' to use it – and what would *that* be? Did 'a way to use' differ from 'a way of using'?) On the other hand, we compared and contrasted such substantives as 'tool', 'instrument', 'implement', 'utensil', 'appliance', 'equipment', 'apparatus', 'gear', 'kit' – even 'device' and 'gimmick'. Here I remember Austin inviting us to classify *scissors*; kitchen scissors, I think we thought, were utensils, and garden shears were probably tools (or implements?), but the sort of scissors used in, for instance, dressmaking were something of a problem. (Sewing 'materials' would probably *include* scissors, but that is not quite an answer to the question.) And I remember that he asked why, awaiting an operation, one would be disconcerted if the surgeon said 'Right, I'll just go and get my tools.' Then once – I am really not sure why or in the hope of what – the logician's use of 'class' led us on to a string of such words as 'group', 'set', 'collection' (what sort of thing does one have to do, to be a *collector*?), 'assemblage', 'range', even 'crowd', and 'heap'.

I must confess (no doubt it is a sign of changed times that I use the defensive word 'confess') that I always found this sort of thing enormously enjoyable, exactly to my taste. I did not believe that it was likely to contribute to the solution of the problems of the post-war world; I did not believe that it would contribute, certainly or necessarily, to the solution of any problems of philosophy. But it was enormously enjoyable,[4] it was not easy; it exercised the wits; and those who think they know that it cannot ever be valuably instructive have simply never tried, or perhaps are no good at it. H. P. Grice once said, when he and I had been looking in this manner at some parts of the vocabulary of perception, 'How *clever* language is!' We found that it made *for* us some remarkably ingenious distinctions and assimilations. That, incidentally, was not on a Saturday morning; regrettably, and perhaps surprisingly, we never, I think, took up problems of perception then at all (except for Merleau-Ponty). I remember Peter Strawson saying that he wished we would, that being just the sort of thing that Austin did best. But probably he did not particularly want to go on about topics on which, throughout this period, he regularly lectured.

The second sort of occasion, though a curiously different sort, which was no doubt highly characteristic of Austin, is best exemplified by our grapplings at one time with aesthetics. Here, as one would expect, Austin was determined to keep us away from generalities about Art and Beauty and Significant Form; we were to find out what sorts of things people *actually* say, and why, in aesthetic appraisal, when the topic is not so grand as to inhibit good sense, or too obviously complex and controversial to admit of any sort of consensus. We looked at an illustrated handbook of industrial design, containing a wide selection of confident aesthetic pronouncements on humble objects of domestic use such as teapots and jugs. (Can it have been in this connection that he offered, as a possible aesthetic maxim, 'If thine enemy shave one side of thy head, turn to him the other also'?) What was curious about this occasion was that Austin, though of course not uninterested in the particular terms used, seemed to be looking for a *standard form* into which all our specimens could be fitted – a form that would mention some physical and some more aesthetic 'quality', and say how the latter was somehow resultant from the former. (A bell will be rung, for those who were present, by the *schema* 'The w of the x makes the y look z' – e.g. 'The shape of the handle makes the pot look stable.') I was puzzled at the time, by this, as I thought untypical, interest in a uniform formula. But perhaps Austin had a *theory* here, in the background: it ought to be remembered that, though he regarded very general theories with instinctive suspicion, and thought that they were often launched into the

[4] I could even take – though some felt that it was going too far – the question of the difference between 'highly' and 'very'. Why can one be highly intelligent or highly interesting, but not highly stupid or highly dull?

world prematurely and recklessly, he very often did have such theories at the back of his mind – and very often kept them there.

Thirdly, and differently again, we spent at least one term in the surprising activity of discussing, in an absolutely ground-floor, first-order way, actual moral problems. No doubt the object here was, typically of Austin, to get us at least temporarily to stand back from the theories, and to remind ourselves not how people are said or supposed to think and talk about these matters, but how they (in this case we ourselves) actually do. But what was curious about this occasion was that, so far as I can remember, practically no philosophical conclusions were ever explicitly drawn, nor did I get any impression that Austin had, even at the back of his mind, any particular philosophical lessons that he hoped we should learn. The only explicit impingement on philosophy that I recall was that Austin seemed to regard with a certain irony R. M. Hare's attachment to 'principles', and seemed not to think much of what were offered as examples of such things. (I recall the words 'a tatty little principle'.)[5] But of course it may be that we were all simply diverted from philosophy by the absorbing interest, of quite another sort, of the things people said; it was indeed fascinating to see, in colleagues with some of whom one was only, so to speak, professionally well acquainted, both what they would come up with as palmary instances of moral dilemma, and what stands they would take when it came to considering solutions. In those decorous old days, propriety set certain recognized though unmentioned limits to the range of moral problems that were openly canvassed, nor could Austin – or perhaps any of us – have endured excursions into actual autobiography; even so, the things people said were interesting enough, both when they were unexpected and, in a different way, when they were not. One question we discussed at length was this. A personal friend has confessed to me, in strict confidence, something that would be regarded by most people as much to his discredit; subsequently, and unexpectedly, he becomes a candidate for election to a Fellowship at my college and I, as a member of the electing body, am asked by my colleagues for my candid judgement of him. What do I do? We considered variants on this theme – What exactly is it that he has told me? Would the discredit be moral or intellectual? (What is that distinction?) Do I think that my colleagues would be *right* in thinking him, if they knew all, disqualified from election,

[5] How would one respond, say as an examiner, to the offer of a bribe? Hare (if memory serves) said that he would say 'I don't take bribes, on principle.' Austin said: 'Would you, Hare? I think I'd say "No, thanks."' I hope that Hare will forgive me if this recollection is inaccurate – or even, perhaps, if it is not.

or that they would be *wrong*? Would he, if elected, do research or teaching? How good is he at his subject anyway? And so on. One of us, I remember, averred that he would speak as follows: 'I happen to know something about this man which most of you would probably regard as disqualifying him from election, but I regret that I am not in a position to tell you what it is.' We did not think much of that. Austin, I remember, attached great importance to the fact that one had 'admitted to one's friendship' the imparter of confidences – a transaction of which he seemed to have an oddly (or perhaps characteristically?) formal conception; and I believe he did not contemplate, under any variant, that the man's confidence should thereafter be betrayed, or even inexplicitly alluded to. When asked what he would do if his colleagues should subsequently find out the truth and reproach him for his silence, he replied that he would 'brazen it out'. In another connection – a case about the use of 'tainted money' for virtuous ends – he was surprisingly insistent that, so excessively ready did he think people were cynically to believe the worst of other people, nothing should *ever* be avoidably done to afford them any pretext for doing so. I am not sure what I learned philosophically during that term, but these discussions too were exceedingly enjoyable.

What was it all for? This was actually a question that I did not much raise at the time, because a good enough answer seemed so very obvious – I expected to learn things that I would not have thought of for myself; and I enjoyed it. But even if no one thought about it very much, there was a formal purpose. Invitation to Sat. mngs. was officially confined to those of Austin's contemporaries and juniors (not all of them) who were full-time tutorial Fellows; and this was not just a handy way of restricting the number of those eligible – the idea, not a bad one, was that full-time tutors were more seriously in danger than others of sinking into the condition of weary, repetitive hacks, their interests straitjacketed by the syllabus of first-degree examinations and their energies sapped by long hours of teaching, and that they more than others needed to be taken out of themselves, to have a weekly shot in the arm. This was why Austin sought, in varying ways and degrees, always to do something new, or, if not that, to try looking at things in some new sort of way; the one thing he did *not* want was to go over, however well he might have done it, just the same ground as we had all been hacking away at in tutorials that week. He did not want us to get set in our ways; and he did not want us to get bored, or exhausted. My evidence would be that he was extraordinarily successful in this aim. If we did not, like fanatical followers of Savonarola, live each week in the light of the sermon of the previous week-end,[6] there were certainly many tutorials of mine that profited at least a little from that borrowed light.

But one can also say something rather less parochial than that; it was not just a matter of refresher-courses for jaded Oxford tutors. As I have said, Austin did not try to use his Saturday mornings – or at any rate, not often – as experimental material for the systematic application of his own ideas about methods. We never, I think, brought dictionaries with us; we seldom made lists. Nevertheless, some of his ideas did operate – inevitably, I suppose – in a sort of guiding role. I think he wanted us to see, not only for our own immediate good but for the sake of the subject, how desirable it was to get out of 'the bogs and tracks' of familiar, time-hallowed, philosophical campaigning. I think he wanted us to see how satisfactory it could be to have before us small, manageable points that could be completely clearly stated and relevantly discussed. I think he wanted to convince us of the possibility of collaboration, and perhaps above all to get us to believe seriously in the possibility of *agreement*. Our meetings were in some ways more like meetings of civil servants, seeking impersonally and anonymously to reach workable agreement on matters of common concern, than like those confrontations of embattled *virtuosi* with which, alas, one is so much more familiar. (That is *really* what was right, and what so often is wrong.) He wanted to accustom us to not getting along very fast, and to not dismissing impatiently, as if we knew *in advance* what was and was not worth looking into, multiplicity of detail – some of which, indeed, would turn out to be of no great significance.

He wanted us to come to think of philosophy as more like a science than an art, as a matter of finding things out and getting things settled, not of creating a certain individual effect. And certainly not as one of the *performing* arts; once, when I saw him in the audience of a very distinguished philosophical performer, he found the spectacle so manifestly intolerable to him that he had to go away – and was not himself play-acting in doing so. He could not bear histrionics.

I remember that he once came back from America – I think in 1956 – a good deal perturbed by what he thought to be the increasing prestige there of Arne Naess. This must have been because he thought he saw the right *purpose* – a more empirical, 'objectivĕ' way of doing philosophy, offering the hope of getting things actually settled by patient industry – in danger of being compromised by what he took to be radically wrong *methods*. 'It's infiltrating from the West,' he said, shaking his head.

[6] A comparison of Isaiah Berlin's, which he may well not remember; the conversation in which it occurred did not have a wholly serious purpose.

I think he disliked above all the perpetual disorder of philosophy, the perennial disagreement and wrangling, the nearly total failure to achieve any solid and permanent advance; and he thought that work in the subject was depressingly under-organized, unbusinesslike, unsystematic – rather as if it were not taken, even by its practitioners, really seriously. He wanted to tidy it up. It does not seem to me at all mysterious that one should feel like that, though it is another question, of course, why he should have minded *so much*.

No doubt I have not made really clear – perhaps in part because I do not really know – why those Saturday mornings seem to me to have been the best of philosophical occasions. It is probably more relevant than I would easily recognize that at that time I was (as were most of us) fairly new to the business and comparatively young, and so quite in general, I expect, more hopeful and impressionable, readier both to enjoy and to be struck by what went on around me. It is perhaps worth remembering that, in the early 1950s, every single person present there, Austin included, was much younger than I am now; most of us had just started, and in a sense the University itself, after the war, had started again. Things are now two decades further along, *nos et mutamur*.[7] It was partly of course a matter of taste. Not everyone, I imagine, found Austin's jokes – including the really silly ones – as funny as I did; nor was everyone immediately attracted (though absolutely no one was unimpressed) by his formidable personality; some even claim not to have believed in his seriousness of purpose, though that complaint itself need not really be taken seriously. Not everyone is fascinated by the endless subtleties of natural languages, or enjoys making lists of words and then putting them through their paces. These were things that gave me, though, much pleasure and satisfaction. But perhaps I am most nearly clear about what I then valued when I ask myself what, now, I am sometimes conscious of missing. Two things come to mind, and they are probably connected. One is that Austin was absolutely first-hand. He was not a purveyor or explainer, however competent or critical or learned, of philosophy; he was a maker of it, an actual origin.

---

[7] On this topic, I remember Austin himself once insisting to me, in the cloisters at Magdalen, that not only is youth – *real* youth – a condition both curious and swiftly transient: is is also, he said, impossible properly to remember, or to characterize retrospectively without falsification. My suggestion of George Moore's *Confessions of a Young Man* he dismissed on the ground that its author was too old (over thirty); his own view was that, in the nearly impossible task of portraying real youth, the most nearly successful contender was Lermontov.

One had the feeling – not always, but often – that those meetings, which were so unmistakably his own, were not occasions on which philosophy was talked about, or taught, or learned – they were occasions on which it was *done*, at which that actually *happened*, there and then, in which the life of the subject consists, and which ensures that the critics and explainers have something to explain. I seem to have that feeling less often nowadays; on occasions when one had it, it was well worth being there. The other thing – unless perhaps it is really the same thing – is that he was not predictable. There are good philosophers whose next book or paper or remark, however good, is more or less extrapolable from the last two or three; sometimes even one may find oneself feeling, presumptuously no doubt, that one could almost have written or said it for them, by a bit of induction on the basis of what came before. Austin was not in the least like that. In what he wrote, and perhaps even more in what he said, one was constantly struck by things which it would never have occurred to one to say oneself, and which one could not possibly have foreseen, either, that he was going to say. That also is something in which the life of the subject consists.

Index